M000233650

vision of the man who threw the curtains wide open on Jesus and his grace for so many of us. This book may very well become a contemporary gospel classic in devotional literature. Want to understand more about the radical implications and transforming power of God's saving grace? Then order Jack's new book soon.

Dr. Scotty Ward Smith, Founding Pastor of Christ Community Church; Teacher in Residence at West End Community Church; author of *Everyday Prayers: 365 Days to a Gospel-Centered Faith*

"Jack Miller was a work of God's Spirit, and the Spirit used him to change my life. When he preached, he had a way of catching you up in his contagious joy—a joy that flowed directly out of the grace of the gospel. These daily doses of his sermons will have that same humbling, liberating effect. Read them and your life will change!"

Charles Morris, Speaker & President of HAVEN Today

"The gospel is simple, but we often write long and complicated books explaining it. Jack Miller's gift is to take the great truths of the gospel and make them sing again to a simple tune. These short devotions are easy enough for anyone to read, but at the same time as profound and heart-warming as the Scriptures upon which they are based."

Iain Duguid, PhD, Professor of Old Testament, Westminster Theological Seminary, Philadelphia

"One of the things that has impacted me the most about Jack Miller's preaching is that he so naturally interweaves our need for spiritual renewal with the expansion of God's kingdom. That message—the gospel needed to restore my heart is the same gospel that is needed to restore the world—is what first brought me to Serge. In the years that I've been the Executive Director of Serge, I have become more deeply convinced that sharing God's love with the nations is intimately linked to how I experience his love as a beloved son."

Bob Osborne, Executive Director, Serge (formerly World Harvest Mission)

"This is a wonderful book. It not only captures the heart of Jack Miller's cross-centered preaching, but it takes us day-by-day back to the cross. Jack urged us to learn to 'preach the gospel to ourselves every day.' I can hardly think of a better way to do that than to wake up in the morning or go to sleep at night with the truth of these readings ringing in our souls."

Stephen Smallman, Author; assistant pastor, New Life Presbyterian Church, Glenside; former executive director, Serge (formerly World Harvest Mission)

"I learned from Jack Miller how the gospel is not just a gate we walk through once but a pathway we walk every day of our lives. And how God takes pleasure in pouring out his power on those who will dare to radically align their purposes with his for the nations. I've never been the same, and neither will you if you prayerfully read and take to heart the riches of the gospel found in these pages."

Dr. Steve Childers, Founder and President, Pathway Learning; associate professor of practical theology, RTS-Orlando

"Like Jacob, who refused to let go of God until he had received a blessing, Jack Miller was tenacious about receiving God's power and grace. And like Jacob, who was permanently wounded by the angel, Jack found out how powerless he really was in himself to accomplish the goals of holiness and faith. Again, like the patriarch, Jack grew from being a somewhat legalistic person to one who could boldly risk everything for the sake of the gospel. These devotions are brutally honest. Jack was remarkably transparent about who he was, and thus he leads us into our own candid self-appraisal. But he never dangles us in guilt. Instead, he rushes to tell us the good news of God's unconditional love in Christ. And then, when we falter, he tells us to stop acting like orphans. Savoring these excerpts and then trying them out in practice ought to make new persons out of each of us."

William Edgar, John Boyer Chair of Evangelism and Culture, Westminster Theological Seminary, Philadelphia; author of *Truth in All Its Glory*

"Jesus keeps on giving us hope to make our own lives overflowing in love, first for him and then for everyone; that we learned from Jack. Left to ourselves, we can't possibly live with hope in our hard and unloving worlds, but Jesus is there for us. Jack kept on learning that and teaching and living it before us, simply and clearly. The overly familiar gospel became the newest and most beautiful part of our lives."

D. Clair Davis, Professor Emeritus, Westminster Theological Seminary

"Jack Miller was, in many ways, a pioneer. It's not that he said anything new, it's just that to many people it seemed new because the message he trumpeted was so old and had been lost for so long. He spoke of grace the way one is supposed to speak of grace: no buts, no brakes, no qualifications, no footnotes. I am forever grateful to Jack Miller for his unwavering commitment to communicate the inexhaustible grace of God to an exhausted world."

Tullian Tchividjian, pastor of Coral Ridge Presbyterian Church and author of *One Way Love: Inexhaustible Grace for an Exhausted World*

"Jack Miller writes: 'Cheer up! You are worse than you think' and 'Cheer up! God loves you more than you know!' And after reading *Saving Grace*, I want to add: cheer up, this is NOT one of those 'of course, I've heard it all before' daily devotional books. If you can reflect on these mini-exhortations and not come out a more effective servant of God with greater joy, you need to read them again!"

Rev. Dr. Greg Livingstone, Founder, Frontiers

Saving Grace

Daily Devotions from Jack Miller

C. JOHN MILLER

New
Growth
Press

www.newgrowthpress.com

New Growth Press, Greensboro, NC 27404
Copyright © 2014 by Rose Marie Miller.

Unless otherwise indicated, all Scripture quotations are taken from the Holy Bible, English Standard Version®. Copyright © 2000; 2001 by Crossway Bibles, a division of Good News Publishers. Used by permission. All rights reserved.

Scripture verses marked NIV are taken from the Holy Bible, New International Version®. NIV®. Copyright © 1973, 1978, 1984 by International Bible Society. Used by permission of Zondervan. All rights reserved.

Scripture verses marked NASB are taken from the NEW AMERICAN STANDARD BIBLE®, Copyright © 1960, 1962, 1963, 1968, 1971, 1972, 1973, 1975, 1977, 1995 by The Lockman Foundation. Used by permission.

Cover Design: Faceout Books, faceoutstudio.com
Typesetting and Interior Design: Lisa Parnell, lparnell.com

ISBN: 978-1-939946-27-0 (Print)
ISBN: 978-1-939946-28-7 (eBook)

Library of Congress Cataloging-in-Publication Data
Miller, C. John.
  Saving grace : daily devotions from Jack Miller / C. John Miller.
    pages cm
  "Selections from Miller's pioneering sermons"—Publisher's summary.
  ISBN 978-1-939946-27-0 — ISBN 978-1-939946-28-7 (ebook)
  1. Devotional calendars. I. Title.
BV4811.M53 2014
242'.2—dc23
                                                    2014026780

Printed in Canada

21 20 19 18 17 16 15 14   1 2 3 4 5

Foreword

There is a story behind my father's preaching. It began during a summer in Spain in 1970, when, burned out from teaching at seminary, he immersed himself in God's Word. By the end of the summer he'd become convinced, in a new way, that the promises of the Old Testament prophets still applied today. As a seventeen-year-old, I remember watching him preach at Mechanicsville Chapel in Bucks County, Pennsylvania, thinking, *God is going do something with my father. You can't be that excited about Jesus and something not happen.*

I say this because Dad is known largely for his Sonship teaching with its emphasis on the gospel. But his passion for the gospel was embedded in his love of the Word and confidence that this is the Age of the Spirit. It was the Spirit of Christ who brought the presence of Jesus to life in the world. Because he believed that, he taught the Word with the expectation that the Spirit would bring change. In the summer of 1971, I remember him teaching Romans 12 to a large group of assorted hippies and church kids. Someone asked him, "When are we going to go on to something else?" Dad replied, "When you start obeying Romans 12!" Then he laughed and continued teaching Romans 12.

No one laughed harder at Dad's jokes than Dad. Most of us were laughing at Dad's laugh, not his jokes, and I'm not sure Dad ever caught on to the difference—but we delighted to see someone who didn't take

himself too seriously, who enjoyed life, and who genu-
inely loved Jesus. It was contagious. I can still see his
smile and hear his laugh when I read these devotions.
As you read, imagine Dad laughing and smiling as he
calls you to repent and obey! A devotional is a particu-
larly good way to hear Dad's preaching. By taking it in
small doses, you'll be able to absorb it better. You'll pick
up a cadence in Dad's preaching on grace as he woos
you and then warns you. As he prods you away from
yourself, the love of God will warm your heart.

The heart of Dad's preaching was the gospel. Dad's
genius was to read Galatians and Romans *through* the
lens of Luke. Dad recognized that Paul and Jesus were
saying the same thing. And before he preached the gospel to us, he preached it to himself. Dad *was* the woman
at Simon's house weeping at Jesus's feet (Luke 7). Dad
was the tax collector crying out, "God, be merciful to
me, a sinner." Dad *was* the returning prodigal; and
he *was* the older brother. He was, as he loved to say,
one beggar telling another beggar where to find bread!
Enjoy the feast!

Paul Miller

Introduction

Through our many years together, Jack was always telling stories about how Jesus had changed people. Now it's my turn to tell you how the gospel of Jesus Christ changed him. Jack wasn't always so in love with the gospel of grace. In the early 1970s, he was a professor at Westminster Seminary in Philadelphia, and a pastor of a small church. After a few years, he became frustrated with his work in both places, feeling that nothing he did was making a difference in people's lives. So he resigned as a seminary professor and a pastor blaming the institution and his congregation. But, as he said in one of his sermons, it turns out that he was better a detecting pride in others than in himself.

God, in his mercy, did eventually show Jack that his struggles started with *his* pride and self-sufficiency, and he turned to Jesus in repentance and asked for forgiveness and help. He said that his conviction of deep sin and his joy in God's love for him through the cross of Christ was like a conversion. It changed his life and ministry forever. He took back his resignations, and we went on a sabbatical to Spain where for three months he soaked himself in the great missionary promises of the Bible. He returned a changed man. His preaching and teaching were now Christ-centered and, instead of just staying in the classroom and the pulpit, he took the message of God's love for sinners out into the streets and parks, to wherever people gathered. Jack said that he saw God change more people in the next two years than he had in his many prior years of ministry.

I began to hear the gospel explained with a new passion and clarity, using words I hadn't understood before: *orphans, sons and daughters, flesh and Spirit, repentance and forgiveness, humility and self-righteousness,* and *faith and legalism.* Jack kept saying, "Believe and you will live." Under his preaching, the new church he planted, New Life, began to grow. We opened our home to all kinds of needy people, including the mentally ill and addicted. Many of these troubled people turned to God and prayed for the grace to live to please him. Eventually the message of God's grace for sinners changed even me—a self-righteous, legalistic, pull-yourself-together-and-then-God-will-love-you kind of sinner.

Ugandan refugees came to Westminster and lived with us too. The deeply troubled world of Uganda under Amin opened up to us and to World Harvest, now Serge—the new mission Jack and others founded on the principles of the gospel.

You have in your hand 366 excerpts from Jack's sermons. They are filled with challenges to understand how deeply broken we are by sin, to go to Christ in repentance and faith, to remember the love of the Father and the gift of the Holy Spirit, and to pray constantly as sons and daughters of the living God. Jack never thought these truths were simply so we could feel better about ourselves or make the Christian life easier. He taught that the gift of the Spirit always overflows to the world and touches others with the good news of repentance and forgiveness of sins. We are the carriers of that gift. It's meant to be shared. Jack shared it with me, the rest of our family, the people at New Life Church, hitchhikers he picked up, men and women he met on the streets, doctors and nurses when he was ill, his seatmates on airplanes, and, eventually with people all over the world. Jack believed and lived the message of the good news of sins forgiven, death destroyed, and life everlasting with the God who loved him.

I was telling a friend about these devotions based on Jack's preaching, and she told me that, after listening to one of Jack's sermons, her thirteen-year-old son went outside to the church parking lot and gave his life to Christ. That was not something Jack did; it was the power of the risen Christ. Jack went to be with Jesus, his faithful Savior and Friend, many years ago. But the power of the gospel to change hearts continues to grow and spread throughout the world. It changed him. It changed me. It can certainly change you. Read these excerpts slowly and prayerfully, asking the Spirit to fill you with the power of the risen Christ. Then go by faith and share the love of Christ with someone else.

Rose Marie Miller

A Note from the Editors

Years ago when I finished putting together my dad's book of letters, *The Heart of a Servant Leader*, I thought our writing partnership was finished. But God had other plans. The opportunity to create a devotional based on his sermons was too good to pass up—Dad's preaching was always the best way to hear the gospel from him.

Dad often has been quoted as saying "Cheer up! You are worse than you think" and "Cheer up! God loves you more than you know!" and as we listened to his sermons and created these devotions that's what we heard—the bad news that we were completely broken by our sins and the good news that the love of the Father sent his Son to die for those sins and give us life in the Spirit now and eternal life with him forever.

Creating this devotional was a joint project with Nancy Winter, Gretchen Logterman, and myself all working together for the last two years. All three of us listened to sermons and created devotions, Nancy and I did the editing, and then Nancy did the hard work of arranging them. In some cases, the devotions consider the same passage of Scripture over several days. At other times, themes and topics are spread throughout each month. I went over the devotions many times to make sure that each one faithfully represents my dad's preaching and the God he loved.

One day when I was talking with Gretchen about listening to the sermons, she said, "Your father's sermons have been God's grace to me." They were also God's grace to me as every morning I listened to my dad talking about the love of God in Christ for weak, needy sinners like myself. Our hope and prayer is that these devotions will also be God's grace to you. If you would like to hear more from Dad, his sermons are now available at newgrowthpress.com.

Barbara Miller Juliani
Nancy Winter
Gretchen Logterman

January 1

Because you are sons, God has sent the Spirit of his
Son into our hearts, crying, "Abba! Father!"
Galatians 4:6

Because God has made you his child, you don't have
to view yourself as an orphan any more, but as an
insider, as someone who belongs. God sent his Son to
set us free from the law and has now enabled us to be
in fellowship with him by giving us his Spirit who lives
inside us and cries, "Abba, Father." We are no longer
orphans, no longer slaves, but sons and daughters who
can afford to be honest because we belong to our heavenly Father. We're part of his spiritual family through
faith in his Son.

Being God's dearly loved child means that we can
start to think spiritually. We learn to think God's way;
to see our experiences—especially the painful ones—
through the eyes of Christ. What are the areas in your
life where you think like an orphan? Where are you living as if there is no God, no forgiveness, no hope, and
no Holy Spirit to change you and others? Identify and
reject an orphan viewpoint in yourself.

Listen to the gospel of Jesus Christ by faith. When
you believe the gospel of Jesus Christ, it changes you.
When you hear by faith, powerful living follows—a life
characterized by faith that expresses itself in loving others in amazing ways.

January 2

And the Word became flesh and dwelt among us, and
we have seen his glory, glory as of the only Son from
the Father, full of grace and truth. John 1:14

Did you know that the way up is down? The idea of the highest becoming the lowest brings with it a view of glory that is hard to digest. We think of glory as ambition realized, fame accomplished. Jesus's glory, however, is revealed in his humility and suffering on the cross.

In the same way, his glory is revealed in you as you suffer and as you are humbled. The idea is that you go down before you go across; that you humble yourself and become Christlike in your love and tenderness and kindness, before you go across to your neighbor or across the seas to anybody else. Only as you get down on your knees in prayer and acknowledge your neediness does God really teach you and use you. Sadly, we often go in the opposite direction. We try to build ourselves up so we can be strong and minister to people out of our strength. Our idea of salvation is to get stronger, clean ourselves up, and get nearer to God, all in our own strength by our own willpower. Instead, the gospel is that Jesus went all the way down to the pit to save you. He doesn't save good people; he saves sinners. There's where the power is: when you know who you really are, you tell him the truth, and he meets you.

January 3

Count it all joy . . . when you meet trials of various
kinds, for you know that the testing of your faith
produces steadfastness. James 1:2–3

Jesus may have been tempted to come down off the cross, but he didn't; he endured to the end. Hebrews 2:10 speaks of Jesus being made perfect through suffering. This does not mean that Jesus went from a sinful state to a sinless state; instead, it means that he went from a less mature state to a more mature state. This involved a strengthening of his character, so he could endure the unendurable experience of bearing away our sins.

If Jesus had to be strengthened, we too have to be strengthened for our particular callings. Perseverance is developed through testing. During the process, you will begin to have joy as you let go of things. One of the reasons we are joyless is that we're afraid of what *might* happen, or we're disappointed by what *did* happen. Sometimes what happened causes me to be afraid of what might happen. But perseverance through the struggle begins to change our whole way of seeing things. As we persevere we begin to let go of the baggage we carry. Sometimes our baggage has to be almost ripped from our hands, but as we release it, joy comes because there are fewer things acting as a barrier between God and ourselves.

January 4

When Jesus saw their faith, he said to the paralytic,
"Take heart, my son; your sins are forgiven."
Matthew 9:2

To the paralyzed man, why doesn't Jesus say first, "Take up your mat and walk"? It's because forgiveness of sins is the biggest thing that Jesus ever does for anyone.

Jesus does see sickness and death as enemies, but he knows that the reason they are in the world is because there is sin. So when he comes to earth and begins to conquer sickness and death, he announces that his kingdom is one of forgiveness. He introduces us to a kingdom of love, and he's inviting you to personalize the passage. You may not want to look at yourself or face the truth, but Jesus knows you through and through. He loves you, and he invites you to believe in him, to receive him, and to believe in the forgiveness of your sins.

Never again look at your sins apart from Christ. You can't handle them. You'll either suppress them and deny that they're there, or if you see how bad they are, they will overwhelm you. Learn to view your mistakes, your failings, and your transgressions in the light of Jesus's forgiveness.

January 5

When the crowds saw it . . . they glorified God, who had given such authority to men. Matthew 9:8

If you know your sins are forgiven, it changes the way you think about yourself and your life. Are you ever troubled by negative thoughts and wonder why things don't work for you? If you know you're forgiven, you can acknowledge that even the most negative thing in your life is under Jesus's blood. You never have to walk in the darkness. Do you believe that? That's where faith responds in praise. The nature of praise is to teach us to look away from ourselves.

What is repentance? Repentance is returning to God as the center. The detached comes back to where it was designed to be. Repentance is simply a way of finding God again, of claiming your Father, of claiming your forgiveness. And what is praise? If repentance is coming to God as the center, praise is lifting up God as the center. Isn't Jesus worth praising? Isn't he worth making the center of your life? He can take fear out of your life and fill you with glory. Doesn't that make you want to praise Jesus, to live for his glory? If you're forgiven much, you'll love much. If you're forgiven little, you'll love little. If you're forgiven little, you'll praise little. So be a big sinner and get a big Savior. You're forgiven; you don't have to defend yourself any longer; now you can have a heart full of praise for what God has done for you.

5

January 6

Blessed is the man who remains steadfast under trial,
for when he has stood the test he will receive the crown
of life, which God has promised to those who love him.
James 1:12

What is the difference between a trial and a temptation? A trial is a situation that you usually don't have any choice but to go through. In the midst of a trial, you may be tempted to think that God is wrong in what he's doing, and to take a shortcut solution to end it. In your desire to find relief from the circumstances that seem so oppressive, you turn to the wrong things. So the trial leads into a test, which leads into a temptation. In response, you make either the right or the wrong decision.

In the Bible we learn that something special comes out of a willingness to endure tough situations. The idea is that when you persevere and endure a trial rather than run away from it, God blesses you. The height of that blessing is that you know your destination is settled. How do you know you really believe what you say you believe? In a trial, if you persevere, humble yourself, and let your pride be broken, you know you have faith. You are living out what you are by your new nature. You are producing the fruit of the Spirit, which gives you increased confidence that you really belong to Christ.

January 7

Blessed is the man who remains steadfast under trial,
for when he has stood the test he will receive the crown
of life, which God has promised to those who love him.
James 1:12

Have you ever experienced a trial that seemed unendurable? As you go through this kind of trial you find God is present with you in a way he had never been before. God brings to you a joy and a peace that is based, not upon what is seen, but upon what is unseen—his unseen blessing and his unseen promise. You begin to know God because other things you trusted in are stripped away. You begin to have a warmth, a mellowness, and a joy. You're not so hard on yourself anymore, and you begin to see that God used even your sin as part of his plan.

Often people look at their past and see sins and failures, and they plan the rest of their lives as though they were failures. They measure their lives by what they did back in some mud puddle. That past sin is certainly something to repent of and turn away from— you don't do it again, and you do everything to make it right—but then you get up and go on, rejoicing that God has forgiven you. You have Christ. You have the Spirit. And if you have these things, you're so rich! You have a purpose. You belong. And you can endure anything, even the present unendurable trial.

January 8

Beloved, let us love one another, for love is from God,
and whoever loves has been born of God and knows
God. Anyone who does not love does not know God,
because God is love. 1 John 4:7–8

The high point of the Bible is in three simple words: God is love. Love comes from God. Everyone who loves has been born of God. If we love, we have moved from a natural state into a spiritual state—we have been born of God. When we've been born of God, we look like God and God is love. Do you love people because God loves you? Those who do not love—those who hate—their brother will not have a part in the things of God, a part in his aggressive love. In other words, if you don't love one another, then you don't belong to God. Ignoring people and being indifferent or callous to them is not neutral; it's hatred.

We can't pretend we don't know what real love looks like because God showed us love by sending his one and only Son into the world that we might live through him. He identified with us in order to bring us redemption. And since God loved us, let us also love one another. Because our sins have been forgiven, we can give of ourselves to others. We have the Spirit of God, we are children of God, and we are free to love.

January 9

No one has ever seen God; but if we love one another,
God lives in us and his love is made complete in us.
1 John 4:12 (NIV)

Everyone who is born into this world is made in the image of God. We have an original dignity, which has been corrupted by sin and disobedience. Sin has touched all of us, made us unclean—like spiritual lepers. But God has given us a new birth, and his image has been made new in us again. We are still imperfect, but in Christ, we are clean, new, and alive. God's love is made complete in us.

Now, I would have said the love of God was complete on the cross and he couldn't go any further than that. At the cross he went down so deep that no matter how depraved we are, he went deeper and brought us up. But God was not satisfied yet. He said his love was not complete until we express that love by loving one another. His love is made complete in you. You are the visible expression of God's work on the cross. Your actions, your deeds, your kindness, your patience, your forgiving others is all part of God's glory in this world. This explains what Jesus meant when he said that his church is his glory in the world (see John 17). You are Christ's glory. You are his radiance whenever you show love to one another.

January 10

There is no fear in love, but perfect love casts out fear.
For fear has to do with punishment, and whoever fears
has not been perfected in love. 1 John 4:18

How do we love others in a way that goes beyond mere words and ideas? It's done by the Holy Spirit who lives in us and fills us with God's love for people. Claim what is there.

What a relief! Are you tied up in knots? Are you afraid of many things? Why are we so selfish? Why don't we just naturally grab all the other spiritual lepers and take them in our arms? We're afraid of getting hurt—afraid of suffering. But if you will not suffer for God, you can't really understand God's suffering for you. What we see in Christ is a suffering, atoning love. Once we see its magnitude and the Spirit teaches us to rely on it, we don't think so much about our own suffering. As we are compelled by God's love, it becomes our privilege not only to believe in him, but also to suffer with him (Philippians 1:29). When we love one another and that love comes to maturity, we are bold because perfect love drives out fear. Most of us have had the reverse experience: perfect fear has driven out love. Do not accept the lies of Satan that you're not loved. Instead enter into the sacrificial love of God for you where there is no room for fear.

January 11

Who is it that overcomes the world except the one who believes that Jesus is the Son of God? 1 John 5:5

The world is strong, but if you believe in Jesus Christ—that he has come in the flesh—you are an overcomer. Intense preoccupation with self is the opposite of faith, but believe in Jesus and you will be filled with the faith that overcomes the world. Everyone who believes that Jesus is the Christ is born of God.

The power of God is the main idea in this victory. Through the powerful work of God in this new birth, we believe in Christ, and because we believe in him we love the Father and, out of that love, we love the children. This love expresses itself in deeds that we call obedience. We believe, we love, and we obey. Remember God's power is yours in the stress, pain, and struggles of life. By faith, you can experience his power, and in the midst of your weakness, struggles, sins, and failures, you will overcome. But note, the emphasis is not on the victorious person, but on the victorious power. If you begin to think of yourself as the victorious person, you could easily go up like a rocket and down like a rock. The glory of what you are is the work of God, and if you're the work of God, you can't ultimately be defeated by the world.

January 12

Everyone who believes that Jesus is the Christ has been
born of God, and everyone who loves the Father loves
whoever has been born of him. 1 John 5:1

Real power is found in Jesus. Believing that he has
come in the flesh gives us the ability to do the
things that defeat the world. Living for oneself, loving
oneself, is the essence of worldliness and brings with it
fear and anxiety. But we don't have to stay stuck there.
This is because we have Jesus, a real Savior, whom we
can meet anytime, in any problem. He is doing a powerful work in our lives. He's never been defeated yet.

When you believe in Jesus, faith produces love and
obedience. Faith unites you to Christ and brings you
into his family—the Trinity—where you really belong.
You look into your Father's face every time you hear
about the love of Jesus and memories are healed. Faith
goes down into the disappointments, pulls them out,
and begins to make a new life that matters. The love
for the world inside you starts to die because your connection to it—your love for it—has been severed. Just
as the love of the world can drive out the love of the
Father, the love of the Father expels the horrible preoccupation with self that dominates us.

January 13

This is he who came by water and blood—Jesus Christ;
not by the water only but by the water and the blood.
And the Spirit is the one who testifies, because the
Spirit is the truth. 1 John 5:6

How does faith grow? When we don't have an assurance of God's love, we don't want to be in his presence because of our sin. We think of God as a tyrant or harsh judge who has never really forgiven us; or maybe he's forgiven some of our sins but not all of them, especially not the habitual ones.

Faith can't flourish when you see God this way because all you see is your guilt rather than Christ's loving forgiveness through his blood. Faith looks at least ten times more at Christ than at your sin. Then you can face sin honestly and say, "Yes, it's really there, and I want to get rid of it." But you do so out of the strength of knowing you are loved. Jesus went to the cross and shed real blood. It was a real salvation that guarantees real forgiveness, a real resurrection, and a real flow of life to us. Because of this, we have the growing assurance that we have life. Part of our growth is to say that my sinful self has been crucified with Christ. The blood of Christ has taken away my sin and guilt, and the dominant rule in my life is now the cross. Faith looks to Christ and finds life.

January 14

[Christ] emptied himself, by taking the form of a
servant, being born in the likeness of men. And . . . he
humbled himself by becoming obedient to the point of
death, even death on a cross. Philippians 2:7–8

Jesus emptied himself—made himself nothing. He took the form of a servant, and he was made in human likeness—a great step down from being equal with the Father. He took a second step down by humbling himself and becoming obedient to the point of death. Then he took a third step down by dying the death of the criminal and the sinner on the cross. He goes all the way down and down and down to redeem you and me.

God proves that he really loves you by the gift of his Son. He's telling you this to melt your heart. He wants you to see that you don't need to be ruled by fear because he controls everything. God's great work of redemption is at the center of history, which is moving toward a great destination. That destination is the glory of the Father in Jesus Christ in which we'll all be enjoying one another and enjoying God throughout eternity. If you're a part of that plan, it can make you so excited that you might even forget to worry for awhile.

January 15

Do nothing from selfish ambition or conceit, but in
humility count others more significant than yourselves.
Philippians 2:3

Be humble. Cultivate unity. Think of others more
than yourself. But tie it to the cross. That's where
we see tenderness revealed, because when Jesus died
there, he died for you and me. He had your name in his
heart. Do you believe that?

When Jesus died on the cross he died for people.
But not just for people in the abstract—he died for me.
He died for you. When he died on the cross and he
cried out, "My God, my God, why have you forsaken
me?" (Matthew 27:46), the answer was that he was forsaken because of my sin and your sin. God's love for us
is a very personal love. When you see that kind of love,
it expels from you the other passions that fill you—
jealousy, envy, and all the rest. He was rich, but he
became poor for my sake. He really loved me, still loves
me, and will continue to love me. He gave up his reputation for me, and therefore I must choose to have a certain mindset, a certain attitude, a certain point of view.
If you think about all issues against this background of
Jesus's redemption and God's plan for the ages, you can
have a new attitude. You forgive and you bless because
you've been forgiven and you've been blessed.

January 16

"Lord, how often will my brother sin against me,
and I forgive him? As many as seven times?"
Jesus said . . . "I do not say to you seven times,
but seventy-seven times." Matthew 18:21–22

Jesus doesn't teach about forgiveness to accuse us but rather to encourage us. He wants us to be alarmed at our own weakness and cry out to him. He's not trying to shake our faith or our confidence; he just wants it to be unthinkable that we would have any lifestyle other than the lifestyle of forgiveness.

Kindness and compassion for one another flow out of the atonement of Jesus. I realized how bad a sinner I was when God in his mercy sent his Spirit to me and convicted me and humbled me. Then I knew that the blood of Christ took away my sin. I received him by faith, and I believed in him. Now I know that God approves of me; I'm under the umbrella of his permanent blessing. That encourages me to daily confess my sins, including the sins of judging, cursing, and condemning others. You may describe it more politely by saying, "I tend to freeze people out when they don't do the right thing." But God encourages us out of his great redemption and the power of the Spirit to live this new life he has given us. We have been forgiven in Christ and we are thankful. Out of that thankfulness, we live a new life of forgiveness toward others.

January 17

If we confess our sins, he is faithful and just to forgive
us our sins and to cleanse us from all unrighteousness.
1 John 1:9

Recognizing and confessing sin is a normal part of the Christian life. God didn't declare us righteous because of Christ and then leave us to wallow in sin. Rather, he has an ongoing strategy for us that involves getting rid of more and more sin. It's like living in a dim room that appears clean, and then pulling up the shades or turning on the light, only to see that it is really dusty and dirty. Even though the room feels dirtier now than before, the dirt was there all along.

When we walk in the light of the Lord and struggle to love people, we begin to see more things wrong with us. What's more, the devil says, "There's no hope for you. God couldn't love somebody as bad as you." The truth is that all along you were this bad, this messed up, and this selfish. It was only as the light came in that you saw all these problems. This is a signal, not for despair, but for hope! Don't be depressed by what you see, but rather learn to own up to your sins by faith and disown them by confessing them. If you confess your sins, they really are forgiven. You can go forward to love others in ways you never dreamed possible.

January 18

[Jesus] said to her, "Your sins are forgiven." Luke 7:48

When you repent and come to Jesus, you come to a risen Savior who is praying for you. When the sinful woman anoints Jesus's feet in the house of Simon the Pharisee, Jesus first turns to Simon and tells him that her sins are forgiven. Because of his coming sacrifice on the cross, Jesus can guarantee that she is declared legally righteous (justified) in the sight of God.

But justification is more than a fact *about* you; it's also a declaration *to* you. So next, Jesus says to the woman—to her very soul—"Your sins are forgiven!" Who is daring enough to contradict Jesus? "Who shall bring any charge against God's elect? It is God who justifies. Who is to condemn? Christ Jesus is the one who died—more than that, who was raised—who is at the right hand of God, who indeed is interceding for us" (Romans 8:33–34). Jesus looks on you and says, "Your sins are forgiven. I have said it! My forgiveness brings you peace with God and peace of mind." Jesus doesn't carry a grudge and neither does his Father. When Jesus forgives your sins, they are completely forgiven. Whenever you repent, whenever you come back to him by faith, you are always in his peace. Do you believe that?

January 19

[Jesus] said to the woman, "Your faith has saved you; go in peace." Luke 7:50

We often think that sins of *commission* are far worse than sins of *omission*. Certainly they often trouble us more. But in this story Jesus wants Simon to understand that what he *omitted* to do for Jesus (no water for his feet, no kiss, and no anointing) was just as serious as the sins that the "sinful" woman had *committed*.

To Simon, Jesus says, "He who is forgiven little, loves little" (Luke 7:47). What Simon thinks of as an advantage (not committing sins everyone notices), Jesus calls a disadvantage. Because Simon isn't aware of his sins and has judged the sinful woman's sins to be worse than his own, he misses out on Jesus's forgiveness and love and on the blessing of repentance. The sinful woman experiences that blessing because of what Jesus does for her. Then he gives her a command that translated literally has the sense of continuing action, "Keep going *into* peace." It is well with your soul because Jesus has died. This blessing of peace for the repentant sinner gives courage to seek forgiveness for all sin. This blessing of peace enables us to listen with love to those who are close to us, to replace judgment with kindness, to apologize and say, "I keenly regret that I didn't affirm you." You can be broken before God and know that as you bathe Jesus's feet with your tears, he loves it and he loves you.

January 20

Let us then with confidence draw near to the throne
of grace, that we may receive mercy and find grace to
help in time of need. Hebrews 4:16

Don't be attached to your own agenda; be attached to Jesus. If you want to be effective, you need to recognize the way pride has a deep hold on your life. Pride can take many different forms. What makes you feel secure? What makes you feel insecure? Do you live for your own glory? Recognizing your egocentricity throws a different light on your sin. You are able to see sin as against God's glory and holiness. When you see how sin and pride has infected your life, then you will also know that you are incapable of changing yourself and God's grace is your only hope.

When you know that the fight with the flesh is not only hard or difficult, but impossible, you will learn to pray. The heart of grace is coming to God in prayer knowing you have nothing to bring—no wisdom, no righteousness. God promises it all for the asking through Jesus Christ. Lay hold of the love of God for you and walk in that love day by day. Then you will find that the Christian life is enjoyable—not a trap or a prison but a fellowship of life. Let us approach the throne of grace with confidence.

January 21

The grace of the Lord Jesus Christ and the love of God
and the fellowship of the Holy Spirit be with you all.
2 Corinthians 13:14

When you first come to Christ, you are justified by faith. God, the Judge, declares you legally righteous. Justification requires no cooperation on your part; you receive it by faith alone. Sanctification on the other hand, the lifelong process by which the justified are made holy, requires your cooperation. In sanctification, God can be thought of as a surgeon whose job it is to cut corruption out of your heart. The power by which you become holy is one hundred percent God's, but it also requires one hundred percent of your obedience. Jesus says, "You therefore must be perfect, as your heavenly Father is perfect" (Matthew 5:48). If you find this command depressing, remember you were never supposed to do this in your own strength. Pray and trust. Where there is trust, God moves in. Believe that God is for you and will help you.

Right where you are, God wants to give you the spiritual power to live a holy life. How beautiful it is to be justified, but don't make it the end of the Christian life! Don't forget that the point of faith, the point of our Christian walk is that we might know the love of God and live in his love for others. God says, "You were made for me and you'll never have peace until you belong to me completely."

21

January 22

Not to us, O Lord, not to us, but to your name
give glory, for the sake of your steadfast love
and your faithfulness! Psalm 115:1

After this first verse, the psalmist goes on to describe
lifeless idols that people worship and concludes,
"Those who make them become like them; so do all
who trust in them" (Psalm 115:8). Those who worship
lifeless idols are themselves lifeless. Sanctification is
about daily putting off idols, our God-substitutes, and
putting on Jesus Christ and his love. We continuously
manufacture new idols. As soon as one is dealt with,
another rears its ugly head. The process of putting off
has to be a daily process—sanctification is a daily walk.

The problem is not just the idols themselves, but
the deeper problem of why we make them. We make
idols—we center our lives on everything except God—
because we have a deep need to be in control. God,
however, wants us to submit to his will and not strive
for our own. God wants you to be holy, to love him
completely, to give all glory to him. Have you gone to
Jesus and asked him to show you your idols? Do you
believe he will give you what you need? Repent for
having loved and served many things other than Jesus.
Repent of making an idol out of control. Accept the joy
of God's presence.

January 23

And he arose and came to his father. But while
he was still a long way off, his father saw him
and felt compassion, and ran and embraced him
and kissed him. Luke 15:20

When a son or daughter goes astray, our first instinct is not to go on a love offensive; instead, our first concern usually is for our own reputation. Next, we obsess over what we see as our own failure. Intense self-analysis is followed by intense discussion followed by intense anger at the prodigal followed by intense—probably shallow—prayer followed by intense condemnation.

There's value in working toward an objective perspective. Remember that you are secure in Christ, that you have been justified by faith in Christ, that you are a child of the King. Knowing this, you can start to see the struggle in a positive light. Prayer is not effective when all you see are the offenses of the other person. You must get to the point where you enlist prayer for yourself! Ask God to take away areas of blindness. Ask God for grace to detach yourself from over-involvement in the situation. Get out of the way and let the Holy Spirit work. Step back and recognize God's plan. After all, the whole relationship, by faith, is under the blood and righteousness of Christ. Work on being a friend to the other person. This is hard for the parent whose orientation is correction not acceptance. Accept the person where they are. Practice ongoing forgiveness and blessing.

January 24

Obey your earthly masters with fear and trembling,
with a sincere heart, as you would Christ. Ephesians 6:5

Holiness begins with your work. Are you cooperating with God's work in the world, or are you fighting it? Even as a Christian, you can be fighting against what God wants to do in your life. Many Christians are unhappy in their work; they fail to see any purpose in it and view it as a dead end. Amidst the daily, sometimes boring, often dull routine, you begin to lose any sense of purpose or glory.

I want to challenge you to consider that holiness begins with your work. The way you do your job and the purpose that you bring to it is where you begin to be holy in your Christian walk. It is great to be fulfilled by your work, but that isn't the purpose of work. Your primary purpose is to glorify God in your work. There's a wide gap between what you would naturally and instinctively do and what you do by his grace. That wide gap is the glory of God. When you do a routine job, whether around the home or in the office, without complaining or bitterness, as unto the Lord, there is glory in it. So go to your job with a holy attitude.

January 25

The Lord your God is in your midst, a mighty one
who will save; he will rejoice over you with gladness; he
will quiet you by his love; he will exult over you
with loud singing. Zephaniah 3:17

Jesus is the mighty warrior who saves you from your self-centered, self-focused, self-justifying life. God delights in you; he looks at you and is content in his love. This liberates you from many sins. How can you not be thankful for that kind of love! His love is not based on anything good that you have done. His love is founded on his free grace alone based on the work of Christ. Christ, on the cross, delivered you from the day of wrath, and now you can bask in the contented love of God.

This powerful, loving God will not condemn you. Sin has been condemned in Christ. You are liberated; you are free to desire holiness. You are free to give yourself to God by faith. The whole point of the phrase, "God is a mighty one who will save," is that God himself is the Savior. You might feel burdened and weighed down by all the things you feel you ought to do for God, or by all of your repeated sins, but remember, God is your Savior. When Jesus died on the cross, your day of wrath was over—it is finished.

January 26

No unbelief made [Abraham] waver concerning the
promise of God, but he grew strong in his faith as he
gave glory to God, fully convinced that God was able to
do what he had promised. Romans 4:20–21

God tells an elderly Abraham and Sarah that they
will soon have a child, together. This announcement elicits laughter of unbelief from both Abraham
and Sarah (Genesis 17:17; 18:12). In essence God is
saying, "Sarah, you're 90; Abraham, you're 100. I know
this and I promise that this is the year you are going
to have a child. This is the year I want your faith to
grow!" God says, "Is anything too hard for the LORD?"
(Genesis 18:14a). This question is designed to build
their faith—to build their confidence in God. God
has tested them over the years, and each test has taught
them more about God.

To fulfill the promise to give these seniors a son,
God will have to overcome the course of nature. This
is a picture of grace as being all of God and nothing
of us. Faith is about resting entirely on God's promise. God often uses his own methods to fulfill his plan.
God made promises to Abraham and Sarah, promises
of offspring, but time stripped away everything they
depended upon to bring God's promises to fruition.
This is how God works: he makes the promises and
then he insists upon accomplishing his work, his way.
This is where faith comes in.

January 27

That I may gain Christ and be found in him, not
having a righteousness of my own that comes from
the law, but that which comes through faith in Christ,
the righteousness from God that depends on faith.
Philippians 3:8–9

Unless you're assured that God loves you, it's pretty
hard to do anything in the Christian life. You set
out to try to change something in yourself, and you
have this vague feeling that you're going to mess it up
anyway. You're convinced that God is always planning
some way to trip you up, and none of your efforts really
lead to anything. There's no freedom, no power, no joy.

What Paul is talking about is getting your roots
down into Christ and his righteousness, so that you can
have the assurance that God loves you and that never
again do you have to try to build your own righteousness. Your foundation is only in Christ. Paul points out
that this is a process. In Philippians 3:12, he writes,
"Not that I have already obtained this." Tree roots are
a good picture of this in that they continue to grow
down into what is unchangeable soil. In the same way,
the foundation of our assurance of God's love for us is
Christ, and we must continue to root ourselves more
deeply in him.

January 28

Not that I have already obtained all this or am already
perfect, but I press on to make it my own, because
Christ Jesus has made me his own. Philippians 3:12

Many people feel that their religion is so right that they have already arrived, and their main job is to criticize those who haven't arrived. But the fact that we have assurance of forgiveness and God's love for us, should not teach us to have contempt for others. Instead we are called to press on, to run to get what we already have.

This is strange, but true. You have already been grabbed by Christ and had your relationship with God changed, but now you're running after the same Christ. He's your supreme value, and you're moving after him. Paul writes very personally about this. He doesn't say we; he says I. He's an apostle of God, charged with speaking the truth of God, but now he's giving a personal example of how he, as a human being, does it. And he says, in effect, I have only the righteousness of Christ for my foundation, for my acceptance with God, but I am giving it everything I've got. He's very emphatic about the personal aspect here, as he shares his supreme value: "Forgetting what lies behind and straining forward to what lies ahead, I press on toward the goal for the prize of the upward call of God in Christ Jesus" (Philippians 3:13–14).

January 29

"I have set before you an open door, which no one is able to shut. I know that you have but little power, and yet you have kept my word and have not denied my name." Revelation 3:8

If I said these words, you might be intrigued for a while, but soon you would know that my words have little power. This is not the way it is for Jesus. In Revelation we see a different Jesus than the one who walked the roads of Palestine. Now he is risen and reigning and fully revealed as the one who is holy and true (Revelation 6:10). He is the Lord of history; he is the King of kings and Lord of lords. Everything is under his sovereign control. This risen, exalted Jesus sets the door of opportunity ajar. What's more, Jesus has the key of David (Revelation 3:7), the key of salvation and power.

We see many doors set before us that we don't necessarily choose; but if we belong to Christ and the open door is there, he can give us the grace and power to walk through it. The door may be at the very place where you think you cannot function, but, nonetheless, it will be open, Christ will hold the key, and it will be a door of power. "I know that you have little power," Jesus says. Do you know this? Revival comes when people acknowledge their weakness. Grace is for the needy. Mercy is for those who cry out to God.

January 30

When they saw him, they worshiped him,
but some doubted. Matthew 28:17

Gathered on the mountain to receive the Great Commission, some doubted. What did they doubt? They doubted the power of God. When Jesus on the cross cried out and gave up his spirit, the curtain in the temple was torn in two from top to bottom like paper (Matthew 27:50). Then came the earthquake. Jesus was crucified in weakness, but don't underestimate his power. Even as he gave up his spirit, the power of his death was changing the course of the natural world.

Eleven disciples go and meet the one who was crucified in weakness but raised in power and who now is crowned King of kings and Lord of lords. Jesus declares, "All authority . . . has been given to me" (Matthew 28:18). This authority is invisible; however, it doesn't mean he is powerless. This is where so many people today go astray. They think Jesus is weak. Jesus brought you to himself. He is in control of all things, and he will close history. "He disarmed the rulers and authorities and put them to open shame, by triumphing over them in him" (Colossians 2:15). Jesus defeated the devil and his minions at the cross. He is Lord over whatever you worship—your idols, your fears. If Jesus masters you, he can change you. If he can defeat all these enemies, he can defeat yours too. He deserves your confidence and your trust.

January 31

Go therefore and make disciples of all nations,
baptizing them in the name of the Father and of the
Son and of the Holy Spirit, teaching them to observe all
that I have commanded you. Matthew 28:19–20

Jesus's instruction to teach others what he had commanded is not legalism. We know this because on that other mountain where Jesus delivered his great sermon (see Matthew 5—7), what he emphasizes is the absolute impossibility of pleasing God without relying on God's grace. The Sermon on the Mount is about giving up your rights through loving others. Fight for truth certainly; but in the midst of the fight trust God to enable you to forgive, put on love, bless your enemies, and show kindness where you wouldn't otherwise.

Jesus, at the Last Supper, talks about how forgiveness is central: "This is my blood . . . poured out for many for the forgiveness of sins" (Matthew 26:28). The last chapter in history is being written by Jesus, and he asserts that it begins with the forgiveness of sins. Our hearts have been melted by what Jesus did on the cross. He has accepted me and made me his child through faith. God calls us to humble ourselves, not to judge, not to be proud or self-righteous. Whatever bad habit you are struggling with, ask Jesus to deal not only with it, but also with the pride and self-sufficiency and arrogance beneath it. Then, because we have been forgiven much, we forgive others and learn to love them from the heart.

February 1

And behold, I am with you always, to the end
of the age. Matthew 28:20b

Jesus didn't give the Great Commission and then
leave us alone to accomplish it. A friend of mine
who fought in World War II told me that his most
frightening day was when the general stood up in front
of the troops in Italy and delivered a powerful speech
about how they were going to smash through to Rome.
As he spoke, the troops, inspired, felt that it was indeed
possible. But then the general got into his staff car and
drove the other way, away from the battlefront. My
friend said that he had never felt so abandoned in all
his life.

Jesus, however, as he sends us, goes with us. Jesus
has left us his Holy Spirit, who now lives in us by faith.
Don't underestimate the power and presence of the
Holy Spirit. There is a big difference between doing
work for God and doing work with God. Take the time
to cultivate a relationship with God, surrendering constantly to his rights, not your own. Allow his authority to become apparent to your mind and heart. The
Holy Spirit makes you alert to the welfare of others. He
gives you a concern for others and for where they are
spiritually. Praying for others is the most meaningful
thing you can do. People who are prayed for are often
the ones who are prepared by God to accept his Word.
Remember: he is with you always.

February 2

Consequently, [Jesus] is able to save to the uttermost those who draw near to God through him, since he always lives to make intercession for them. Hebrews 7:25

God tells Abraham of his plan to judge Sodom. God opens his heart to Abraham, and Abraham opens his heart to God. God wants us to relate to every Sodom—the world—the same way Abraham did, by prayer. Abraham emerges as a man of compassion, a man who prays, a man like Jesus himself. He forgets about himself and prays in the Spirit of Christ giving himself totally to prayer. In Abraham we see a foreshadowing of future intercessors: Moses, Jeremiah, Jesus. Abraham shows concern for the honor of God and urges God to remember his character and not to destroy any righteous person who may live in Sodom. God answers Abraham's prayer by rescuing Lot and his family. In Sodom the deepest issue was self-worship. This is still the issue that lies at the heart of sin today—self-worship.

In worshiping the creature instead of the Creator (Romans 1), we give up the knowledge of God. The glory of God, the purpose for which we were created, has been lost, replaced with a radical devotion to self. Self-worship leads to self-despising when your idol is exposed as flawed. God calls you to humble yourself, forsake self-worship, and seek his will. The only thing you can build your life around that will bring you lasting joy is the glory of God in the face of Jesus Christ.

February 3

By faith Sarah herself received power to conceive, even when she was past the age, since she considered him faithful who had promised. Hebrews 11:11

Finally, Isaac was born. Sarah bore a child by faith and by the power of the Holy Spirit (Galatians 4:29). In the Bible, faith and the power of the Holy Spirit are two sides of the same coin. Faith is a conscious expression of the power of the Holy Spirit. What is the nature of the promise on which Abraham and Sarah's faith was founded? It was God's unconditional promise; as such, it was something that God alone was responsible for. The promise did not depend on them.

An unconditional promise comes as a gift: you do nothing to earn it. The name Isaac means "he laughs." God has been pleased to smile. God has fulfilled his promise. God is with me. God made the promise after, humanly speaking, all possibility of Sarah having a child was past. In fact when God said that the next year Sarah would give birth, she laughed in unbelief. The name Isaac is a constant reminder of how God did it all. In God's unconditional promise, nothing comes by human effort. God's unconditional grace is for the unworthy, for the barren, for the powerless. It's for me and it's for you.

February 4

Who is like the Lord our God, who is seated on high,
who looks far down on the heavens and the earth? He
raises the poor from the dust and lifts the needy from
the ash heap, to make them sit . . . with the princes
of his people. Psalm 113:5–8

This psalm is about the nature of grace: the stooping of the Most High. It has been said that if you don't understand this psalm, you don't understand any of the psalms. In Psalm 113 God is pictured as the Almighty—El Shaddai—who brings praise to his all-powerful name. God's name is so great that it requires that even the enemies of God—the nations (you and me)—be brought in. This is the gospel: those who are far off are brought near by the blood of the cross.

Praise is a form of sanity where you suspend thoughts of the future and dwell in the eternal now lifting up God as the center. True praise involves paying attention to God with a surrendered heart. Even to glance at us requires God's condescension. What we might expect is for the psalm to progress to a glorious vision of the Almighty. But instead we see God visiting the trash heap on the outskirts of town. He visits the destitute—the poorest of the poor, the utterly cast down. God's power is revealed through the weakness of the barren woman (Psalm 113:9), a prominent theme in Scripture. He lifts up the destitute and makes them royalty. This is grace.

February 5

"See that you do not despise one of these little ones. For I tell you that in heaven their angels always see the face of my Father who is in heaven." Matthew 18:10

The worst of our sins is pride. We don't see ourselves as one of the "little ones." But, the less we see ourselves this way, the more vulnerable we are. Our pride leads us to overestimate our ability to be holy. We don't turn to God; we don't rest on his promises. We think we are trusting God, but in reality we are trusting ourselves. Our primary concern is not for God's reputation and glory but for our own. We depend on our own righteousness rather than on the righteousness of Christ.

It is obvious that we need God's divine power, which gives us everything we need for "life and godliness" (2 Peter 1:3). When we are proud, if we feel guilty over a sin, our tendency is to want to clean ourselves up before turning to God. What we don't understand is that if we could make ourselves acceptable to God there would be no need for Christ. The heart of the gospel is that God has given us his Son to take the penalty that we deserve for our sin. Further, God gives us his Spirit—to lead us and to teach us. He makes us *want* to be holy. God does the work as we repent and cling to him. Acting in faith, you don't create something, you claim something.

February 6

"If your brother sins against you, go and tell him his
fault, between you and him alone. If he listens to you,
you have gained your brother." Matthew 18:15

What is our instinct when somebody wrongs us?
Is it to go to that person or to go to someone
else? It's easy to confess somebody else's sin publicly.
However, in the Bible, we learn that gossip is sin—a
lust and an evil passion (Romans 1:29). Don't condemn
others outwardly *or* in your heart—both are sins.

What is God after? God wants us to be holy,
reflecting his character to the world. God's design is
that we "proclaim the excellencies of him who called
[us] out of darkness into his marvelous light" (1 Peter
2:9). God wants to make us a beautiful, holy people,
enjoying him, free, knowing his goodness and greatness. Sin is deceitful. Certain that we are right, we judge
God and we judge people.

But the worst sin is not knowing you have any sin.
When you sin, you move farther and farther from God.
The function of the church is to "exhort one another
every day, as long as it is called 'today,' that none of [us]
may be hardened by the deceitfulness of sin" (Hebrews
3:13).

February 7

"If a man has a hundred sheep, and one of them has
gone astray, does he not leave the ninety-nine on
the mountains and go in search of the one that went
astray? And if he finds it . . . he rejoices over it more
than over the ninety-nine that never went astray."
Matthew 18:12–13

It is easy to forget the attitude we are to have when confronting someone about their sin. The "little ones" (Matthew 18:14) are those who are immature in the faith and prone to stumble. God's care for us is the same as the shepherd's who, when he sees one sheep missing, will go out searching for that one wanderer. The shepherd's heart carries him after that sheep.

This is how we are to view the sinner among us. We are not the judge, but the compassionate searcher. What is hard about all this is that it's not just someone else who is vulnerable; we ALL are vulnerable. We who lead the church are vulnerable. The moment you think you are not is the moment you are the most vulnerable. Just when you think you are ready to serve, ready to bring glory to God, that is when you are in real trouble. Pray for a heart that knows how weak and vulnerable you are. Pray for a heart that forgives and builds up others. Do you believe that all that you need is found in Christ? Come to him. He will rejoice over you.

February 8

We want to know God's will about what we should do or where we should go, but God's will for us is to love and pray for our enemies. When we do this, we show ourselves to be his children. Jesus doesn't tell us to look within ourselves for the strength and power to love; he tells us to look at him and at how he treats sinners. We are to look at the sun and the rain and be reminded of how God blesses everyone. We are then to do the same: love and bless and forgive, continuously.

Jesus's admonition to "Be perfect," isn't only for the exceptionally holy, but for everyone who has been justified through Christ's blood, shed on the cross. Matthew 5 begins with, "Blessed are the poor in spirit." The poor in spirit reach out for what they don't have from a rich God. This is what we have done by accepting the work of Christ on the cross. We need a total humbling to keep these commands and to love our enemies. The perfection of God is that although he hates sin, he continues to show love. We are to let God love through us. Through God we have the power to love, to pray for, and to forgive our enemies. This is God's will for us.

February 9

So you are no longer a slave, but a son; and if a son,
then an heir through God. Galatians 4:7

Do you pretend to have your self-centeredness, your sinful desires (what God calls "the flesh") under control? When I believed in Jesus, I had no idea that I would have such a struggle with sin. Even when we start with the best motives, our self-centeredness can (and does) take over and we can easily self-destruct. There's something compulsive within us that has the capacity to master us.

The reason more people don't experience deliverance, liberation, and progress is that it's standard in evangelical Christianity to pretend that our flesh is under control. We're not so much moral as moralistic. We're not so much obedient to God as obedient to our own rules. And we're much more satisfied with the appearance of being near to God than actually being near to God. Have you ever had this experience: You cried out to God to help you with a problem, and you were delivered? Afterward you thanked God lightly and patted yourself heavily on the back? To begin thinking like a son or a daughter of God instead of like an orphan, you must have a heart of faith that knows you are loved of God, and a heart of humility that recognizes how weak and poor and stumbling and far from God you are. Jesus didn't come to save the half-lost, but to reach into the very pit for us.

February 10

But to all who did receive him, who believed in his
name, he gave the right to become children of God.
John 1:12

Faith is an action word, a verb, that means receiving,
depending upon, needing. It has the idea of weakness in it, of neediness, of constantly going to Christ.
But there's something more in it that you might miss.
Not only is it passive in just collapsing on Christ, but
it's aggressive in that, in your need, you constantly go
to Christ for fullness. It's aggressively seeking Christ.
So when you read the Bible, don't be satisfied unless
you've had something of Christ come to you through
the passage. Come to the Word hungry for Christ. You
have nothing, you need everything, and faith is the way
you go aggressively into Jesus. You want more of him
because he died for you and nobody else did. Jesus loves
you, he lives for you, and he gives you life.

In the midst of suffering and struggle, God meets
you. In your short time on earth, don't be afraid to suffer. Die every day for Christ, wherever you are. You
know who suffers the most in life? The people who are
determined not to suffer. The people who do not want
any pain are the ones who go through the most agony.
There's no place for that in Jesus. You're safe; you're in
the Eternal. The Most High has become the lowest in
order to lift you up to the heights. You're free!

February 11

Now the man Moses was very meek, more than all
people who were on the face of the earth.
Numbers 12:3

While they were slaves in Egypt, more than any-thing Israel needed a deliverer. But their deliv-erer could not have a slave mentality; what's more, he had to be a person of stature, courage, and dignity. In being plucked out of the Nile, adopted by Pharaoh's daughter, and given the best education, Moses was pre-pared to be the deliverer of his people.

Moses who identifies with his brothers in slav-ery and sees himself as the avenger, one day kills an Egyptian guard who is beating a Hebrew slave. Then Israel rejects him as their deliverer, and he flees into the desert where for the next forty years God retrains Moses to make him a fit deliverer for Israel. These forty years are a time of loneliness for Moses. But he isn't only lonely; he is deeply disappointed at his early prom-ise and fading potential. During this time of aloneness in the dust and dirt of the desert, however, God does a great work in proud Moses; God humbles him. In preparation for the exodus of his people, Moses is on a personal exodus, learning to be God's shepherd—God's faithful servant. God is the one who humbles; it's not something we can do for ourselves. God's leader needed stature, courage, and dignity—but more than anything else, he needed to walk humbly with God.

February 12

Where is he who put in the midst of them his Holy
Spirit, who caused his glorious arm to go at the right
hand of Moses, who divided the waters before them to
make for himself an everlasting name? Isaiah 63:11b–12

After leading God's people through the parted Red
Sea, Moses declares, "Your right hand, O LORD,
glorious in power. Your right hand, O LORD, shatters
the enemy" (Exodus 15:6). A long time before this,
while still a young prince in Egypt, Moses had raised
his hand to kill an Egyptian. After this, Moses spent
forty years being retrained by God in the desert. During
this retraining, Moses had to learn that what he needed
to deliver his people was God's right hand and not his
own.

What Moses had to learn, and what God taught
him, was that Moses's hand was powerful only because
he was an instrument of the all-powerful God. God
wields the sword; Moses does not. Moses had to be
trained not to take God's glory for himself. When you
wait and wait and wait, when your problem seems too
great, what God is doing is breaking you so his power
might be visible. By his sacrifice on our behalf we are
redeemed. We can then go to others with mercy and
compassion, humbly, in full knowledge of our own sinfulness. Then God will gain for himself "an everlasting
name." What a splendid reputation he has!

February 13

Grace was given to each one of us according to the measure of Christ's gift. Therefore . . . "When he ascended on high he led a host of captives, and he gave gifts to men." Ephesians 4:7–8

The subject of spiritual gifts conjures up thoughts of abilities, capacities, talents, careers, education, success, and rewards. But these are all byproducts of the grace of Jesus at work. Grace is an inward power that enables us to do what we would not ordinarily want to do. The discussion of spiritual gifts in Ephesians starts off with their origin in the grace of Jesus Christ. We are mostly interested in what our spiritual gifts are, however, the emphasis here is on the power and the authority of Christ, the giver of gifts. The giving comes from outside ourselves.

Grace is a gift; its power is demonstrated in the vast triumph, the massive victory, of the Lord Jesus Christ. Paul emphasizes inward grace to show us that it's not just about what we do; it's about who we are. If you get the "you" straight, then the doing will come straight too. But if you don't know and taste of grace, you're going to be confused in what you're doing. It ought to be tremendously encouraging to think of inward grace as power from the heart of Jesus to the hearts of his people.

February 14

Grace was given to each one of us according to the
measure of Christ's gift. Ephesians 4:7

Christ meets you when you are weak—when you are forced to be honest and say, "I can't handle this." The word *grace* is given priority in the text so that God might meet you in your loneliness and get you to see that what's happened to you is part of your training for his service. The awareness that God loves you in the midst of your hurts is a precious thing to know. We who believe in the Lord Jesus have grace, an inward presence of the Holy Spirit.

We have the power of the Son of God living inside us. But that doesn't mean we can (or have to) do everything. Christ gives us sanity through limits; that is, when Christ gives us grace, he doesn't give all the grace or all the spiritual gifts. The Holy Spirit is unlimited in his distribution of grace, but each of us is limited in our expression of it. That has in it a healing, clarifying, cleansing sanity. We often think that we have to be able to do what someone else can do or that we have to do something very visible. This passage reminds us that we are creatures, made in the image of God, and what he has given us is enough. Isn't it wonderful to be sane and not pretend that you're more or less than you are?

February 15

"First take the log out of your own eye, and then you will see clearly to take out the speck that is in your brother's eye." Luke 6:42b

In Luke 6 Jesus teaches us how to shepherd one another, and specifically how to correct others. Do you criticize others but remain unteachable yourself? If you have a strong desire to fix others, Jesus exhorts you to first fix yourself. However, when you are a leader, it is difficult to correct yourself or even to see your own faults. Taking Jesus's words to heart, I once asked my wife to tell me what one thing she would change about me if she could. Without hesitation she replied, "Jack, you don't listen." I thought I was a good listener! If you dare, ask someone close to you to tell you what one thing they would change about you if they could.

You cannot correct others in love without first being humbled. God can (and will) change you, but you have to start by listening to his Word—allowing your heart to be searched by God's Word. The cross tells us what God had to do to deal with our evil hearts—it exposes us. But the cross also exposes the love of God for us. Ask God to show you the "plank" in your own eye. Correcting others needs to be done out of a humble heart filled with the love of God.

February 16

Jesus told his disciples, "If anyone would come after
me, let him deny himself and take up his cross and
follow me. For whoever would save his life will lose
it, but whoever loses his life for my sake will find it."
Matthew 16:24–25

When Jesus was baptized at the start of his ministry, God publicly declared him to be his Son. Immediately after, led by the Spirit into the wilderness, Jesus faced Satan's testing for forty days. Jesus then "returned in the power of the Spirit to Galilee" (Luke 4:14). Notice the progression: Jesus's identification as God's Son is followed immediately by suffering. His victory over Satan is followed by a release of the Spirit's power. He is matured and goes in the power of the Holy Spirit toward his great purpose—saving his people from their sins.

By shying away from suffering, by rejecting God's will, you may be short-circuiting both your knowledge of God and your growth. If you've told God that there are certain things he can't do with your life and certain sufferings you won't go through, you are cutting off the ministry of the Spirit to you. Power is being unleashed in history, and it only works through those who deny self, take up their cross, and follow Christ.

February 17

"For God so loved the world, that he gave his only Son, that whoever believes in him should not perish but have eternal life. For God did not send his Son into the world to condemn the world, but in order that the world might be saved through him." John 3:16–17

Knowing the Father's will, Jesus does the Father's will and cleanses the temple. Jesus knew why he was on earth. He said, "My food is to do the will of him who sent me and to accomplish his work" (John 4:34). On the cross, Jesus knew his death was accomplishing his Father's will, "When Jesus had received the sour wine, he said, 'It is finished,' and he bowed his head and gave up his spirit" (John 19:30).

Jesus knows the will of his Father; he zeroes in on it; and he completes it. Do we flit from one work to another? My wife says that often I talk about successes but neglect to talk about the hard work and failures along the way. If you don't stick to things, if you don't prepare, if you don't persevere through difficulty, you'll always be frustrated because deep down what you really want is your own way. You want the success, but not the blood and mud that goes with it. Whose will are you doing? There is a Father who loves you so much that he punished his own sinless Son for you. He welcomes you as righteous just as his Son is righteous. Give him your will.

February 18

Have mercy on me, O God, according to your
steadfast love; according to your abundant mercy
blot out my transgressions. Psalm 51:1

David knows that repentance has to do with God first of all. The first part of Psalm 51 talks about grief; the second part, about joy. Repentance includes putting off sin—grieving—and putting on joy—accepting God's forgiveness through Christ's work. Living in sin is insanity. It is about going away from God. Repentance is a return to sanity—an awakening to your desperate need for God's mercy.

Repentance is not only about grief over your sin; it's about turning and heading back to God. David admits that he has sinned, that he is the one who had no mercy, no compassion. David cries out to God acknowledging that he is in desperate need of a God who is not like himself. David desperately needs a compassionate God. God had embraced David, taking him from being a lowly shepherd to a great king. David knows there is nothing in himself to commend him to God, and his opening words in this psalm plead God's character—his steadfast love and abundant mercy—on which David knows he can fully trust. He begs God to blot out his transgressions. David may have once thought he himself was the Messiah; but now he knows he is not. David knows now that he is a sinner in need of the Messiah. Mercy must come to him from without, from God alone.

February 19

Restore to me the joy of your salvation.
Psalm 51:12a

Sin is about giving your heart to something other than God. David's adultery started as an adultery of his heart. If you know the evil in your heart, then you know you need mercy. In Psalm 51, David has a clear-eyed view of his sin. He is not defensive. He doesn't just see his sin and feel half-guilty about it and stew over it; he turns from it. This is the essence of repentance. We don't experience joy, because we don't really repent. We don't turn from our sin and cry out to God for mercy.

Come to God asking him to show you the truth about your rebellious heart. Allow God to make you sane through and through. Along with David, know that God is able to wash you and make you whiter than snow. Don't underestimate the power and glory of the Lord Jesus Christ. The blood of Jesus cleanses from the deepest sin. No matter what you have done, you can have the confidence that God blots out your sin for the sake of Christ. Never again do you have to protect yourself or defend yourself. You can admit the very worst about yourself and turn from it because of Jesus. As you repent daily, you can celebrate and live a life of obedience and fruitfulness.

February 20

Jesus said to him, "Go; your son will live."
The man believed the word that Jesus spoke to him
and went on his way. John 4:50

If we want to see God do a new and mighty work, we're going to have to start by facing our unbelief. Do I really believe when I pray to the Father in the name of Jesus? And, if I believe, do I act on the basis of that belief? Or do I say, "I believe in the name of Jesus," and then walk into my closet and hibernate there bearlike, waiting for the summer to come, waiting for answers to arrive. No, we should pray in our closets with our eyes on Jesus—on his power and promises—believing that his name will cause our prayers to be heard; that the blood of Jesus has made a way for us. Then we step out into our world in faith and express love and kindness to our friends, neighbors, enemies, and strangers.

Even though we are sinners by nature, Christ's blood has cleansed us and made our prayers acceptable. There is no problem you have that won't yield to prayer in the power of that Name. When we have prayed in the name of Jesus, then we can walk forward, obey Christ by faith, and love others by faith. That's how we put feet to our prayers.

February 21

Sometimes my own prayers are pretty feeble. But one thing I don't do. I don't just tack Jesus's name onto the end of them. I try consciously to make the heart of my prayer in Jesus's powerful name. Do you do that too? When you pray, do you rest your case in the reality that the Son of God is interceding at the Father's right hand for you? Do you know that he bears your nature, and that he really understands you, welcomes you, loves you, and wants to hear those prayers?

If there's selfishness and sinfulness in your prayers and you haven't bowed to his will, you can pray about those things and say, "Lord, I don't know how to pray. Please teach me." Is your heart deeply comforted by the kind of assurance that brings? This is the way Jesus himself wants you to pray in his name about your faith struggles and your real troubles. Then believe that he sees you and hears you and is going to act according to his will out of his great love for you and the world.

February 22

"Holy, holy, holy is the LORD of hosts; the whole earth is full of his glory!" Isaiah 6:3

Moses has much to learn about God's holiness and about his own unholiness. Moses sets out on God's mission carrying God's staff along with God's message for Pharaoh: "Israel is my firstborn son, and I say to you, 'Let my son go that he may serve me.' If you refuse to let him go, behold, I will kill your firstborn son" (Exodus 4:22–23). Thinking that his special relationship with God entitles him to special treatment, Moses neglects to circumcise his son. On the way back to Egypt the Lord threatens to kill Moses. To save his life, Moses's wife hastily circumcises their son and throws the bloody foreskin at Moses's feet. Now they learn the significance of that bloody rite: their religion is based on blood.

Moses knew that the message to Pharaoh involved the death of the firstborn, but he didn't see that this same thing applied to him. God the righteous Judge cannot overlook sin: sin is paid for by atoning blood. Circumcision couldn't be ignored or overlooked; it was a prophecy of the atonement of Jesus. Without an understanding of the requirements of God's holiness, Jesus's cross represents what a half-angry God did to reconcile himself to partial sinners. Only against the backdrop of God's holiness do we see the immensity of Christ's work on the cross.

February 23

"I will redeem you with an outstretched arm and with great acts of judgment. I will take you to be my people, and I will be your God." Exodus 6:6b–7a

In response to God's message through Moses, Pharaoh says, "I do not know the LORD, and . . . I will not let Israel go" (Exodus 5:2). To make matters worse, Pharaoh withholds straw from Israel and their brick-making becomes even more arduous. Moses is crushed; Israel hates him and his God.

How often do we feel like we are doing God's work God's way only to be faced with obstacle after obstacle and barrier after barrier? You pray for God's leading, work hard, and then have to face one disappointment after another. How often do we feel that our lives are summed up by this: bricks without straw? But God's holiness is not only about his righteousness, but also about his power. The job we have to do, we cannot do in our own power. We work hard, but we must realize that we also are spectators watching from the sidelines to see what God is doing. Our work will never be about ourselves as conquerors; it will only be about God, the Conqueror. This is how it was for Moses, and this is how it is for us. You can't build a life of power by your own effort. You can only do it by trusting in the great I AM. You are not the great I AM—God is.

February 24

But that is not the way you learned Christ!—assuming
that you have heard about him and were taught in him,
as the truth is in Jesus. Ephesians 4:20–21

God can make beautiful compositions out of our
lives. It's in that light that Paul exhorts us to put
off and put on (Ephesians 4:22, 24). Paul says, let
Christ shape your mind. Learn Christ. Grow in knowing him. Don't think that you have to do this yourself.
Tie together the whole passage (Ephesians 4:19–24):
the strength of Christ and being made new in the attitude of your mind.

If you have a small view of Christ, as you think
about putting on a new self, you will often see only
your limited resources. But Christ alone has the power
to change you—you can't change yourself. He can
show you how to wake up, how to fight, and how to
put off your old ways of thinking. Putting on the new
self means going to Jesus more and more to get a life
of truth without secrets, and to abandon manipulat-
ing others. As you do this, you begin to see the people
around you as individuals who are worth a great deal
to God, and you are able to treat them with kindness,
forgiveness, thoughtfulness, and love.

February 25

The people who walked in darkness have seen a great
light; those who dwelt in a land of deep darkness, on
them has light shone. Isaiah 9:2

The plagues one by one dethrone the gods of Egypt. Their supreme god is the sun and the pharaoh was the sun god's earthly manifestation. So the Lord sends total darkness to defeat Pharaoh and Egypt. Moses is a weak man, and yet he stretches out his weak hand and darkness spreads over Egypt. What an amazing result God produces from a weak, but submitted servant! The darkness, however, covers only Egypt; where the Hebrews live there is light. God uses a powerful, hard-hearted pharaoh to show his surpassing glory.

The world is full of bondage, full of darkness. When Jesus comes, light pierces the darkness. "The sunrise shall visit us from on high to give light to those who sit in darkness," Zechariah says (Luke 1:78b–79a). How often we forget how strong sin is—what a bondage! Beneath all our sins lie our stubborn hearts filled with darkness that want their own way. Jesus dies on the cross taking our darkness on himself. Jesus enters the darkness on the cross and melts our hearts. We want God to show us the "practical" things. Who should I marry? What career should I pursue? We want guidance, but Jesus wants to give us himself. Jesus is the light of the world: he is the answer. He wants to show his glory in our lives.

February 26

Let no corrupting talk come out of your mouths,
but only such as is good for building up . . . that it
may give grace to those who hear. . . . Be kind to one
another, tenderhearted, forgiving one another, as God
in Christ forgave you. Ephesians 4:29, 32

Are you helping others by the way you talk? Or do you constantly voice unbelief, fears, and doubts? There's an appropriate time for these, but if they dominate your conversation then you don't know Christ very well. Does Ephesians 4 sound like a burden? If so, you've forgotten the power source, the Holy Spirit, who has a tremendous investment in you. The day God called you to himself as a believer is the day he planted in your heart a Cooperator, who teaches you that you are adopted and that you belong to the Father. You not only possess the Holy Spirit; even more, he possesses you.

Stop listening to yourself and listen to God. Confess your negativity and complaining to God in prayer. Take these things to the cross and leave them there. In Christ, be compassionate and forgive. The very heart of prayer is coming to the end of self and giving up your pride. Pray and let God work in your heart to dig out all that's wrong and clothe you in love. Jesus got dirty with our sins; he shed real blood for your real sin. He will help you to forgive as you have been forgiven, to hate sin and love righteousness, and find peace in Jesus.

February 27

Blessed is the one whose transgression is forgiven,
whose sin is covered. . . . Be glad in the LORD,
and rejoice, O righteous, and shout for joy, all you
upright in heart! Psalm 32:1, 11

When people were asked to read the Ten Commandments and estimate how many sins they commit each month, the average estimate was 4.6 sins per month. In Psalm 32 David speaks of his transgressions, e.g., adultery with Bathsheba, life of deceit, arranging Uriah's murder. How can he be a man after God's own heart (Acts 13:22)? But in knowing he is a transgressor, David shows that he knows himself. To transgress means to step over a forbidden boundary. And here the stepping over is done with a rebellious, self-centered heart that has forgotten God's glory. The rebellion centers on self. David doesn't run away from the truth; he admits it and rejoices in God's forgiveness. His repentance is what qualifies him as a man after God's own heart.

We try to hide from God. But the normal Christian life is one where sins are confessed daily on the basis of free justification through faith in Jesus. Do you know your sins? You may think you are a "good" person, but do you gossip and complain? Do you look down on others? Only when you know you are a sinner, is there hope that you will find grace. If you don't know you have a debt, you can't be happy when it is paid.

February 28

God sent forth his Son, born of woman, born under the
law, to redeem those who were under the law, so that
we might receive adoption as sons. And because you
are sons, God has sent the Spirit of his Son into our
hearts, crying, "Abba! Father!" Galatians 4:4–6

When praying, honest confession is where spiritual power begins. In the Christian church there
are too many "good" people who do not go to God.
Why should you go to God if you think you just need
a little tweaking, a little propping up? People like this
pray with self-effort, with insecurity, with guilt, and
with little sense of forgiveness. But these are not the
prayers of a child of God.

Remember, God has undertaken a great rescue
operation in history. Jesus was born under the law
of God and took on himself the condemnation we
deserved for our sin. Now the full legal rights of adoption are given to us who are in Christ by faith. What
does our position as God's child teach us about praying? What you need to pray is: "Lord, I'm going to be
in shambles today. I need your grace desperately." You
won't pray this way unless you see your need. You can't
pray effectively without confidence that God loves you,
hears you, and is interested in and wants to answer your
prayers. Do you pray with full knowledge of your position? Are you confident that God loves you? Do not
underestimate the glory of the cross.

February 29

And because you are sons, God has sent the Spirit of
his Son into our hearts, crying, "Abba! Father!" So you
are no longer a slave, but a son, and if a son, then an
heir through God. Galatians 4:6–7

The very essence of talking to God, is talking from your heart. Ask God to give you the Holy Spirit to pray for you (Romans 8:26–27). Ask for the Spirit of wisdom to be with you as you pray. When we pray and cry out, "Abba Father," the Holy Spirit too cries out, "Abba Father."

When you pray, the Spirit prays in you and through you, teaching you how to pray. Do you think God doesn't hear his own Spirit when he cries out? Praying Abba Father is the deepest prayer of faith. It can't go deeper than when you know the significance of God being your Father. The very word *father* carries with it hope, love, forgiveness, faith, and acceptance. In prayer you surrender to God's will. Thank him for the answers to your prayers before you even get them. Thank God for delayed answers knowing that these help faith to grow. God wants a fuller identification of your heart with his. What pulls it all together isn't this answer and that answer; it is you becoming a son or daughter. He wants your whole heart. Hand everything in to God. Our hearts in tune with his heart is the center of prayer. Ask God to teach you how to pray. He will do just that.

March 1

"Give us each day our daily bread." Luke 11:3

The essence of this phrase is: give us sufficiency, give us enough. But what is it that we are asking for? We are asking for the Holy Spirit—the Spirit is our daily bread. Fellowship is the priority in the Christian life—not doing things for God, but being with God. The cry for the gift of the Holy Spirit should be from that pre-supposition: that the Holy Spirit is what we desperately need. Often we want God's power without the burning fire and humbling presence of the Spirit. Miracles like healing are all well and good, but they really have an impact when done in the attitude of dependence and weakness that comes when the Spirit is present. When we ask in weakness, God is willing to give himself—and give abundantly.

Ask for the gift of the Spirit for specific things: ask for fellowship; ask for the Spirit of wisdom and love; ask for his control and for grace to abandon your own desire for control. Abandon the search for your own bread. Admit that you don't have it. If you never ask for the Spirit, you are going to be pretty hungry. But to those who ask, the Spirit is given abundantly. Remember: the Holy Spirit is our daily bread.

March 2

Be imitators of God, as beloved children. And walk in
love, as Christ loved us and gave himself up for us, a
fragrant offering and sacrifice to God. Ephesians 5:1–2

Wake up: you are called to be a child of God!
When you believe in Jesus Christ, you move
from being under God's condemnation to being under
God's blessing. You are legally forgiven and a part of
God's family. God is no longer angry with you because
Christ paid for your sin.

Now, as a child of God, you are being made into
an image of Christ. Jesus's work has already begun in
you. Did you know that whenever you forgive someone
who has wronged you, you are imaging Christ because
that is the way God relates to you? This is the hour to
wake up to what God is calling you to. Walk in love,
just as Christ loved you and gave himself up for you.
The sense of the verb *walk* is "do it now, and keep on
doing it." The only way to walk is "in love." Don't think
of anything else. This is who you are in Christ: become
who you are. Fulfill your calling by loving and loving
and loving. You are called by God the Father to wake
up to the awareness of the immeasurable love of God in
Jesus Christ our Lord and then to walk in that love as
you relate to others.

March 3

Therefore be imitators of God, as beloved children. And
walk in love, as Christ loved us and gave himself up for
us, a fragrant offering and sacrifice to God.
Ephesians 5:1–2

When you sin and focus on yourself, the only thing you can remember is guilt and fear. Fear and love can't go together; guilt crowds out love. The whole point of the grace that runs through Ephesians is that you will not find love within yourself. Love comes in when you acknowledge that you can't manufacture it yourself. The Holy Spirit makes you know the power of the Father and helps you cry to him.

People who know they are weak are the ones whom God helps. He runs to the cry of those who know they need grace. He doesn't pay much attention when we come in our self-dependence, self-satisfaction, and self-righteousness and ask for a gentle wake-up touch. God loves honest, broken hearts. When we cry out for help in this way, he begins to wash away the anxiety and the fear. He makes us see how deep our sins are and shows us where to bring them—to him. He wants you to walk in love, but he wants you to see that love is found in his Son. Faith looks away from self to the cross and to Christ and to what the Father has done. When you look to Jesus, a holy love spreads through your life.

March 4

> I will say of the Lord, "He is my refuge and my fortress,
> my God, in whom I trust". . . . He will cover you with his
> feathers, and under his wings you will find refuge; his
> faithfulness will be your shield and rampart.
> Psalm 91:2, 4 (NIV)

God loves clingy people. You can cling to God, and he won't mind at all. Cling to him in love, and you will have his strength. That's a pretty nice trade. You bring to him your weakness, and he gives to you his strength. He will be your shield and your rampart. He will cover you. That's how faith works. If you believe that, you're pretty well on the way to having your joy fulfilled and your joy restored.

It's very easy to *presume* and think you're *believing*. Presumption and faith are often very close to the same thing. Both are characterized by confidence. But presumption is confidence in yourself or in some human resource. It never has submission to God in its makeup, but instead is always trying to get God to submit to your will. Faith has trust in it, reliance on God—on Christ's death on the cross—and submission to the will of God. That's what brings you into fellowship with God. It's not your power to be religious, but rather that you have a God who has drawn near. And he has come in the person of Jesus Christ. Because he has drawn near, he is drawing me nearer through Jesus.

March 5

For freedom Christ has set us free; stand firm therefore,
and do not submit again to a yoke of slavery.
Galatians 5:1

Christ has set us free from the chains of the law.
But we have the tendency to create new circumcisions—new rules, new duties. We become burdened
with obligations. Are you trying to fulfill your obligations by heading back to slavery, back to Mount Sinai,
back to that place of no mercy? Remember it is all or
nothing. If you put yourself under obligation to one
part of the law, then you are responsible for keeping
the whole law.

You can't have justification by faith in Jesus Christ
plus something else. You might think that you believe
that salvation is by grace through faith alone, but think
about the obligations you are burdened by. Think
about how you unconsciously live as if the fulfillment
of your Christian responsibilities earns you God's favor.
Almost anything can become a new circumcision: your
approach to tithing, your Christian duties, an orderly
home, and the list goes on. Think about what drives
you. Do you live under the law at Mount Sinai or have
you joined the celebration of the justified on Mount
Zion? Remember, for the believer, the judgment day
has come and gone. God has set you free to be his own
dear child!

March 6

For in Christ Jesus neither circumcision nor
uncircumcision counts for anything, but only faith
working through love. Galatians 5:6

The Greek word *working* is a very strong word—
supernatural working. Our justification—our
being declared righteous through the finished work of
Christ—has tremendous significance for daily life. It is,
in fact, an overarching reality that manifests itself in a
life of love.

What does this kind of life look like? What exactly
is this faith working through love? When faith works
through love, your life will look like a cross. We get a
stream of life not from Mount Sinai where God gave
the law, but from Calvary where Jesus died on the cross.
The very heart of this kind of love is that it will enable
us to love others the way we ourselves have been loved.
That's how we will reach the world. We are not judges
on Mount Sinai, we are sinners saved by grace. You
don't reach people by being a judge, but by being a sinner broken at the cross. Our tone and touch and tears
reach others. Have you been to the cross?

March 7

"For everyone who exalts himself will be humbled, but
the one who humbles himself will be exalted."
Luke 18:14b

In this parable, two men go to church. Both want to be accepted by God and both pray. But the Pharisee *avoids* knowing his need by seeing himself as better than others and by despising others. He prays, "Thank you that I am a fine servant of yours. I am not a robber like this tax collector here, who is a cheat." As long as he compares himself with others, the Pharisee cannot know God because he cannot know himself. Also, the Pharisee avoids knowing his need by doing something extra to earn God's favor. Going beyond the law gives him a basis for feeling proud of himself.

The tax collector, however, stands far off and beats his breast in prayer. It is clear that he understands the temple's purpose as a place where blood is shed for the atonement of sin. He cries, "God, be merciful to me, a sinner." Literally translated, he cries, "God forgive me because of sacrifice. God be merciful to me *the* sinner." In that culture one might confess to being a sinner *along* with everyone else, but to be *the* sinner would draw upon oneself a negative indictment that was unheard of. Unlike the Pharisee, the tax collector acknowledges his need for grace. Grace is for those who know they have a need. Do you wonder why you don't know God better? Do you know your need?

March 8

"For God so loved the world, that he gave his only Son, that whoever believes in him should not perish but have eternal life." John 3:16

The Law of Moses demands a perfect righteousness—perfection. Every detail must be obeyed perfectly. Perfection is not only about outward obedience, but about the giving of everything in you—your whole heart—to God. "You shall love the LORD your God with all your heart and with all your soul and with all your might" (Deuteronomy 6:5).

The Old Testament is the story of Israel failing to keep the Law and eventually being moved out of the Promised Land, which was a picture of God's heaven. John 3:16 teaches us the gospel—both the depth of God's condemnation of the world and the extremity of his remedy for sin in sending his Son to die. God himself took on flesh and lived a perfect, righteous life. Jesus's perfection went below the surface of his life to his soul—he loved God with his whole heart. Thus the requirements of the law were fully met in his life. Jesus experienced utter separation from God for our sake. When we grasp the import of Christ's sacrifice, we understand the full extent of the Law's demands. God so loved the world that he gave. God turned on his Son the wrath that we deserved for breaking his holy law. What was due us was poured out on Jesus. God gave so we might live.

March 9

Beloved, let us love one another, for love is from God,
and whoever loves has been born of God
and knows God. 1 John 4:7

I believe the greatest sin among Christians today is underestimating the holiness of God and the greatness of the work Jesus did on the cross to fulfill the demands of that holiness—to make us righteous. This is why there is so much self-effort in the church. This is why there is so much fear and hesitation and downheartedness. We think there is an inner circle of real Christians who are God's favorites. We don't grasp the fact that if we believe and trust we are in Christ; we are God's own dear children. Period.

Are you broken before God? Are you lifted up to unutterable joy because of the greatness of the blood of Christ? As Charles Wesley wrote: "Arise, my soul, arise; shake off thy guilty fears; the bleeding sacrifice in my behalf appears." Are you unwittingly looking to the law for your justification forgetting that on the cross, Jesus met the demands of the law fully, for you? Knowing God's love for you enables you to love others. You can be free to lay fear aside and take risks for God. Pray that God would open your eyes to see your sin and confess and forsake it. God will enable you to live out the meaning of the law—to love God and love others. He will fill you with love and power to go and love others.

March 10

"The Lord is my strength and my song; he has become
my salvation. He is my God, and I will praise him, my
father's God, and I will exalt him." Exodus 15:2

Witnesses to an amazing miracle, the Israelites
cross the parted Red Sea and move quickly
from fear to praising God. Terrified, they had huddled
at the shore of the Red Sea as Pharaoh's army closed in
on them. They had cried to Moses about how he had
brought them to face certain death. But Moses at God's
command had stretched out his hand, and God had
sent a wind to part the water, enabling Israel to pass
through on dry land. Egypt's army in hot pursuit followed God's people into the sea. Screams, yells, roaring
wind, crashing waves . . . then silence.

How does Israel respond? "The people feared the
Lord, and they believed in the Lord and in his servant
Moses" (Exodus 14:31). The silence is broken by singing. As slaves Israel had little to sing about. But now
they sing—they worship. Israel celebrates what God
has done; they celebrate God himself, and they celebrate that this God is theirs. "The Lord is my strength
and my song; he has become my salvation." He gives
me joy! God didn't come to me and say fix up yourself
and then I will love you; he loved me just the way I was.
Praise him who loves us and has freed us from our sins!

March 11

Peter [said]: "I now realize how true it is that God does not show favoritism but accepts from every nation the one who fears him and does what is right."

Acts 10:34–35 (NIV)

Wake up to the opportunities before you. God has opened the door of grace wide and there's room for everybody. There's no reason for prejudices against anyone. God is seeking all kinds of people to come to himself. Whom do you struggle to accept? People who are different from you? The unpleasant people who live with you? Does the gospel have power to really change all kinds of people? Does it have the power to change you? The gospel teaches everybody to love, even if they are not loved in return. Jesus says, "I'm going to teach you how to love the self-righteous, the unwashed, your enemy." The power is for us to change, and then for us to go to others.

When Jesus tells Peter, "I will give you the keys of the kingdom of heaven" (Matthew 16:19), the keys are the gospel. Later, Peter who is struggling with his prejudices against Gentiles, discovers that the power is in the gospel. While still speaking—and he probably thinks he has more to say—Peter is interrupted by the Holy Spirit who comes and works faith in the hearts of all who are listening (Acts 10:44). The keys are being used whenever the gospel is preached. Jesus emphasizes that you die as you do it. In the dying, the gospel flows.

March 12

For I am not ashamed of the gospel, for it is the power
of God for salvation to everyone who believes, to the
Jew first and also to the Greek. Romans 1:16

What is one of the greatest hindrances to sharing our faith? For many Christians it's not a lack of knowledge or method, it's a bad conscience, a feeling that they are not qualified spiritually to witness. But throughout the centuries, when the church of God has recovered the gospel, people are liberated for outreach. If you are not convinced that both your justification and sanctification is by faith and flows out of your relationship with Christ, it's going to be hard to live with authority and confidence.

But if you are assured that whatever he asks of you, he also gives you the resources for, and that you have his love with you, then no fight is too big to take on. The gospel is the power of God unto salvation. Is there any greater power than that? You can't say that the law is the power of God unto salvation. The law is the will of God, but it is certainly not the power of God to save people. It tells people what they should and should not do, but only the gospel tells people what God has done to save them. Know Christ and know his gospel. It's the power of God to change the hardest heart—yours and your neighbor's too.

March 13

Then he touched their eyes, saying, "According to your faith be it done to you." Matthew 9:29

God can use you to grow disciples. When you have faith in God, people sense his presence. When you believe that God is alive and doing mighty things, people are convicted. The power of God is at work wherever there is faith in the risen Christ. Things are going to happen because he is the Lord of the resurrection, and he cannot be present without changing people. He raises the dead. They hear the voice of the Son of God and live.

It's not up to you to create something by faith. It's already created. You don't have to put Christ in the heavens. You don't have to make the gospel strong. All you have to do is recognize how strong it is and act on it. The King is already moving. Ask him to help you to be obedient in your life and witness, but then believe that he will bring about the results. You can be confident that the gospel will be working as a great scythe cutting down the harvest. It will bring in the lost. As you step out in faith, you will find that God has already begun to speak to someone. When you pray in faith, you will find that the kingdom has already moved before you.

March 14

And I said, "Who are you, Lord?" Acts 26:15a

In the miracle of conversion the believer moves from darkness to light—from the insanity of serving self to the sanity of serving God. Conversion means to put your weight on Jesus. Are you hovering, or are you leaning on Jesus? Is your weight fully on him? In conversion we come to know more than abstract ideas about Jesus. We come to know Jesus himself. We trust Jesus and then submit to him. As humans, we bristle at authority; we do not want to submit. But the Bible makes it clear that insisting on one's own way is treason against God. God made us to want his way and his will and not our own.

Paul's conversion may feel remote to us—far removed in time and space. But we need to surrender to God in the same way. On his face on the road, when Paul says, "Who are you Lord?" he is worshiping. In effect he is saying, "You are sovereign, Lord. I give myself to you." The principle is the same for us. When we turn to God, it is only because God has first revealed Christ to us. When we are converted, we submit to God and are filled with security, significance, and joy. That's the miracle of Jesus Christ coming into your heart and life—the miracle of conversion.

March 15

By this we know love, that he laid down his life for us,
and we ought to lay down our lives for the brothers.
1 John 3:16

When we meet Christ, we begin to see ourselves
in a new way. We see all our so-called virtues
in a new light. The light that blinded Paul is like the
light that Christ sheds in our hearts to reveal sins that
are deep and habitual. Paul was trusting in the law and
he thought he was doing a good job keeping it. But his
self-righteousness led him to murder.

You can know that you have been converted if
God is free to convict you of sin. Is God free to go
into the dark recesses of your heart and drag out secret
sins? Paul the Pharisee judged and condemned others;
he was unable to move toward God and others. When
he was converted, God gave Paul the power to move
toward others. Knowing God's love, Paul can love others. He becomes a dying man. When we are converted,
God gives us the power to move toward others and the
power to forgive. Seeing your own sin gives you the
power to forgive those who have sinned against you.
Jesus laid down his life for us, and he gives us the power
to lay down our lives for others.

March 16

"I have appeared to you . . . to appoint you as a servant
and witness to the things in which you have seen me
and to those in which I will appear to you." Acts 26:16

Paul is converted, but now what? Does God place
him on a throne behind protective glass to be
admired by the masses? No. What Jesus says to Paul
is this: "I'm sending you in my stead." The words that
applied to the Messiah in the prophets now apply to
Paul—and to all God's people. We are not apostles, but
we are still sent.

When we are converted, Christ moves in; he lives
in us and goes with us. Our conversion is not only for
us but also for the nations. You can't evangelize on the
basis of how you feel. If you wait to feel up to it, you
will never go. You only get grace when you're stretched
beyond what you do normally—grace will be yours
when you need it. Jesus said, "As you go, I will give you
the grace that you need." Where do you begin? Pray
and pray some more. Ask God to break you, change
you, and help you love others. Set goals; don't just drift.
Lying like a dead log is not faith, it is presumption. Ask
God to show you what he wants you to do. Ask him
to send you forth with courage, discernment, wisdom,
and joy. Commit to giving God the glory.

March 17

But the fruit of the Spirit is love, joy, peace, patience, kindness, goodness, faithfulness, gentleness, self-control; against such things there is no law.
Galatians 5:22–23

Notice how the fruit of the Spirit are arranged. The first three—love, joy, and peace—are attitudes; the others are relational qualities. When asked which fruit they lack, many people say patience and self-control. What people really want is a life that's under control. They want the end product, not the love, joy, and peace that creates it. Patience and control cannot be built on a self-centered life. The whole point is that faith working through love is the foundation for all the fruit. How can you be patient with a person you don't love? The Spirit of Jesus—the Holy Spirit—is the originator of love. All the others flow out of that.

What's the difference between a work and a fruit? A work is something I make. A fruit is something that grows, largely apart from my interference. I can't make a tree: it grows. The root of the Spirit's ministry is love. The fruit of the Spirit doesn't mean anything if you have no sense of direction. The fruit of the Spirit is for export—it's not just for ourselves. Christ honors himself by producing fruit in us to bring glory to himself. He will not rest until he gets that honor. This is your calling.

March 18

But he gives more grace. Therefore it says, "God
opposes the proud, but gives grace to the humble."
James 4:6

After the flood, God had commanded the people to spread out and fill the earth. Preferring the security of living together, they ignored God's word, settled in one place, and built a city. They made the mistake of looking on God's word only as good advice. What they didn't understand is that if you don't obey God's word, if you don't allow God's word to humble you and break you, you are rebelling against God. Out of the passive rebellion of delayed obedience comes a more active rebellion. The city becomes their strength, their source of power, and their way to control God. *Babel* means gate of God. For God to enter the city, he would have to come through *their* gate.

Have we adopted a similar attitude? Do we listen and obey God when he speaks, or do we secretly pray that our *own* will would be done? When God comes to us he brings salvation as a free gift. But in our pride, we always try to reach God on our own merit; we try to control God. So often we want to manage God while refusing to let God manage us. In the human heart there is a tower reaching for control even over God. But in his mercy, God dethrones us so we can learn about the Holy Spirit. Abandon your power plays, humble yourself, and repent. See and live in the love of God for you.

March 19

Jesus . . . said, "It is finished," and he bowed his head
and gave up his spirit. John 19:30

"It is finished" means that Jesus has completed the conscious suffering involved in paying for our sins. What exactly did Jesus suffer? Over what has he gained victory? We say he has been the victor over sin and death. It's great to hear these grand, eloquent words in the funeral home or cemetery. These words bring us comfort, but we don't think through what they mean. Sin is the breaking of God's law. Death results from sin, and eternal separation from God is the punishment. When Jesus died, he took the sin away and paid for it. He took death away and brought life instead.

The point is, "For God so loved the world, that he gave his only Son, that whoever believes in him should not perish but have eternal life" (John 3:16). In response to being forsaken by the Father for us, Jesus on the cross cried out, "My God, my God, why have you forsaken me?" (Mark 15:34). That forsakenness was tied in with his actually bearing the punishment for our sins. He finished all of it—sin, death, and punishment. God went that far in caring for us on the cross. He overruled evil and brought good from it. He took the greatest crime in history and made it his greatest victory.

March 20

When Jesus had received the sour wine, he said, "It is
finished," and he bowed his head and gave up his spirit.
John 19:30

The hardest sin to confess is my pride—my stubbornness and coldness of heart. I need to be broken and have other people correct me. I need to be told sometimes, "Jack, you're not doing very well today." When that happens I don't immediately go and thank the person for pointing it out because sin makes us inherently self-centered and unteachable. But God wants us to be Christ-centered. How can we bring our pride to Christ when we don't want to be taught and we don't want to be exposed? The only way is to be convinced that God loves us—all the way, unconditionally, forever. The only thing that can soften a heart is the absolute finished character of God's love, as represented in the cross. In other words, we can afford to go to a God who understands us in Jesus Christ, most perfectly, and bring to him ourselves as we really are.

The principle of alienation lies deep within us, and we naturally want our own way. But God in his overmastering love looks at us and says, "I know all about you, and I love you just as you are. And I gave my Son to finish a work for you." When we really hear and understand this, we can acknowledge the truth about our pride-filled hearts and in humility invite others to speak the truth to us.

March 21

We were buried therefore with him by baptism into death, in order that, just as Christ was raised from the dead by the glory of the Father, we too might walk in newness of life. Romans 6:4

As the sun rises on the first day of the week, three women bring spices to the tomb intending to anoint Jesus's dead body—to bid him a final farewell. As they walk, downcast and discouraged, they wonder aloud who will roll away the stone to give them access to the body. But when they arrive at the tomb, the stone has not only been rolled away, but it lies off to the side as if it's been given a giant heave. When the woman enter the tomb and see the angel, they are alarmed, terrified. The resurrection power of the living God has come down.

The Ten Commandments were written by the finger of God (Exodus 31:18), and now the strong hand and arm of God (Luke 1:51) has reached down and brought resurrection to the Son (Romans 6:4). The empty tomb and the angel's words point to the fact that death is not king, Jesus is. Jesus has mastered death. Jesus's death and resurrection is the fulfillment of a plan and a program designed by God in eternity. That plan had at its heart the mercy of God in that the Son agreed to come to die for our sin and by his blood to bring us into friendship with God. Now, by faith, we too walk in newness of life.

March 22

And they went out and fled from the tomb, for
trembling and astonishment had seized them, and they
said nothing to anyone, for they were afraid. Mark 16:8

Your ability to live the Christian life depends on whether you believe in this big Jesus. He has awesome power! Your perception of how big Jesus is will be how big your faith is. If your faith is scrawny, you have a poor understanding of who Jesus is. Don't think Jesus sends you somewhere he hasn't already gone. According to the Bible every human must face death. Through Jesus, however, God's justice is satisfied and those who believe in him are no longer under the penalty of death. Death now is the door through which the believer passes to enter into the presence of God. Know this with certainty: The stone is rolled away for you! The tomb is empty for you! Jesus died for you and he rose for you!

Do you know this in your heart, or do you live as if Jesus died, rose again, and then evaporated? Have you let God deal with your fear of death? Have you taken that fear to God? Have you seen the reality of the empty tomb? The One who emptied that tomb is using his same power in your life to carry you through whatever you face. The same power that was at work in Jesus is at work in you. Ask Christ to come and work in your life. Ask God and he will break your heart of stone.

March 23

"Do not be grieved, for the joy of the LORD
is your strength." Nehemiah 8:10

The joy of the Lord is something that God gives, and the heart of it is God being present. When he is present, he does three things: convicts of sin, forgives sin, and offers personal joy and intimacy. The center of joy is being able to love God because he loves you so very, very much. Revival comes from what God alone is giving. Revival comes from what God alone is doing. The joy of the Lord comes from the outside. The joy of the Lord is your strength. God is for you and he is present. He is Christ crucified for you, he is living in you, and he supervises all things for your benefit. If you can't be joyous over that, I don't know what you can be joyous over!

What Nehemiah is saying here is not that you shouldn't grieve over sin and repent of it, but that the heart of holiness, the heart of the Old Testament law, is always found in joy. To please God, to be holy, to have God near, you have to have joy. God is the God of wonders and miracles, and he's making the dry bones live. The joy of God is God present with people. And when God is present, you can't be the same old you. Something new must happen.

March 24

All the people wept as they heard the words
of the Law. Then [Nehemiah] said to them, "Go your
way. . . . Do not be grieved, for the joy of the Lord
is your strength." Nehemiah 8:9b–10

It is always best to start with Christ before getting into confession and repentance. You can only have healthy sorrow when you have healthy joy. That is the priority of defending, maintaining, and building up the joy that God has given you. You can't build up what you don't have. But if you are a believer in Jesus and he has made you part of his church, then you are alive, you have the Holy Spirit, and Christ is in you. He is no longer your judge, condemning you, but he's your Father, wooing you to himself. Now, as a Father, he will certainly need to forgive you, as you confess your sins, but he is no longer your judge so you have the platform for joy.

How did you get here? Behind everything that happened, Jesus was drawing you—bringing you to his joy, to his conviction of sin, to a knowledge of his forgiveness—and inviting you into his intimacy. That's his priority for you. Yield to it; respond to it by faith. When you open the Word and pray, when you love people and are kind to them, you do so in the knowledge that the power is from above.

March 25

Those who had returned from the captivity made
booths and lived in the booths, for from the days of
Jeshua the son of Nun to that day the people of Israel
had not done so. And there was very great rejoicing.

Nehemiah 8:17

You don't worry, you just have concerns. The problem with your "concerns" is that you're trying to get control of something. You want a career, a family, a better job, a better spouse, better kids, or better health—all the usual things. When we focus on these things, we're putting cement in the ground, trying to make things permanent.

The whole point of the Israelites celebrating the Feast of Booths was to remind them that they were pilgrims. Jesus is the first pilgrim who is really obedient. He comes into the world and doesn't fall in love with it or with his own ambitions. He endures the cross, despising its shame, for the joy set before him—obeying the Father and rescuing you and me. Because of this, the rest of us are on a pilgrimage to the second coming. We've been raised from the dead, we're alive, and we're headed to Christ's return. And because our focus is on that, everything else takes on a different significance. We love Jesus, we're waiting for him, and that's the heart of our pilgrimage. We don't need to complain that we don't have what we think we should in this life. Once you see that, you are free to live without fear or anxiety.

March 26

Elijah said to Ahab, "Go up, eat and drink, for there is a sound of the rushing of rain." 1 Kings 18:41

On what does Elijah's faith rest? It rests on God's promise to him. Elijah tells Ahab that he hears the sound of rain. But it wasn't raining. Where was the sound of rain? Was it out to sea on the Mediterranean? Did Elijah have the latest weather report about a storm coming? No, he gave Ahab God's weather report by faith because he believed in the promise of God. God had said to Elijah, "Go, show yourself to Ahab, and I will send rain upon the earth" (1 Kings 18:1). God says that he is going to end the drought; he is going to bring a revival of life.

What is Elijah thinking and believing as he prays: "O LORD, God of Abraham, Isaac, and Israel, let it be known this day that you are God in Israel, and that I am your servant, and that I have done all these things at your word. Answer me, O LORD, answer me, that this people may know that you, O LORD, are God, and that you have turned their hearts back" (1 Kings 18:36–37)? Down in the depths of his heart he believes the Word of God. God said it. God promised it. Elijah took it to heart and stepped out in faith. That's how God builds faith—your faith and mine. He wants us to believe his promises, and then act on them.

March 27

And Elijah went up to the top of Mount Carmel. And he bowed himself down on the earth and put his face between his knees. 1 Kings 18:42

When you are with God, that is what you are; you are no more and no less. Who you are with God defines all the rest. Elijah climbed to the top of the mountain and there he met his God. If you have trouble praying, it is probably because you've never learned how to go up a Mount Carmel, meet with God, and be nothing before him. If I can't stand to be alone with God, I have to ask, "Lord, what's wrong with me?" His reply is always the same, "Jack, you need a heart for me. You need to want me."

If you have experienced hard things recently, consider that God is using these hard things to get you alone with him. He wants you to stop so that he can speak to you. And once you get alone with God, you begin to discover that being with God—that knowing him and his love for you—is the best and most beautiful thing in the world.

March 28

And in a little while the heavens grew black with clouds
and wind, and there was a great rain. 1 Kings 18:45

Elijah, bowed down on Mount Carmel, isn't just acknowledging how small he is; he is acknowledging how big God is. When you get alone with God and begin to pray, you learn your insignificance. You see how big and powerful God is, and suddenly, the whole of your life becomes worship and praise. The Spirit comes, and you pray for revival. If you are praying for someone who is sick, then you just naturally also begin to pray for that person's revival. You enlarge your sphere because you know how big your God is.

When your God is big, your faith takes on new power. Powerful faith is never found by looking inside yourself. It's found by looking at God and his promises—at his powerful atonement and powerful resurrection. When my faith is in God, in Christ, in Christ's work on my behalf, my faith is powerful. I may feel weak right down to my knees. And I may be as scared as everyone else, but nonetheless I have the resurrection power of God working in me and in my weakness. The same power that brought torrential rain to Israel, that brought Jesus back from the dead, is at work in my life and in the lives of those for whom we pray.

March 29

Without faith it is impossible to please him, for whoever
would draw near to God must believe that he exists and
that he rewards those who seek him. Hebrews 11:6

Jesus is not coldly looking down on us wondering
what he can catch us doing wrong or how he can
trip us up. The One who is in heaven has taken on a
human nature and a body like ours. He understands us;
he sympathizes with our weakness. Jesus was tempted
like we are, yet never sinned. Therefore, he has a throne
of grace where we can come and pray and find mercy,
help, and strength (Hebrews 4:15–16).

Your response to all that Christ is ought to be confidence in him. The very definition of Christianity in
Hebrews is confidence in Christ, and I cannot do anything unless I abide in him. Faith is the ability to see
the invisible—seeing with the eyes of the heart what
God is and what God has for us. The anchor of our
faith is the returning Christ. Jesus is not a passive lord
on a throne or a high priest who's doing nothing, but
he is constantly coming and will come at one final hour
to close history. We haven't seen Christ's return, and we
don't see him interceding for us and ruling over us, but
faith is the power to see what is invisible. It is the work
of the Spirit in our hearts, convincing us of what we
could never believe if left to ourselves.

March 30

"No servant can serve two masters, for either he will hate the one and love the other, or he will be devoted to the one and despise the other. You cannot serve God and money." The Pharisees, who were lovers of money, heard all these things, and they ridiculed him. Luke 16:13–14

The Pharisees thought they were doing a good job of serving both God and money. Loving money means to have a tightfisted attitude toward money. They were not necessarily greedy in the sense that they were trying to take in more and more, but they were greedy in the sense that they were holding tightly to what they had. We all tend to be tightfisted unless we realize what is ours in Christ. When we have Christ, we can let go of anything and everything because we are immensely rich. "For you know the grace of our Lord Jesus Christ, that though he was rich, yet for your sake he became poor, so that you by his poverty might become rich" (2 Corinthians 8:9).

The Pharisees couldn't release their grip on money because they didn't have a grip on the true treasure, the wealth of Christ. In their minds, they probably acknowledged that all they had came from God, but in their hearts God got his ten percent tithe and the rest was theirs. For that reason, they didn't see that we are only managers of God's money. You don't own anything—not even your mind, your intelligence, your body, your ministry. It's all Christ's!

March 31

Every time you hear God's Word, you have a choice: strive for control or submit. What a blessing it is to submit, realizing that we are only stewards, only managers; we are not the lords of the world.

Wherever there is stewardship, the owner is going to call for an accounting, and God's accounting is different from ours. As Jesus says to the Pharisees, "You are those who justify yourselves before men, but God knows your hearts. For what is exalted among men is an abomination in the sight of God" (Luke 16:15). Their whole consciousness was wrapped up in what other people thought, and the reason they had been faithful in their tithing and good works was that it made a good impression. Is this how you approach the good things you do? On the other hand, perhaps you think of yourself as poor and not having much. Don't you see: you have the riches of Christ! Be bolder—not stupid or rash—but don't be stingy. You have a rich Father and you then are also rich. Repent of living before people rather than God. Open your eyes to see the magnitude of what God did for you at the cross. When he gave his Son, there wasn't anything left that he had to give.

April 1

The LORD is near to the brokenhearted and saves the crushed in spirit. Psalm 34:18

What does it mean to be brokenhearted and crushed in spirit? In the Bible, Cain, Esau, King Saul, and Judas are all examples of people who seem to fall into this category. But when you look at them closely, you see that while they were certainly depressed and despairing, they were not actually brokenhearted and crushed in spirit. They don't believe that God loves them or is concerned about them. But their basic problem was that they were all still trusting in themselves, not God.

The brokenhearted and crushed in spirit, on the other hand, have submitted to the breaking of their pride. The blessing, presence, and work of God are evident in their life. They see God as he really is; they trust in him. Humility and confidence characterize their lives. They have the humble heart of a son and daughter who are able to be honest with their father. The humility of the broken heart is never to be separated from the assurance that God is watching over you. The Lord is near those who are broken and crushed.

April 2

The eyes of the LORD are toward the righteous and his
ears toward their cry. Psalm 34:15

Do you really believe that God hears you when you cry out to him in prayer? Or do you pray and then walk away and worry about the very thing about which you prayed? These are prayerless prayers. But you don't have to pray like that. God has given you the Spirit! You are a child of the King; you belong to him. Are you praying like you're a stranger to God? As a child, you come in prayer to your Father with your real needs, expressing your real emotions. You cry out to God, and trust him to deliver you. And even if you find yourself doubting, God still cares for you.

Parents don't disown their children every time they're naughty, and God doesn't either. He invites you to pray with confidence because you're a son or daughter. His eyes and ears are open to you. Prayers of faith flow from the heart that knows it is seen and heard by God.

April 3

God said to him, "Fool! This night your soul is required of you, and the things you have prepared, whose will they be?" So is the one who lays up treasure for himself and is not rich toward God. Luke 12:20-21

Jesus says that a person who lives only for this life is blind, because nothing material—no possession, no achievement—can fully satisfy, and certainly can't be taken into the next life. This life is so short; how foolish to live as if only this life matters. What is of utmost importance is becoming rich toward God. Therefore the aim of life is to come into fellowship with God in such a way that you have a life of joy that is in some measure independent of circumstances. This joy comes to you because you know and love God, not as a result of whether you are rich or poor. This joy does not come to you because of what you possess in material things, which are fading. The most important thing is to enjoy God and to delight in him. If you don't enjoy and delight in God, now is the time to start investing properly—not in material things, but in your relationship with God.

April 4

[Jesus] said to them, "Take care, and be on your guard
against all covetousness, for one's life does not consist
in the abundance of his possessions." Luke 12:15

My freedom, my fulfillment, my rights: we are
obsessed with self-centered concerns. Instead,
invest in being rich toward God. If you want to be
rich, be aware that you're here only on temporary loan,
and that Christ is coming. Christ rules; Christ is king;
Christ is everything. Sometimes we have little joy in
knowing Christ because we are hedging our bets. We're
willing to be brave right up to the point where we might
be hurt. Our concern is with our own safety. What we
forget is that our safety is already established. No one
can hurt us. We have already died and been raised with
Christ. Who can ultimately harm us now?

Often the root of the problem is that we act more
like orphans without faith in God's providence than
like sons and daughters who trust their heavenly Father.
Jesus gives us the Spirit of adoption (Romans 8:15).
God is no longer our condemning judge but our holy
Father in Jesus Christ. If we know that we are God's
dear children, we will be used by him.

April 5

"Ask, and it will be given to you; seek, and you will find; knock, and it will be opened to you. For everyone who asks receives, and the one who seeks finds, and to the one who knocks it will be opened." Matthew 7:7–8

Do you ever feel completely defeated in your struggle against sin? What we often do in that situation is to take stock of our resources, which often look so small when compared with the looming threat against us that we just want to quit. What the devil wants us to do is to lose sight of Christ's part in the change process. He wants us to forget that Christ's honor is at stake in your growth. If you lose, Christ loses. God is not going to permit his ark to be taken into captivity by the enemy and kept there (see 1 Samuel 4–6). He's going to win. Therefore, any change, any victory over sinful habits, has to start with you exercising more faith in your sovereign Senior Partner. I am persuaded on the basis of Scripture (see, for example, Hebrews 4:15–16) that, if you do that, your life will begin to move forward in a new way. You'll be able to face the real weaknesses and sins in your life, cry out to God for the Spirit's help, and begin to make good choices that are consistent with your calling.

April 6

"Judge not, that you be not judged. For with the
judgment you pronounce you will be judged, and
with the measure you use it will be measured to you."
Matthew 7:1-2

What do we do when we judge? We ignore our own sin and focus on the sins of others. It's much easier to spot and remember other people's sins than our own. Only when you begin to see the truth about your own heart and admit that you are the one with the problem, can things start to change.

But just when you are starting to grasp the extent of your own sin, the devil will try to convince you that the problem is too big to be solved, even for Jesus. When this happens, remember that Jesus is the master teacher, and he only teaches to help. Jesus never wants to destroy anyone; he always wants to build. Jesus is not the accuser, Satan is (Revelation 12:9–10). Jesus wants to deliver you from the blindness that makes you unable to see your own sin and prone to judge others. Blindness to your own sin leads you to think that *you* are righteous enough to condemn people and cast them out. But you are not the judge; you're a servant and friend. As Christ brings his grace into your life, enlightens you to your own sin, and teaches you how to give up judging others, you will find a new freedom to live life with transparency and joy.

April 7

"Ask, and it will be given to you; seek, and you will find; knock, and it will be opened to you. For everyone who asks receives, and the one who seeks finds, and to the one who knocks it will be opened." Matthew 7:7–8

This passage about continually asking, seeking, and knocking is familiar to us. Here and in the following verses, though, Jesus's intent is to counter the devil's suggestion that God doesn't like us very much. He's pointing out the readiness and willingness of God to respond to you amid the mounting pressures of life when you know you're incapable of putting on a forgiving lifestyle.

The asking, seeking, and knocking are for "good gifts" (Matthew 7:11); but what exactly are these gifts? The parallel passage in Luke 11:13 tells us that God wants to give us the Holy Spirit. The good gifts in Matthew, then, are simply the outworking of the Spirit's presence. You are called to continue to ask for the gift of the Spirit and his fruit: love, joy, peace, patience, kindness, goodness, faithfulness, gentleness, and self-control (Galatians 5:22–23). God wants you to talk with him about where you really are, and he wants to bless you with the Holy Spirit.

April 8

"Everyone to whom much was given, of him much will be required, and from him to whom they entrusted much, they will demand the more." Luke 12:48b

Jesus assures us that the world to come will not be a dull place. Look at the line of Jesus's thinking in Luke 12. Now you are called to be a wise steward who does his or her job faithfully no matter how big or small. Then, when the master returns, the wise steward will get a bigger job as a reward. Most of us might not think of that as a reward, so we might not immediately see this as a great promise. The point is that when Jesus returns on the clouds of heaven with glory on that last day, it won't be a Hollywood version of heaven that's light and misty with see-through people. There will be a new heaven and a new earth. When Christ returns, anything good on earth will be made even better, and anything bad will be removed.

In heaven we will not be so transformed that there won't be any work or any adventure. If you're faithful with this little job that Christ has given you to do now, he will give you a great big job in heaven—a job that you will have a lot of fun doing throughout eternity.

April 9

"Who then is the faithful and wise manager,
whom his master will set over his household, to give
them their portion of food at the proper time? Blessed
is that servant whom his master will find so doing
when he comes." Luke 12:42–43

If you think about God and how he saved you, he exercised a lot of creativity. God sent the best of heaven, his own Son, to earth to become like you, except without sin. Christ had to obey God perfectly, and he had to die on a cross to take away your sin and guilt. Who would have thought of faith as a way of receiving this and repentance as a way of seeing your need of it? God is always surprising us. Who would have thought that in actually changing you and me, God would do it from the inside by moving into our lives?

The great work of the Holy Spirit is to fill us with faith and make us faithful servants, so ask the Lord to give you a mind that thinks by faith. Even though Jesus is now invisible, presently he will be visible. He stands at the door and knocks. As you live and work, be faithful—be full of faith. Hang in there. Don't just show up, but begin to show up with a smile.

April 10

"Who then is the faithful and wise manager,
whom his master will set over his household, to give
them their portion of food at the proper time? Blessed
is that servant whom his master will find so doing
when he comes. Truly, I say to you, he will set him over
all his possessions." Luke 12:42–44

Jesus says, "Don't just talk about faith; express it by your deeds." Give up your self-centered life, lifestyle, and way of thinking. Jesus is overcoming the kingdom of this world, which is a kingdom of "me first." Become Christ's servant, where the great word is *others*. Love others deeply, as you have been loved.

Your eyes can't be opened to a glorious future unless you know what you have in Christ right now. If what you know of Christ now is weak and insubstantial, then it's going to be difficult to lay hold of his return. When Jesus warns about the wages of the servant who forgets (Luke 12:47), he's making a case for faithfulness. He's also showing himself as not just a teacher, but a lover who is first of all the great faithful one—the one who did something for you. If there had been no one else in the universe but you, he would have still done it for *you*. He was the faithful servant who was faithful unto death—death for you. He was the one who endured, and the one who went to the cross for you when you were an enemy.

April 11

He withdrew from them about a stone's throw, and
knelt down and prayed, saying, "Father, if you are
willing, remove this cup from me. Nevertheless, not my
will, but yours, be done." Luke 22:41–42

In Jesus's day, the typical way of praying was not to get down on your knees, but to stand up. When Jesus falls to his knees, he is saying something about the surrender of his life. He's saying that he depends on God and is seeking his will. In prayer, we get in touch with God. We begin to understand ourselves and our weaknesses. When we're under attack, always our best defense is surrendering to the will of God.

Think about how you pray: Are you praying for *God's* will to be done or are you praying for your *own* will to be done? Do you perhaps assume that your will is the same as God's will? One of the reasons prayer is so hard is that we have made up our minds that we have nothing to learn when we pray. If you are anxious, isn't it possible that you are not surrendering your life to Christ? This is why we need to pray constantly—and pray together. Pray about everything, asking God to help you know and do his will.

April 12

He withdrew from them about a stone's throw, and knelt down and prayed, saying, "Father, if you are willing, remove this cup from me. Nevertheless, not my will, but yours, be done." Luke 22:41–42

Do you fight God, or do you surrender your will to him as you pray? You've been asking him to show you what career to follow or where to live or whom to marry, but have you really surrendered your will to him? Have you ever prayed, "God, I'm willing to let you do anything with me"? Are you willing to see the whole Christian life as a life of prayer?

You must pray and watch, and you must not be taken by surprise by Satan's attacks. Rather you must go to God, praising him and being filled with thankfulness, knowing that he will be with you and there is nothing to fear. Then he introduces you to the supreme joy, the contentment, the satisfaction of knowing that what matters is not how you feel or even so much what you do, but that you be constantly and in everything like Jesus. Love your Father because you are loved by him. You have seen the cross; you have seen what love has done for you. You are on the verge of God's reviving you, of joy inexpressible coming into your life. But here's the hard part: Do you want it? Are you willing to seek it?

April 13

Jesus said, "Father, forgive them, for they know not what they do." Luke 23:34a

What a vast comfort that Christ prays for us! On the cross, Jesus, prays his love and forgiveness, surrenders his perfect life, thereby taking control of history and conquering the world. The criminal hanging beside him hears Jesus pray and sees him forgive. His own heart is convicted, he believes in Jesus, and asks Jesus to remember him. A little later Jesus gives up his life. The temple veil is torn from top to bottom; the earth shakes; and the centurion cries out, "Surely he was the Son of God!" (Matthew 27:54).

What a prayer intercessor is our Jesus! This mediator, this great high priest, goes about his work and what happens? Pentecost follows in answer to Jesus's prayer. When the Spirit comes, people learn to pray. And when they are in prayer and visited by the Spirit's presence, the Word goes forth. Peter preaches—this man who was so weak he denied Christ three times—holding up Christ as Lord. Peter's hearers are convicted in their hearts, and in answer to Jesus's prayer, three thousand people are made children of God (Acts 2).

April 14

Jesus said, "Father, forgive them, for they know not what they do." Luke 23:34a

W e're not called to judge or condemn people; we're called to forgive and bless them. Through his death on the cross, Jesus has ushered in a time of mercy and love, forgiveness and intercession—a time of repentance. When he was crucified, the hearts of people were revealed in all their rebellion and sin. "He came to his own, and his own people did not receive him" (John 1:11).

God the Father has appointed Jesus to be judge. But that's in the future. Jesus is not judging humankind in that final sense yet; rather he is now their intercessor and seeks to bring them to himself. Look at Jesus on the cross. He's not standing over you in judgment; he's taken your judgment day on the cross. In a real sense, the judgment day is over for the believer. We know with confidence that we'll get through it because of Jesus's work. You and I are not judges, either. Are you enthusiastically giving up your right to judge? Are you praying for people with compassion, perceiving their ignorance?

April 15

Therefore do not be ashamed of the testimony about
our Lord, nor of me his prisoner, but share in suffering
for the gospel by the power of God. 2 Timothy 1:8

Paul gives two reasons for putting away your fears. First, the gospel is worth dying for. Second, the Holy Spirit in us is the Spirit of confidence, authority, and love, and has nothing to do with fear. Therefore, we should not be "ashamed of the testimony about our Lord." You don't need to be ashamed of any part of the gospel.

When we think about witnessing, we wonder how *we* will do it. But the more you focus on yourself, the less you do it. Take your eyes off yourself and see that the gospel is worth *everything* to you. It does for people what nothing else can. When you witness, you are harmonizing yourself with the movement of the kingdom. The King is working, which means you don't have to sweat it out by yourself; rather, you can rely on the gospel. Our problem is that suffering is a part of the kingdom program. We say, "God, make me a witness, but protect me from suffering." Abandon your self-focus and see the truth: you have nothing to fear.

April 16

Share in suffering for the gospel by the power of
God who saved us and called us to a holy calling . . .
because of his own purpose and grace, which he gave
us in Christ Jesus . . . who abolished death and brought
life and immortality to light through the gospel.
2 Timothy 1:8b–10

What are you afraid of? Pain? Suffering? Death? Do you know that Jesus has taken care of all that? He died for our sins and rose again, bringing with him immortality and life. This is the Lord's answer to our fears. It is not just an intellectual answer, but an answer that fits reality. The living God, the Judge of the universe has declared us "not guilty." We are accepted as righteous in Christ, therefore we are forgiven and no longer subject to death as the penalty for sin.

Now we have passed from death to life. We are freed; we are justified; we have the Spirit. We have every reason to see the gospel as worth a great deal. Therefore, we should be willing to suffer for it. Paul calls us to take our "share in suffering for the gospel" because Jesus "abolished death and brought life and immortality." It's easy to say in the abstract, but in the places you live and work, you ought to be willing to bear witness. It will always cost something, but the tremendous worth of the gospel and what has been given to you through Christ is worth the cost.

April 17

For God gave us a spirit not of fear but of power and love and self-control. Therefore do not be ashamed of the testimony about our Lord. 2 Timothy 1:7–8a

God will bless the lives of those who are committed to him and seek to obey him. Power comes as you go. It can be quiet power, but it only comes as you obey. I could give you a guilt trip by saying, "You don't witness because you don't love people." That would be true, but it wouldn't help you very much. The point of this passage is not that you witness or stand for Jesus when you *feel* like it. That's not the kind of love it's talking about. Rather, it's an intelligent, clear-eyed love in which you talk to the person whether you feel like it or not. You do it because it's the duty of love.

This is where self-control comes in. In humility you recognize your limitations, and yet still obey. That enables you to set aside your fear of other people. I suspect that for most of us, our biggest problem is that we are not really controlled by the Spirit as we seek to obey. We're far too worried about how we feel. We must guard against the familiar fears that creep in, build up, and sap the Spirit's power, making us timid. Strength comes as you bring your fears to Christ. Then you will be empowered by his Spirit to love others and share the gospel with them.

April 18

Love is patient and kind. 1 Corinthians 13:4a

The word for *love* in this passage is not the word meaning *affection*. It has more to do with decisions, a reasoned choice, and carries the idea of showing or proving one's love. Christian love is love that thinks; love that sees into the heart of things and persists. This love is not naïve, nor is it unwilling or unable to see evil. It is compassionate, steady, and persistent. Instinctively, when we think about love, we think about who will love *me* that way. But the thought here is about the love *you* are called to show to *other people*! Patience and kindness have to do with how you relate to other people.

The word for *patience* literally means that the mind is far from getting angry quickly. "Love is patient" means that you put away passionate anger, and because that anger is put away, you can be kind. The word *kind* here can be translated as *good*. It has the idea of goodness that is constantly expressing itself in relationships. These two words together carry the idea of comforting others. Comfort means to strengthen others. You don't show love to—comfort—others in their weakness only to leave them in weakness; you show love with the intent of making them strong.

April 19

Love does not envy or boast; it is not arrogant or rude.
It does not insist on its own way; it is not irritable
or resentful. 1 Corinthians 13:4b–5

Love does not envy—it does not compete with others. Envy is when you compare yourself with others and are unhappy because they have something that you don't have. Basically, envy indicates dissatisfaction and unthankfulness with what God has given you, especially as compared with others. We, like the Corinthians, are a competitive bunch. As we look around at the other folks at church, we don't think of ourselves as one body, and we don't see gifts and graces in other people as gifts to us from God.

If you don't see other believers as also belonging to Christ, as your blood brothers and sisters, you will judge and condemn them. If you don't see them as those for whom Christ died, you will compete with them incessantly. From a competitive spirit come all the other things listed: boasting, arrogance, rudeness, insisting on your own way, irritation, and resentment. Beneath it all is pride that elevates us to the throne of self-worship. God calls us to turn away from—to repent of—all these prideful, self-seeking attitudes and behaviors.

April 20

[Love] does not rejoice at wrongdoing, but rejoices with the truth. Love bears all things, believes all things, hopes all things, endures all things. 1 Corinthians 13:6–7

Love has confidence in others. This doesn't mean that love is blind or that we don't talk to people about things they do wrong. It means that we come alongside them in love. Love believes and hopes in what God will do in another person's life—in what God will make of that person in the future.

Having this frame of mind is crucial for effective prayer. You can really pray when you have a vision of who that person is going to be when God has finished the work. The problem is we are convinced that we alone know what is right; and, thus, we try to dominate situations for the so-called good of other people. When they don't do what we think is right, we condemn them. This is a sign that we don't know how to pray with confidence. You don't know what God will begin to do in your life if you begin to pray with confidence. The devil's greatest attack on believer and unbeliever alike is to say, "God cannot change you, and God cannot change others." Maybe one reason our prayers are so feeble is that we don't ask God for confidence as we pray, that as we meet people throughout our day they would be changed.

April 21

Love bears all things, believes all things, hopes all
things, endures all things. 1 Corinthians 13:7

"Love bears all things" literally means that love always covers. Even though we see people with their weaknesses, we cover over them. This doesn't mean we don't confront people with truth. It means we're not vicious or malicious, but kind. This idea of covering leads back to the cross. We wonder how we're going to love all the people in our lives, and we think that what faith does is create love for other people in us. This is partly true, but faith does something much bigger. Faith shows us God's love for people and claims that love; it does not create it. Once you see that, you can pray for God to show you his love for the people in your life.

Doesn't that take a burden off your shoulders? You don't have to worry about how you're going to love everybody. You can simply pray that God will bring you into his love. Reread John 3:16 and remember again how God loved us so much that he sent his one and only Son to die for our sins. He sees all of our sin and rebellion against him and our ungratefulness for what he provides, and instead of turning his back on our poor record, he covers it over with Christ's perfect record. Every believer has that covering over them. God has that heart for all of his children.

April 22

But I say, walk by the Spirit, and you will not gratify the desires of the flesh. Galatians 5:16

What does "walk by the Spirit" mean? There's a difference between walking and taking a step. When you're walking, you have a progression. You keep at it. It's not floating or drifting, which has a sense of randomness to it. With this idea of walking, you have a sense of destination and direction that's continuing. It's a habit, something you do every day.

Another way of putting it is simply that it's a matter of obeying. You are obeying the lordship of Christ every day, not out of your own resources, but out of fellowship with the Spirit, who supplies the power. This is not a matter of indifference or something you can opt out of; this is a command. You are commanded to walk by the Spirit, and there's a promise that accompanies it: "you will not gratify the desires of the flesh." This is very strong, very emphatic language. Basically, Paul is promising you a win in the fight against the flesh if you will walk in the power of the Spirit. He's talking to you as a son, as a daughter of God, whom Jesus has died to redeem and set free to obey, and the heart of being a child of God is enjoying your Father and learning to enjoy doing his will.

April 23

> For the desires of the flesh are against the Spirit, and
> the desires of the Spirit are against the flesh, for these
> are opposed to each other, to keep you from doing the
> things you want to do. But if you are led by the Spirit,
> you are not under the law. Galatians 5:17–18

Maybe you don't know much about walking by the Spirit because you don't know how much you need him. You haven't realized how tenacious and mean your flesh—your old sinful nature—is. The minute the flesh sees the Spirit urging you, as a renewed person, in a new direction, he immediately moves in ready to fight. An intense conflict breaks out between the flesh and the Spirit. The result is that you feel like you're making no progress whatsoever.

Are there areas in your life where you can't seem to make any forward progress? This is where God wants to meet you. Paul is telling you that you are no longer under the law—under the curse. "Christ redeemed us from the curse of the law by becoming a curse for us . . . so that we might receive the promised Spirit through faith" (Galatians 3:13–14). It is the Spirit who takes away the power of sin. As you're led by the Spirit, you discover you're not condemned, you're not cursed of God; instead, you are free. So when you get into the battle, cry out for help like a child to the Father!

April 24

"Blessed are the merciful, for they shall receive mercy."
Matthew 5:7

Being merciful toward others starts with knowing how much we need mercy from God. Once, Jesus was passing by two blind men who called out, "Have mercy on us, Son of David!" (Matthew 9:27). I don't think they said this quietly. If you needed help and your only hope was passing by, you would be yelling, "Lord, if you have ever listened, listen now!" The blind men cried to Jesus out of the depths of human emotion and need. And their deep need was met by Jesus's deep compassion.

When you know you are spiritually blind and your only hope is Christ's work on the cross for you, then you too will have mercy on others who are spiritually blind. The pattern is this: I myself have been very weak, miserable, and in need of God's pity. I'm like the blind man spiritually. I go astray instinctively. My record of mercy is not good. God showed grace to me by giving his Son, Jesus. Jesus had pity on me and died for me. And because he had pity on me, I show pity to others.

April 25

"Blessed are the merciful, for they shall receive mercy."
Matthew 5:7

Did you ever have the sneaking feeling that God might not be happy with you? This passage says that you can know that God is for you if you are showing compassion to others. If you are being kind and merciful, you will receive mercy. It's a promise. Happy are the merciful for they shall obtain mercy from God. With every act of kindness, we also are receiving mercy from God.

This doesn't mean we earn God's forgiveness and our justification by our deeds of mercy. That's getting the Christian life backwards. Instead, it's because we have been justified and forgiven by Christ, that we can be merciful. Mercy is the fruit that shows you are rooted in Jesus Christ. If you have no fruit, you have no root. Jesus is saying that we can be assured we are redeemed and God's mercy is with us because the fruit of sharing God's mercy with others is on display in our lives.

It's said that people who live together for a long time begin to look like each other. I don't know how true this is of others, but it is true of you and Jesus. When you live with him long enough, you begin to look like him. Because you have been freely given mercy, you share mercy with others. Because you have been pardoned, you know how to pardon others.

April 26

"I tell you, though he will not get up and give him anything because he is his friend, yet because of his impudence he will rise and give him whatever he needs. . . . If you then, who are evil, know how to give good gifts to your children, how much more will the heavenly Father give the Holy Spirit to those who ask him!"

Luke 11:8, 13

Effective praying must include a kind of desperation. The man who knocks on his neighbor's door at midnight is desperate to fulfill his responsibility to provide for an unexpected guest. The host is in danger of shaming himself along with his entire community by his lack of preparation. His desperation drives him to impudence—to a shameless boldness.

The point is this: Crying out for the Spirit has something to do with a desperation that drives us to forget about our pride and about what anyone else thinks. It's about abasing yourself, falling on your face, and crying out from your heart. Know your absolute helplessness—that you can do nothing, you have no resources, you're poor, you're a beggar, and you must have what only God can give. The passage is about learning to pray that way. If the man in bed would not get up and go help his friend until he was shaken by the urgency and persistence of the noise he made, how much more will the heavenly Father willingly give you the Spirit?

April 27

What causes quarrels and what causes fights among you? Is it not this, that your passions are at war within you? You desire and do not have, so you murder. You covet and cannot obtain, so you fight and quarrel. You do not have, because you do not ask. James 4:1-2

When I was growing up in Oregon, we went on a school picnic near a deep, swift river. We were all playing on a large rock overlooking the river when one boy pushed another into the water, knowing he couldn't swim. I will never forget hearing him cry as he went into the water. We raced over and rescued him. After that we called the spot "murder rock." This passage is saying that we too struggle with that kind of murderous rage. We murder people in our hearts in all different ways. We gossip, slander, avoid people, and sometimes mix it up face-to-face.

James points out that these relationship problems come from desires deep within us. Instead of taking these desires to God in prayer for him to reshape, we try to get what we want from others. When we do this, we are assuming that if we can't handle a problem, then no one can—including God. We go through life feeling miserable, without hope for real change in our relationships. For us, grace often means getting the best job, healing, or help with a problem, but that's so shallow. It doesn't have anything to do with God's healing grace that goes deep into the desires of the heart.

April 28

God opposes the proud, but gives grace to the humble.

James 4:6b

What defines our visible conflicts and the invisible envy and selfish ambition that underlie them? It's pride. It's okay to have dignity about what you do or accomplish, but James is talking about a way of life where I'm self-sufficient and everything is centered around my will.

How do we move from the problem to the cure? It's very simple: "God opposes the proud but gives grace to the humble." God opposes the self-sufficient—those who don't pray, or who pray self-centered prayers. But he gives us hope. He will give us the Spirit of grace. God's grace introduces us to a whole new way of thinking and feeling, a whole new way of choosing based on what Christ has done and who Christ is. Christ came down to us who were the lowest that he might raise us to the highest. But the exalting of the Christian comes through Christ on the cross paying the terrible price that made grace worth something. Grace is costly grace. It cost Christ everything that it might be free to you and me. When we receive grace, we are so inspired by the wonder of it that we say, "Lord Jesus, there are some things about me that even I don't like." And just as Jesus humbled himself for us, to exalt us, we say, "I want grace now to humble myself before you." Interact with Jesus—humble yourself, ask for that costly, free grace to change your proud heart.

April 29

*Submit yourselves therefore to God. Resist the devil,
and he will flee from you. James 4:7*

Are you trying to be saved while still on the throne? Don't you know that God only saves people who fall on their face? How can you expect God to hear your prayer when you are trying to do his job and get his glory? When you are trying to build your own record and be so perfect that no one could ever criticize you? The great call here is to think of grace as God-centered—Father, Son, and Holy Spirit—all of God and a willing God. That's to whom we submit.

But submitting to God has to be spelled out in how you relate to other people. We need to submit to one another as well. Do you listen to people? Or are you so defensive that there can't be revival? You are so sure that you have it all together that you don't need grace? Grace comes when we submit—to God and others. When you do so, when you humble yourself, the devil will be on the run, not just walking, but fleeing. Is there some area of your life where the devil has tempted you? Perhaps in sexuality? Addiction? Fears that grip every part of you? The answer has to be this: Submit yourself to God and to others. Take your stand on the cross of Christ. The devil has no claim over you.

April 30

Draw near to God, and he will draw near to you.
Cleanse your hands, you sinners, and purify your hearts,
you double-minded. Be wretched and mourn and weep.
Let your laughter be turned to mourning and your joy
to gloom. Humble yourselves before the Lord, and he
will exalt you. James 4:8–10

A husband and wife were driving together, and she said to him, "Why don't you sit close to me anymore?" As he held on to the wheel, he looked at her and said, "I haven't moved." God is saying the same thing to us here, "I haven't moved. Come near to me. I will surprise you and be there." Remember these words: "Come near to God and he will come near to you."

Do you think your fears, lusts, and desires cannot be overcome? When you surrender to God, he will come near—you will change. On the one hand we let go of all self-effort and rest only on Christ for our growth, but as we do that we get on the move. Notice the action language: We wash, grieve, and mourn. We don't need a tune-up; we need to be remade. We, fault-finding, defensive, desperate sinners, need Jesus to do a deep work and give us grace. Do you want God to meet you today? Come near to God and say, "I want Jesus. I want the Holy Spirit. Deal with my desires and my self-centeredness." Commit yourself to getting into this passage and moving out in love. Don't let the cross be powerless in your life.

May 1

From the rising of the sun to its setting, the name of
the LORD is to be praised! Psalm 113:3

The audience in Psalm 113 is everybody, all over the world, from the place where the sun rises to the place where it sets. Notice that this audience is expected to do something, not just sit and listen. They are expected to join together, like a choir, in praise. Praise is about celebrating the greatness of God with other believers. You want everyone to praise the Lord! To hear about the greatness of Christ and not say *hallelujah* and to not have a life of praise is to miss everything.

The omnipotent God has come in the person of his Son, Jesus Christ, and won a victory that none of us can take in. Catch the inexpressible glory of it. The very nature of praise is to celebrate the great reality of God's working in lives, in history, in his government of the future, in however he may use you. God uses everything—even your weaknesses and your failures. Ours is a very great God, and it is his "God-ness" that makes us happy.

May 2

The Lord is high above all nations, and his glory
above the heavens! Psalm 113:4

Jesus delighted in the will of someone else, in pleasing another person. We tend to fight the wills of other people, and we especially fight the will of God because we don't trust him. The mark of the maturity that God gives is that you enjoy his will and submit to it. Sometimes you do the wrong thing, but God loves you anyway and is delighted by the heart attitude of giving yourself to him.

We praise him because he is worthy of it. When God demands our praise, he is not being megalomaniacal. His glory is above the heavens, and he is simply living the truth and demanding that people recognize the truth. If you asked people to worship you for your glory, you'd be living a lie. You are not all-glorious; you're just like the rest of us. But God is all-glorious. "Who is like the Lord our God, who is seated on high, who looks far down on the heavens and the earth?" (Psalm 113:5–6). Our God is so exalted that he has to look down to see the galaxies. He's infinite, majestic, and qualitatively different from us. His name is Yahweh, the Lord, the self-existent One, the Creator of all, who upholds it all and has committed himself to people. We are to delight in him. He is worth it.

May 3

He raises the poor from the dust and lifts the needy
from the ash heap. Psalm 113:7

Do you feel like you're on the ash heap? Perhaps a lot in your life has gone wrong—you've had hurts, disappointments, failures, habitual sins. You're afraid to get too close to God; afraid he might expose and ruin you. Maybe you have little hope that you can change. Deep down you doubt that anyone would love you if they really knew you. Because you don't want to be hurt, you keep your distance.

But here's where grace comes in. God, who is so exalted that he has to look down to see the galaxies, sun, moon, and stars, stoops even farther than that. He stoops right down into the ash heap where you and I live. The ash heap represents poverty, helplessness, and death. God comes down to this ash heap and lifts us up. This is the height of what we should celebrate. We are all much worse sinners than we know. What God has done is to plant the Holy Spirit inside us to bring us onboard this rescue operation. The Holy Spirit is eager to show you God and his power in the midst of your ashes. He wants you to see how even the ashes and broken things in your life can be openings for God's grace.

May 4

My son, give me your heart, and let your eyes
observe my ways. Proverbs 23:26

Many children from Christian families have not given their hearts to God. Why have parents lost the hearts of their children? One reason is that often parents have not really given their own hearts to God. We are asking our children to be something we are not. When God says, "Give me your heart," he is asking for the whole person—not just outward behavior, but the inward bent of our lives. That really puts a tight shoe on the foot. Because we all have a tendency to fake it—not just preachers like me—but all of us.

Giving your heart to God means a deep surrender to the will of God, which is not easy. We quickly discover that we are already committed to our own will—to not doing anything dangerous, embarrassing, upsetting, or uncomfortable. But God says, "My child, I want you to know my character and my person and my promises so well that you can trust me as I lead you through darkness. You may not be able to see in the dark, but you can be confident because your hand will be in my hand and I know every step of the way." Give your children the gift of seeing you walk with your heavenly Father. Give them the gift of seeing you surrender your desires to Christ. Then watch, pray, love, and wait in faith for God to be at work in their hearts.

May 5

My son, give me your heart, and let your eyes
observe my ways. Proverbs 23:26

Often we go back and forth between thinking we are doing okay and then, if we make a mistake, deciding we are hopeless failures. But God tells us to stop that way of thinking and see the possibilities he has in you. He wants us to see ourselves as potential missionaries. We are not in this world just to survive. We are here to be warriors for Jesus Christ and to carry his gospel to this confused generation. Give your heart to God and then give your life to follow him.

But how do we get the courage to do this? The end of this verse can also be translated, "let your eyes delight in my ways" (NASB). As you delight in God, you will grow in courage and faith. How does this happen? Take time to meet Jesus. He kept the law. He delighted to give his will to the Father. And now, having atoned for our sins, he lives in us and for us. Jesus wants to meet with you. His office is always open. You can knock and go in anytime. Out of your relationship with him you can be strong in dealing by grace with others. You can have a backbone. You can do right when it's hard. But the only way is to meet with Jesus. Tell him where you are messing up. Let him clean it up. He will.

May 6

Jesus said to him, "Today salvation has come
to this house. . . . For the Son of Man came to seek
and to save the lost." Luke 19:9–10

On his way to Jerusalem for the last time, Jesus meets Zacchaeus. When Jesus stops, calls Zacchaeus, and says that his mission is to "seek and save the lost," he is giving us a picture of what the cross is all about. When we think of being lost, we might think of losing our way, but Jesus is going far deeper. He is talking about a life lost for all eternity—a life disconnected forever from the love of God. He is going to Jerusalem to take upon himself our eternal lostness.

We often are unaware of our own lostness—much less that of our lost neighbor. But how can you grasp the greatness of the love of God if you don't understand your lostness? If there was nothing much wrong with you when Jesus died—if Jesus died on the cross for little sinners with little sins—then why the agony and the darkened sky? Why does Jesus cry out, "My God, my God, why have you forsaken me"? Jesus died alone and in agony because the Father is utterly just and must punish sins. Without Jesus, we are lost for eternity. Jesus brought out the depths of the love of God, by going so deep into suffering that he emptied all the wrath of hell. What a salvation! What a Savior! What a message to share with the lost!

May 7

Jesus said to them again, "Peace be with you. As the
Father has sent me, even so I am sending you." And
when he had said this, he breathed on them and said to
them, "Receive the Holy Spirit." John 20:21-22

Jesus defines the church as "the sent ones." Jesus handed his commission on to us, and then he gave us the Holy Spirit so we would have the power to live out his commission. I don't know exactly how the Holy Spirit was transmitted by Jesus's breathing, but something powerful was going on. The emphasis is on Jesus's strength and authority coming upon poor stumbling humans so much like us.

After they received the Holy Spirit, we see in Acts that the apostles lived with joy-filled passion, and died with courage. Their boldness is shocking; we, on the other hand, can't even share Christ with a friend. We have the same Spirit, but somehow we miss the connection. In that moment, Jesus breathed the Holy Spirit into the church. Do you believe that? Then fan into flame the Spirit because that's the connection with the authority of Jesus. We have the power of him who rose from the dead, and who is now seated at the right hand of the Father, ruling all things by the word of his power. Move toward others with the good news of salvation knowing that his power is on you and in you.

May 8

Jesus said to them again, "Peace be with you. As the Father has sent me, even so I am sending you." John 20:21

Many of us have decided that we are saved to sit and sleep and be safe. We're secure—but also self-indulgent. Has the devil stolen the Great Commission from our hearts? A young Count Ludwig von Zinzendorf stood before a painting of Christ on the cross. At the top of the painting was the inscription, "Behold the man." At the bottom were the words, "This I have suffered for you. What have you done for me?" His heart's cry was, "I have done very little." That changed his life. We have something even better than a portrait to change us. We have the living Savior. We can go to Jesus and ask, "Where are you leading me? To whom do you want me to go?" Meditate on Christ's death, resurrection, and gift of the Spirit. You will "behold the man" and be filled with a commonsense, sane love for other people, with brokenness over sin, and self-forgetting love.

Once I was in a taxi with a Spanish-speaking driver. I thought about sharing the gospel, but I don't speak Spanish very well. So I prayed and asked the Holy Spirit to help me with my Spanish. At the climax of my gospel presentation, I made this powerful statement, "Christ died for our fish." The man roared with laughter—and then he was my friend for life. Don't try so hard—just be stupid along with me. The lost are out there. Let's love them from death to life.

May 9

I rejoice, not because you were grieved, but because
you were grieved into repenting. For you felt a godly
grief, so that you suffered no loss through us.
2 Corinthians 7:9

When we think about grief, we don't usually think of it as being good. But the apostle Paul says that a certain kind of grief can be good. And Jesus says, "Blessed are those who mourn for they shall be comforted" (Matthew 5:4). A more literal translation of the word *comfort* here is "empower." Our word for comfort originally meant not just having tears wiped away, but being strengthened, fortified. So the Scripture tells us that grief can be a source of comfort or happy change. This is a little puzzling to us. But this kind of grief brings strength to your soul because it is a grieving over your sins. This is a good grief that moves you away from thinking about yourself and moves you toward loving Christ and others.

Good grieving over our sins is a way of breaking down the isolation in us. Good grief is like a resurrection. Self-centered grief—"worldly grief" (2 Corinthians 7:10)—is like rigor mortis. Godly grief brings repentance and change, and leaves no regret. What a wonderful thing to have no regret for past sins and mistakes! What's the secret to a life of no regrets? It's godly grief over our sins combined with faith that looks to the cross of Christ for forgiveness and hope.

May 10

For godly grief produces a repentance that leads
to salvation without regret, whereas worldly grief
produces death. 2 Corinthians 7:10

If you want to know what worldly grief over sin looks like, look at Judas (Matthew 27:3–6). After realizing that he had betrayed an innocent man, Judas, seized with remorse, threw the money down in the temple, and went and hanged himself. Here was a man whose grief over his sins was not combined with faith. He had been with Jesus, but had never trusted himself to his Lord and Savior. There is nothing more dangerous than grieving for your sins without faith in Christ.

But Peter—also a denier of Christ—went to Jesus with his sins. Imagine the scene: The rooster is crowing; Peter is loudly denying his best friend; and the Lord turns and looks Peter in the eye with love. When Pentecost came and the Spirit fell upon him, Peter preached grief over sin and repentance in a way that no one had ever done before. Of the people who heard his sermon that day, three thousand were pricked to the heart. They grieved over their sins and turn to Christ in faith. The link? Peter believed. Peter saw his sins and went to his faithful Savior and Lord Jesus for forgiveness and help. Good grief for one's sins is believing grief—believing in the love of the Father, the saving grace of his Son, and the power of the Holy Spirit. This is the kind of godly grief that brings salvation and leaves no regret.

May 11

For godly grief produces a repentance that leads
to salvation without regret, whereas worldly grief
produces death. 2 Corinthians 7:10

How can you tell the difference between good (godly) grief and bad (worldly) grief over sins? One way is to look for self-pity. If you are filled with regret, check your heart for self-pity, because the sorrow that accompanies self-pity is self-focused and not focused on the work of Christ on the cross. Another difference between good and bad grief is that good grief leads to confession, but bad, self-centered grief leads to a desire for vindication.

You can see that in Job. He was looking for vindication from his three accusing friends (who were wrong!). He doesn't find vindication, but he does meet God and is broken before him (Job 42:5–6). Before he met God in his majesty and holiness, the center of his life was wanting to be seen as righteous. This desire is in every human heart, but fulfilling it means relying on yourself for salvation. You have to vindicate yourself by getting on the cross and taking care of your own sins. But through faith in the Savior who would one day come, Job was transformed and became a type of those who persevere until they get to know God, who trust God for their vindication, and who are strengthened as they mourn for their sins. "Blessed are those who mourn for they will be comforted" (Matthew 5:4 NIV).

May 12

For godly grief produces a repentance that leads
to salvation without regret, whereas worldly grief
produces death. 2 Corinthians 7:10

How do you get a "good" grief over your sins? You get it by faith—by going to Jesus and asking for forgiveness for your sins. Most of us are good at seeing others' sins. And often we are indignant over them. Remember when the prophet Nathan told King David about the man who took the little sheep from the poor man, killed it, and ate it? David replies indignantly, "Let me at him. I'm going to kill that man." Then Nathan said, "You are the man!" (2 Samuel 12:7).

God says we are all "the man." We have all sinned and come short of the glory of God. We were made for glory, not for fighting and attacking one another. We were made to be free children of God. But we have an innate coldness toward God. Even so, God loves you so much that he gave his one and only Son for you. Look at the cross and see his love for you. Let its message break you so that you grieve over your sins, which pierced Jesus through. This conviction will change you. That's the power of the cross. Have you seen Christ on the cross for you? Have you asked for forgiveness in his name? Turn to him in faith. Ask the Spirit to warm your cold heart with a godly grief.

May 13

He chose us in him before the foundation of the world,
that we should be holy and blameless before him. In
love he predestined us for adoption as sons through
Jesus Christ, according to the purpose of his will.
Ephesians 1:4–5

As a young man, I was restless and confused. I thought I was a Christian but there was no change in my life. One afternoon I read the first chapter of Ephesians. It made me angry and I thought, *Who does God think he is?* The answer from Ephesians was clear, "God is God. Who do you think you are?" I was cut to the heart and realized I wanted my glory; I wanted to say it was my will that chose Christ; I wanted to save myself. I saw how evil it was to live for my glory, so I said to God, "I don't even know if you want me, but take me." And he took me.

When I saw what Jesus had done for me on the cross, I wanted to dance for joy. Immediately I wanted others to know the joy of surrendering to Christ. I was only twenty years old, but I went door-to-door and said to whoever answered, "Have you heard about Jesus and how he can save you and fill your life with joy?" Before, I had been afraid of people, but once I saw the glory of Christ, I understood that others were just like me— nothing to be afraid of. Are you still living for your own glory? Surrendering to Christ can free you to live for something much bigger—the glory of God.

May 14

Blessed be the God and Father of our Lord Jesus Christ, who has blessed us in Christ with every spiritual blessing in the heavenly places. Ephesians 1:3

We think of heaven as something ghostly and unreal, but heaven isn't like that—the heavenly realm is the power center of the universe. Jesus is there, and we are right there with him. You are with him in glory! God chose us to be holy, chose us to be his sons and daughters (Ephesians 1:4–5). No matter who you are or what you have done, when you are in Christ you are made beautiful. Paul calls us God's workmanship (Ephesians 2:10)—his work of art.

Consider what it means that you are in Christ. Every blessing is yours in Christ. You are being made beautiful in Christ. You belong to God for eternity. You are at the center of power with the Lord of the universe. If you are not excited that he has made you his holy, blameless, precious child and work of art, then you might have forgotten what you are really like. That's my fundamental problem: I don't feel that I'm elect, but that I'm elite. Know this: we didn't start out as the best, but as the worst. And left to ourselves, we are still not very far from that. When you see that, then there is a humility and gratitude in you that attracts others to Christ. Jesus doesn't really like the elite. He didn't choose the best. He is the best.

May 15

He chose us in him before the foundation of the world,
that we should be holy and blameless before him. In
love he predestined us for adoption as sons through
Jesus Christ, according to the purpose of his will.
Ephesians 1:4–5

When God looked down the long corridor of history, he didn't look at us and say, "There's some wonderful people who will want to receive my Son." Instead he saw us—the perishing and the lost—and adopted us into his family. We didn't have to do anything, he found us. That was a good thing, because underneath the mess that was my life was a core of self-dependence.

When I first read, "In love he predestined us for adoption," I was angry. But then I realized I had to respond—either to surrender or to turn away. You can't have it both ways. Either you let God be God all the way or you choose your own way and try to save yourself. That doesn't mean I didn't choose Christ. I did. But who was at work showing me my sin? Showing me my need for Jesus? The question is: who is the first mover? The answer has to be God. The God of the Bible is Yahweh, literally "the God who saves." Salvation is of the Lord. And when salvation is of the Lord, what are you worried about? You can trust that your heavenly Father has your life all in hand. He knows the beginning from the end.

May 16

*Forgetting what lies behind and straining forward to
what lies ahead, I press on toward the goal for the prize
of the upward call of God in Christ Jesus.*
Philippians 3:13b-14

In the movie *Chariots of Fire*, Harold Abrahams, in an effort to improve his racing technique, hires a coach, who teaches him how to strain forward when nearing the finish line to gain the couple of inches necessary to win the race. This is the image that comes to mind when Paul writes about, "forgetting what lies behind and straining forward." He's talking here about his mind and his heart—what he thinks about and what he loves. Christ is his goal; Christ is everything to him.

In a race, there's glory along with tremendous tension. The racer, before even leaving the starting block, pictures the race from start to finish. For Paul, and for us, when we know we're going to win Christ, everything we do works toward that end. There are certain habits to be put off and others to acquire in order to win the race. Paul is talking about how you live in this present world, focusing everything on gaining Christ. Meditate on this; be challenged to do the same.

May 17

But whatever gain I had, I counted as loss for the sake of Christ. . . . forgetting what lies behind and straining forward to what lies ahead. Philippians 3:7, 13

What does Paul mean by "forgetting what lies behind"? Earlier in this passage, he listed his reasons for having confidence in the flesh, before denouncing them as rubbish compared to Christ. He wants not his own righteousness but the righteousness of Christ. In other words, he discards all the things that made him noble in the eyes of the world, because they weigh him down as he runs the race.

When I first started preaching, one week I would preach a sermon that was strong and fiery, but the next week I'd come back so weak that my congregation wondered if I was the same person. After praying and searching my heart, I discovered that every time I preached a strong sermon, I viewed it as something by which I earned God's favor—something to boast about. Without fail, the following week God would withdraw his Spirit, and my sermon would be weak and powerless. When I repented of my boasting, God humbled me. This is the way it is with many people. They become tangled up with their virtues, offend God, and consequently have no strength. In their pride, they don't have any real need for Christ, except as an occasional prop. Do you ever do that? Paul is calling us to repent, to forget what is behind and press on toward Christ.

May 18

Jesus said, "Leave her alone. Why do you trouble her?
She has done a beautiful thing to me." Mark 14:6

Mary (John 12:3) anoints Jesus, who responds by saying these remarkable words: "She has done a beautiful thing to me." This is in stark contrast to some there that day who were indignant that she had "wasted" a year's wages. Cutting across attitudes, values, and ways of thinking as he often did, Jesus had the habit of upsetting his hearers.

But when Jesus's words are jarring, that is when we most need to listen. Here he is telling his disciples—and us—what it is that counts most in life. The principle the disciples are working with is what you give away you lose. That might have some truth to it in some situations, but not here for Mary. The reason Jesus calls what she did beautiful is because she gave all of herself to him. Every area of your life ought to involve a giving of yourself to Christ. As you do that, God will bless you and bless you and bless you. Can you compare yourself with Mary and say, "I have given everything to Jesus"? "I'm not in this for my glory, but Christ's"? You won't ever lose what you give to Christ. You will be blessed beyond measure.

May 19

"She has done what she could; she has anointed my
body beforehand for burial." Mark 14:8

How well do you listen to Jesus? The disciples are with Jesus, who is reclining at the table with the shadow of the cross over him. Because the disciples have not listened to Jesus, they fail to see the glory of what he is about to do. Further, they don't understand why Mary is anointing him.

Why haven't they been listening? Why don't we listen? This kind of listening calls for a deep humbling. It begins by going to Jesus and saying, "Lord, I am completely distracted, preoccupied, and self-absorbed. Instead of being like Mary, who sat at your feet listening, I am much more like her sister Martha. I don't know how to sit at your feet, and I don't know how to listen." If you want to know Christ, he will reveal himself to you. He is the one, after all, who put that desire in your heart. Go to Jesus, sit at his feet, and say, "Lord, teach me to listen to you. Show me yourself. Show me that you love me. Give me faith. I know that you are the Son of God who loved me and gave yourself for me." Come to Christ and say, "I need your blood; I need your righteousness; I need your Spirit to flow in me and blot out my sins. I am the needy one today." Then when you see Jesus, give everything to him, just as Mary did.

May 20

If anyone comes to me and does not hate his own
father and mother and wife and children and brothers
and sisters, yes, and even his own life, he cannot be
my disciple. Whoever does not bear his own cross and
come after me cannot be my disciple. Luke 14:26–27

Jesus wants to free us from our tendency to try and own his kingdom work. We should work hard, of course, but not for our own glory. We say we want to succeed for Jesus's sake, but often underneath is the desire to prove ourselves, to get our security from our success. When that happens, our work for God owns us. We become defensive, fragile, and vulnerable, emotional prisoners of our work. Then, if someone attacks our ministry or if it seems to be failing, we're shattered, our identity in tatters.

Being free from all that is as simple as giving up everything—our reputation, success, glory—and following Jesus. When we lay it all down to follow Jesus, then the success of our work is up to the Spirit, and our identity isn't tied to our success or failure. Jesus calls his disciples to give up everything and follow him. He calls us to the freedom of being attached to Christ and his kingdom. How liberating it is to discover grace afresh!

May 21

He also told them a parable: "Can a blind man lead a
blind man? Will they not both fall into a pit? A disciple
is not above his teacher, but everyone when he is fully
trained will be like his teacher." Luke 6:39–40

Jesus says that the basic principle of discipleship
is this: those around you will become like you. If
you are following Christ and becoming like him, then
Christ will be reproduced in others. But if you are
blind, those following you will also be blind, and you
will all end up in the ditch together.

What blinds us? What leads others into a pit with
us? It's our pride. If the Spirit is going to use you to
reproduce Christ in others, you have to deal with the
various ways that deeply rooted pride has a hold on
your life. In his letter to them, Paul wants the Galatians
to see that relying on the law to get near to God is arrogance, and their only boast should be in the cross of
Christ (Galatians 6:13–14). The Spirit wants to make
us people of grace who draw others to God. That begins
with seeing we have nothing and Christ has everything.
It's only as you face up to this that you can do what God
is calling you to do.

May 22

"For God so loved the world, that he gave his only Son, that whoever believes in him should not perish but have eternal life." John 3:16

When you know God's great love for you and the whole world, you go from being *self*-conscious to being *Christ*-conscious. First John 4:7 says, "Beloved, let us love one another for love is from God." Since love is "from God," as we come to know God, we are filled with his love. God's love softens our cold, stony hearts; he makes us human. For this to happen, you must know your identity as a child—a son or daughter—of God.

Many Christians are preoccupied with questions about what they should do, or how they should act, or where they should go. But the deeper questions have not been resolved. Deeper questions like: who am I? Do we grasp that God loves us with a love that is so big we can't take it in? We are not orphans out in the world just trying to survive. We are God's dearly loved children. So many Christians are just trying to figure out how to cope with the next bruising that is coming their way. But when you understand God's love for you, then you have the power to love the world. God wants to do great things *for* you and *through* you.

May 23

"You therefore must be perfect, as your heavenly
Father is perfect." Matthew 5:48

Be perfect. We don't usually take these words seriously because we grade ourselves on a curve. Some people are worse, some better. We'll be accepted because God will average it out. But God's law demands perfection, which means loving God with all your heart, all your soul, and all your might. Only one person ever loved God like this: his own Son, Jesus—one hundred percent man and one hundred percent God—whom God sent out of love for us.

Jesus is like us except for one crucial difference: he loves God from the heart. In him the law's demand for perfection is met. In the agony of real history, fighting real forces, he is separated from God for our sake. God the Father turns on his perfect Son the wrath our sins deserve. This great sacrifice moves us to cry out with the tax collector, "God, be merciful to me, a sinner!" (Luke 18:13b). When we underestimate the holiness of God and the greatness of God's love, then it's easy for us to worry, to be full of self-effort, to compare ourselves with others. But Jesus gives us a new name: "child of God." By faith your new consciousness is son of God, daughter of God, loved by God. Be broken before God because of your sins. But don't stay there; be lifted up in unutterable joy because of the greatness of God's love for you in Christ.

May 24

If I speak in the tongues of men and of angels, but have
not love, I am a noisy gong or a clanging cymbal.
1 Corinthians 13:1

In Christ, we have freedom (Galatians 5:1). But our
freedom is not for serving ourselves; it's for serving
others. How does that work? Because of what Jesus did
at the cross we are cleansed from our sins and released
from condemnation. At the cross, God shows how
much he loves us, how personally he loves us. His love
shapes us into new people. How these new people think
and act is illustrated in 1 Corinthians 13.

As a struggling sinner, I know how easy it is to put
on counterfeit love—to be nothing but a noisy gong.
But God always gives me the grace to notice my lack
of love and go to Jesus for help. There is grace for you
too. Because you are God's dearly loved child, you don't
have to judge, compete, or use others. Your conscience
is free, and you can look on others with love. Jesus says
you will do greater things than he did. Do you believe
it? Don't look at yourself any more as unimportant. You
are worth so much. Ask God to open your eyes to see
your sinfulness—to confess it, to forsake it, to be driven
to the cross again, and to be filled with love and power
as a child of the living God.

May 25

Restore to me the joy of your salvation, and uphold me
with a willing spirit. Psalm 51:12

As a youngster, I had a cow to care for. In the pas-
ture, there was a spring where I took the cow to
drink. Once, the spring was so clogged with leaves and
dirt that there was no water. A friend, using a shovel,
dug into the spring and cleared out the debris. At first,
it looked worse than ever; mud and leaves were every-
where. But when the water was released, the spring
once again flowed clean and clear. In Psalm 51 David
says that his joy in knowing God had been reduced to
a trickle by sins for which he had not repented. David
needed joy restored and the way forward was through
repentance.

When we first meet Christ, we are overwhelmed
by joy. But often, the spring from which the joy flows,
gets clogged up by sin. If we have a superficial view of
our sin, then we will not turn daily to God for grace
and forgiveness; and we won't experience the joy of
our salvation. But if we come to Christ moment by
moment, the dominant theme of our life will be joy.
This joy is more than mere ordinary happiness; it's what
Peter calls "inexpressible and filled with glory" (1 Peter
1:8); and it flows freely when our sins are confessed.
How glorious to know the love of the Father and the
forgiveness guaranteed to us because of the death and
resurrection of his Son.

May 26

Blessed is the one whose transgression is forgiven,
whose sin is covered. Blessed is the man against whom
the LORD counts no iniquity, and in whose spirit there
is no deceit. Psalm 32:1–2

Conviction of sin doesn't have to leave you in a black hole. In fact, here David is full of joy that his sins are forgiven. They are covered; they are not counted against him. David doesn't know exactly how this will be accomplished; he speaks by faith through the Spirit. But from the vantage point of the cross and the resurrection, Paul quotes this passage in Romans 4:7–8, and applies it to the righteousness of Christ that is ours through faith. Because Jesus shed his own blood for your sins, you can be sure they are covered. God no longer sees them. You are counted righteous before God because of what Jesus has done.

How does this work? Our relationship to Jesus is compared to a marriage (Revelation 21:9). Because we are "married" to Christ, everything he has is ours. That's how marriage works. When my wife and I, as students, were married, I had nothing, but she had $85 and a typewriter. I needed both! And because we were married, we shared them. The same is true of you and Jesus. Everything he has and did is yours.

May 27

Blessed is the man against whom the Lord counts no
iniquity, and in whose spirit there is no deceit.
Psalm 32:2

What brings change to someone lost in sin? Change starts when the sinner is introduced to God's love and forgiveness. When the assurance of God's love is interjected into the atmosphere, the hope of change comes with it. This is because when you know you are forgiven and welcomed by God through Jesus, you can face the truth about yourself.

A child who is afraid of his parents will lie and lie and lie some more. Only the assurance that he is loved will coax the truth out of him. That's what David expresses in Psalm 32. He is learning about the love of God, and on that basis he can tell the truth and have his sincerity restored. If we have really seen how holy God is; if we really understand what Jesus did to pay for our sins; then we are so overwhelmed with joy that we can come clean. We don't have to lie anymore. Our sin is forgiven, covered, not credited to us anymore. With joy in knowing God's forgiveness, we confess, turn from our sins, and teach other sinners to do the same.

May 28

Do not grieve the Holy Spirit of God, by whom you were sealed for the day of redemption. Ephesians 4:30

Paul's command not to grieve the Holy Spirit, stated positively, is an invitation to guard your friendship with the Holy Spirit. Paul is echoing Isaiah's lament that God's people turned from his love and his Spirit is grieved (Isaiah 63:10). But Paul also has the marvelous love of God in view that is broken open to us in the previous chapters in Ephesians. Paul is talking about a friendship so amazing and a plan of salvation so great that you wouldn't want anything to hinder it. A friendship with the Holy Spirit is so intimate and wonderful that you want to be on the alert and sensitive to what God has started in you. The gift of the Holy Spirit is the climax of God's plan of redemption. The Spirit of grace is in your heart, a Spirit of sealing, so you know that Christ is coming again. You know the inheritance is yours. You know you are a child of God. It's not a rebuke, but an encouragement to go deeper into the love of God. That's why you need to guard yourself against lying, bitterness, stealing, and unwholesome talk because these all affect your love relationship with God (Ephesians 4:25–32). Come often to the living Christ so you can be cleansed and your friendship with God renewed.

Do not grieve the Holy Spirit of God, by whom you were sealed for the day of redemption. Ephesians 4:30

How can you tell when you have grieved the Holy Spirit? The answer is simple. The Holy Spirit is a person who, like us, is wounded when people turn on him and ignore him. As a Christian you are, of course, sealed, but you do, nevertheless, feel the loss of the Spirit's presence as well as the restlessness that comes from not being in fellowship with him.

My wife's mentally disabled sister, Aunt Barbara, loves to bring her toys to friends' homes for the children to play with. If the children fight over the toys, she gives them a warning or two. Then, if they don't listen, she packs her bag and heads for home. That gets their attention and gradually they learn to act better, because they like her to visit. That's like the Holy Spirit, isn't it? He does you a favor when he withdraws. He gets your attention. You are still friends, but his absence is felt. His strategy is to let you get so sick of yourself that you turn again to the Father and rediscover the freshness and beauty of the forgiveness of sins. He wants to remind you how much you need the cross, how much you need to be a little child at the feet of Jesus. The Spirit is sensitive to you being clean on the inside. He's there to help you grow in holiness, in kindness, and in love for others. Invite his help.

May 30

When you heard about Christ . . . you were taught . . .
to put off your old self, which is being corrupted by
its deceitful desires; to be made new in the attitude of
your minds; and to put on the new self, created to be
like God in true righteousness and holiness.

Ephesians 4:21–24 NIV

You are in a struggle as you cling to the things from your old life before Christ. Paul wants you to deal with this problem, so that you don't drift into living a double life, where you claim to be a new person in Christ, but still live like the old you. He reminds you that you have learned something about Christ, so you can lay aside the old, corrupt desires, which don't belong to you anymore. When Christ died, all of your old sinful ways died too. He paid for them by his blood, and he broke their power. So now you can count yourself dead to them and put on your new self.

You might say, "What a minute. That news is too good to be true. My sins are still there." Yes, you still struggle with sin, but now the crucial difference is you are dead to sin and alive to Christ. Sounds too simple? Remember: because you are alive to Christ, you are now God's friend and his Spirit lives inside you. The Holy Spirit is the person who is most important in keeping you from leading a double life. All of his resources are yours as you live in humble reliance on him.

May 31

"These I will bring to my holy mountain, and make them joyful in my house of prayer." Isaiah 56:7

Being a Christian is about joy: the joy of forgiveness, the joy of the resurrection, the joy of seeing others come to Christ. How do you get this joy? By understanding both the law *and* the gospel. Both are good and holy. Both are from God and deal with our standing before God. But they have radically different functions. The law demands perfection—not just external, but loving the Lord with all your heart (Deuteronomy 6:5). The law says, Do this and live. In response, we try to make ourselves acceptable to God by obeying his commands and we fail.

But the gospel says, Christ has kept the law from the heart. He has paid the penalty for your sin on the cross and through faith in him you shall live. We have so little joy because we water down the law so it doesn't really mean what it says, and we water down the gospel, so our salvation isn't really as big as it is. You have to accept the full demand of the law along with the full glory of the gospel. In Christ, God's love for you is unconditional and unchangeable. When you are shocked by your sins and shocked by God's love in Christ, then you will be full of joy—joy you will want to share with others.

June 1

"For God so loved the world, that he gave his only Son, that whoever believes in him should not perish but have eternal life." John 3:16

How can you experience the joy of knowing Christ? Read and reread John 3:16. God's love for you is far greater than you can imagine. God's law demands perfection. The penalty for imperfection is death. But the Father gave his one and only Son for you. Christ died for you. He perished, so you can live. Are you trying to work out your own salvation? That will take away your joy. Are you lifted up in pride so this doesn't mean anything to you? That will take away your joy too. Only the love of God in Christ will fill you with joy and carry you through the weariness, the boredom, the shame, and the weakness. It will carry you through today and tomorrow.

If you would like a little joy today, then come to Christ. If you see yourself as imperfect, self-centered, with a heart far from God, turn from your sin and trust in Christ. When you open your heart to Jesus and ask him to take away your sins, when you trust that his righteousness will make you acceptable to God, then his Spirit will fill your heart with deep and abiding joy.

June 2

The title "Son of Man" shows us two things about Jesus: his humanity and his deity. The first thing it shows is his humanity. Jesus really knows you. He doesn't call you by name to scare you, but to show that he loves you deeply. He suffered on a real cross, in his humanity, to take away your sins. The second thing the title Son of Man shows us is that Jesus is Lord of the universe. The picture is of the Father, the Ancient of Days, giving to the Son of Man all authority (Daniel 7:13–14). He is Lord of All, and he can change us wherever we are.

He gets a lot of glory in that, doesn't he? The One who died on the cross died in weakness, but he was raised by the power of God! He now lives, and the wind of his Spirit now moves across the world. He's no longer walking the earth on sandaled feet, but he's moving invisibly inside hearts—convicting of sin and showing the love of God. He says, "Come and I'll change you. I'll give you a new life. My blood will take away all your sins. Will you have me?"

June 3

"Blessed are those who hunger and thirst for
righteousness, for they shall be satisfied." Matthew 5:6

Jesus didn't say, "Blessed are those who *are* righteous,
for they shall be satisfied." His whole Sermon on the
Mount is about how obedience to the law is not only
about behavior, but also about heart orientation. What
God calls us to is not a pharisaic self-righteousness. The
Pharisees were nice, decent people, but they missed the
inward and upward and outward relationship of Jesus's
teaching.

If you are a true believer, your response to Jesus's
words should be "Help!" Those who know their inability
to be righteous, and ask for help, will be blessed.
The very idea of eating and drinking is that what you
need comes from outside yourself. You don't have the
righteousness God requires, and, therefore, this is what
you long for. Jesus wants us to have an appetite for, to
long for, what we do not have—the righteousness that
comes from him. It is blessed to long for what Jesus
wants to give you. It is blessed to be dissatisfied. It is
blessed to aim for perfection. You are not going to be
perfect in this life, but you *aim* for it because that's what
Jesus commands. You work for it, you long for it, and
you put off your sins. That's what it means to have an
appetite for God.

June 4

"Blessed are those who hunger and thirst for righteousness, for they shall be satisfied." Matthew 5:6

Christ is in the business of meeting your need, but you may have to discover that your need is much greater than you ever imagined. You may have thought of your need very superficially; that somehow you could get your act together if the Lord could just put a few things in place for you. Very soon after, your act fell apart, and you thought this Christianity thing doesn't work. But it does work, and it works exactly when your act falls apart.

When you hunger and thirst, what do you think about? Usually, you think of something good. It's fulfilling, certainly, but you also enjoy it. That means the food must become attractive to you. Jesus is the host who invites you to the table, but he's also the bread. Remember that Jesus loved you without limit in order to satisfy the justice of God. When you see that his blood was shed for your sins and failures, what an appetite you have for him!

June 5

Have mercy on me, O God,
according to your steadfast love;
according to your abundant mercy
blot out my transgressions. Psalm 51:1

Faith and a pure heart go together. David's cry of repentance is also a cry of faith. Even though David had committed adultery and taken a man's life, and must have been in the depths of despair, he steadfastly believes that God's mercies for him are abundant. He cries to God out of real darkness, "Have mercy, cleanse me, purge me, wash me." And then he prays, "Create in me a clean heart, O God, and renew a right spirit within me" (Psalm 51:10).

Faith reaches up and claims the mercies of God. It asks by faith for God to cleanse and renew the heart. David is not asking for a little spot cleaning; rather, he's asking for God to create in him a whole new heart. What David longs for and cries out for are mercy and a cleansed heart. If you get this, then no matter what struggles you go through, you will realize that you can claim God's mercy for a pure heart because that's what God wants.

June 6

"Blessed are the pure in heart, for they shall see God."
Matthew 5:8

Faith does not create realities; it recognizes them, acts upon them, and depends upon them. Faith is simply opening your eyes to see what God has done, what God is doing, and what God is wanting to do in your life. I promise you, in the name of Jesus, if you believe that, you're going to grow. Your heart will be cleansed by faith, and it will happen again and again.

If you want to be really depressed, take an hour and look inside yourself for faith. Now, don't look for faith, look for Jesus. When you look for Jesus, you have faith. This is the mark of a Christian, the mark of one who believes, the mark of one who has the Spirit. And the more you cultivate a singleness of vision, to have your eyes turned toward Jesus, the more you will develop purity of heart.

June 7

Draw near to God, and he will draw near to you.
Cleanse your hands, you sinners, and purify your hearts,
you double-minded. James 4:8

Let the name of the Lord go deep into your consciousness, soak into your very being, and touch
all you do. Let people know that you've been with
him. The enemy of this is to be double-minded. It is
tempting to hold some things in reserve that you don't
want to give up. This is very foolish since God reads
your heart. Focusing on God is the beginning of air-
ing out those closets where you've been hiding stuff.
One common result of withholding areas of your life
from God—of being double-minded—is burnout. You
serve God here, serve yourself here, and serve someone
else here, and you let your life go into a thousand frag-
ments. The truth is that we all do this. The question
is whether by faith we're dealing with it or letting the
Lord deal with it.

The main difference between a strong Christian
and a weak one is that the latter is hiding things in her
heart that she doesn't want to get rid of, and the former,
the stronger Christian, is the one who opens the door
and invites God in to clean house. It's that simple.

June 8

"Blessed are the pure in heart, for they shall see God."
Matthew 5:8

A pure heart is a heart that by faith lives in God's presence and serves him and him alone. This world has yet to see what God could do with you if you would abandon halfhearted service to God and serve him with your whole heart. A pure heart will see God because the whole life will be oriented toward serving him. In other words, if you're serving yourself, you're not looking toward God. To see God you would have to turn around and go in the other direction.

Maybe you get stuck on the fact that you obviously *don't* have a pure heart. You know for a fact that your thought life is anything but pure. But consider this: the things that bother you most of all may not be the things that bother God most of all. If you don't recognize that you're headed away from God, then what you see as your most basic sins will only scratch the surface of the real problem. What's really wrong is the whole selfish, self-centered course of your life. Therefore God says, "Turn around and serve me. If you do that, you'll see me." What we're really talking about is loving others more than yourself and viewing service to others as an opportunity to glorify God.

June 9

When the disciples saw him walking on the sea, they
were terrified, and said, "It is a ghost!" and they cried
out in fear. But immediately Jesus spoke to them,
saying, "Take heart; it is I. Do not be afraid."
Matthew 14:26–27

Christ's presence can make us uncomfortable. He refuses to adjust to our preconceived notions about who he is and what he should do. Here in Matthew he demonstrates his mastery over creation and his sovereignty. Very soon the crowds are going to melt away, and the disciples will be faced with the decision about whether to follow Jesus. Will they, will you, be able to say, "Lord, to whom shall we go? You have the words of eternal life" (John 6:68)? Walking on the water, Jesus is giving the disciples a basis for faith. His messianic identity as the Son of God is being disclosed to them. And it is awesome.

When Jesus comes, often things become uncomfortable and unpleasant for us. Our sovereign Lord knows our hearts and the things in them that need to be dealt with. He speaks to us in our suffering and weakness. Therefore, if he begins to search you and get you to face up to things in your life you don't want to admit are there, the temptation is to be afraid of him. But when we submit to his testing, we find that his goal is always to do something beautiful and glorious and absolutely loving in our lives.

June 10

"Take heart; it is I. Do not be afraid." And Peter answered [Jesus], "Lord, if it is you, command me to come to you on the water." He said, "Come." So Peter got out of the boat and walked on the water and came to Jesus. Matthew 14:27–29

A practical way of expressing faith is through courage, boldness, daring. Christ's command to the disciples is to put off fear and put on courage because of who he is. We usually think that Peter is being presumptuous by jumping out of the boat. Jesus said to take courage, but Peter was rash and did something he wasn't ready for. But consider this: Peter loved Jesus, and he longed to be with Jesus. So when he hears that familiar voice, Peter asks Jesus to tell him to come. And then he acts on Jesus's invitation. The focus here is not walking on water but coming to Christ. Rather than presumption, this is faith working through love.

For a Christian, all of life is like walking on water. Everything about the Christian life is impossible. Just persevering is impossible. Humbling yourself is impossible. Having relationships is impossible. You can't do any of it. But you can because God, in Christ, causes the depths to congeal enabling you to walk on the water by faith. Faith is depending on nothing but Christ and his invitation.

June 11

> [Jesus] said to Thomas, "Put your finger here, and see
> my hands; and put out your hand, and place it in my
> side. Do not disbelieve, but believe." Thomas answered
> him, "My Lord and my God!" John 20:27-28

Repentance and praise are two sides of the same coin. Repentance relinquishes the center of your world to God; praise makes God the center of your world. When we return to God as the center, and we praise Jesus as our Lord, our owner, our sovereign, our King, our everything, we are confessing the glory of God. Jesus says, "All things are possible for one who believes" (Mark 9:23). Why? Faith lays hold of God. It lays hold of Christ's righteousness so that you have what God has.

This is why, when Thomas exclaims, "My Lord and my God!" he has the one thing needful in the Christian life. We often have long lists of needs, but the one thing we really need is God. When you recognize this and surrender to him, giving him control of your life, you are praising him. You believe that Jesus is raised from the dead, and because you know that, you praise and you praise and you praise. What's more, you can join with other believers in praise. God has come, and he meets with his church. Where two or more are gathered in his name, he will be with them—he will be working, he will be changing, and he will be giving you life!

June 12

[David said], "Leave him alone, and let him curse, for the
LORD has told him to. It may be that the LORD will look on
the wrong done to me, and that the LORD will repay me
with good for his cursing today." 2 Samuel 16:11b-12

It is important to see God's grace and chastening hand in
the critical words of others, even when the critic is wrong
in his charge. When accused by Shimei, David says,
"Leave him alone and let him curse, for the LORD has
told him to." David had not done what Shimei, a slan-
derer, was accusing him of. What can David learn from
this criticism? The fact is that Shimei's accusation holds
some truth. David is not responsible for the death of Saul
or his family, indeed there are several who expect to be
killed to whom he offers life. However, the truth in the
accusation that David is a "man of blood" is that he *is*
responsible for the death of Uriah, Bathsheba's husband.

God used Shimei, an evil man, to drive home the
truth that everyone who has power tends to abuse it.
David used his kingly power to take another man's wife
and, subsequently, his life. Often we repent of past sin
and think it's done, but God wants to show us how
to hate it when the seeds come up again. We all have
favorite sins that crop up in different ways, and God
sends people to help us continue to repent of them.
The next time someone accuses you of something, even
if what they're saying isn't true, look behind it and see if
there is something that you can learn.

June 13

But while he was still a long way off, his father saw him
and felt compassion, and ran and embraced him
and kissed him. Luke 15:20b

Before we consider what repentance is, think about what it isn't. Repentance does not pay for sin. It's not about being plagued with guilt. True repentance does not lead to a deeper mire. It doesn't refuse to give up what's been repented of. Repentance is not a legal thing or an emotional thing.

So, what is repentance? According to the parable of the prodigal son, there are two aspects of repentance: the first is waking up, coming to one's senses, regaining sanity. It is insanity to live for this world as if it were eternal when it's not. The parable of the prodigal is a parable about the Father's riches of love. You can't live as though God's world or anything in it is yours; it all belongs to him. In fact, the best and only real thing to own is the Father himself. The second aspect of repentance begins with being truly sorry for your sin and recognizing that your sin is ultimately against God. In this change of heart, you confess the whole truth about your sin and unworthiness. The only way you can do this is if you have a Father who loves you like the father in the parable loved his son. Repentance cannot be separated from the amazing love of a holy God.

June 14

Do you presume on the riches of his kindness and
forbearance and patience, not knowing that God's
kindness is meant to lead you to repentance?

Romans 2:4

Even good, moral people are sinful and under God's judgment. The Pharisees of the Gospels fall into this category and so do we. Because we think we look good on the outside, we have little sense of need. We are self-righteous and perfectionistic; we feel superior to other people; and we have the habit of, inwardly if not outwardly, judging others all the time. Paul declares, "The wrath of God is being revealed from heaven against all the godlessness and wickedness of men who suppress the truth by their wickedness" (Romans 1:18 NIV).

If you want to understand the gospel, you have to see that you deserve God's wrath. The gospel tells us that Christ, when he died on the cross, took on himself the hell that we deserve. God is so holy that he must punish every sin ever committed. The magnificence of the gospel is that we, who were under the wrath of God, have the righteousness of Christ placed to our account through faith. God's glorious forgiveness, acceptance, and love are ours. This rips the heart out of self-righteousness and moral strength. Faith is not about trying harder or human willpower, or self-effort. It's about abandoning all hope of being righteous and collapsing on Christ as your only hope.

June 15

Now we know that whatever the law says it speaks
to those who are under the law, so that every mouth
may be stopped, and the whole world may be held
accountable to God. Romans 3:19

The great message of the law of God is to fall on your face and be quiet. No one yet has talked his way out of hell. In Romans, Paul says that our hypocrisies, big mouths, judging spirits, gossiping, slandering, and divisiveness are all to be silenced. Every mouth must be silenced before God, in order that we may find grace. You can't find grace as long as you're talking and not listening. The Bible says, "Be quick to hear, slow to speak, slow to anger" (James 1:19). And we reverse it: we are slow to hear, quick to speak, and quick to anger.

We reverse it, because we don't appreciate what happened to us in the death of Christ. Emmanuel, God with us, came into the world and died to take away our sin and guilt. But when we see what Christ did for us, we are quieted. Then you can recognize your sin and admit your guilt, and be cleansed through Jesus Christ. See the connection between Christ's atonement, his righteousness freely given to us, and a radical life of humility in which we are broken before God for our pride and self-centeredness. Are you willing to go with Jesus all the way, or is it just words? Let's be quiet and listen to his Word. Let's run with his Word and not our own.

June 16

"Blessed are the pure in heart, for they shall see God."
Matthew 5:8

Here's another way to say it: Blessed are the pure in heart, for they know what their priority is—God himself. When you take the time to meet with God and listen to him, then you are not controlled by other people's demands but by what God wants. The pure heart is the heart surrendered to God and to his will.

The person who had the purest heart was, of course, Jesus, who says, "I delight to do your will, O my God; your law is within my heart" (Psalm 40:8). He volunteers to come into the world, live as a human, and sacrifice himself. He surrenders his whole self to God, and he delights to do so because it is God's will. Now, we do not go to crosses ourselves and die on them for the sins of the world, but we are told to take the gospel message to people right where we are and from there to the ends of the earth. The most glorious thing that ever happened in the universe is that the love of God was revealed in Jesus Christ. It must be our overmastering purpose, as people of God who are pure in heart, to live this out and to tell others about it.

June 17

O Israel, hope in the LORD! For with the LORD there is
steadfast love, and with him is plentiful redemption.
And he will redeem Israel from all his iniquities.
Psalm 130:7-8

How do you get to be pure in heart? By faith. When you trusted in Christ, you were given a new heart. Now you are part of Jesus and one with him. You died with him and were risen again with him. Your sins are not only pardoned, but you have a new life in him. Therefore, you are dead to sin and alive to God. Psalm 130 starts, "Out of the depths." The psalmist starts out in the pit, but rises through the forgiveness of sins by faith to the place where he is certain that with God there is plentiful redemption.

An impure heart is a result of holding fondly to bad habits and sins. How does one change? As you dwell on your sin you slide into the depths with the psalmist. But if you believe in God's forgiveness, you can ascend out of that pit. Believe you have a heart cleansed by faith, throw off your sin, and then act without any doubt that your heart is now his and is pure. That's what the psalmist does here. The longer he looks at God's great redemption, the stronger his faith grows. This is what makes it possible to give yourself over to God's priorities. Faith in Christ really does cleanse hearts and make them pure.

June 18

All these with one accord were devoting themselves to
prayer, together with the women and Mary the mother
of Jesus, and his brothers. Acts 1:14

The disciples had run away when Jesus was arrested, but here, after the resurrection and ascension, they are devoted to praying together. How do you see God? You see God by waiting on him, and the new covenant way of doing this is by praying together. "Blessed are the pure in heart, for they shall see God" (Matthew 5:8). A characteristic of the pure in heart is that they pray together.

How devoted are you to praying with others? It is in corporate prayer that we must come to God about everything in the church—the family, the Sunday school, the home, the elders, the worship. I'm afraid that we don't pray enough, and we don't pray enough in the right way. There are many who pray a great deal, but pray ineffectively. You can tell when you've prayed effectively because your heart is pure, full of faith, and wants God's priorities. Ask God to teach you how to pray and learn what his priorities are. To do this you have to give up being a loner. You have to give up doing your own thing. You must pray together.

June 19

"Those whom I love, I reprove and discipline, so be
zealous and repent. Behold, I stand at the door and
knock. If anyone hears my voice and opens the door, I
will come in to him and eat with him, and he with me."
Revelation 3:20

Some people interpret Revelation 3:20 like this:
Jesus stands at the door of your life and knocks;
you're on the inside and, of your own free will, you
open the door and welcome him in. There's some truth
in that. But really, how it works is that Jesus stands at
the door and knocks. You hear the knocking, put three
locks on the door, and move the furniture up against it.
Then the Holy Spirit slips in a window, goes into the
basement, turns the furnace on full blast, and sets a few
fires while he's at it. It starts to get really hot and smoky
in the house, and in desperation you begin to move the
furniture away from the door. As you gasp for air you
open the locks and fling open the door. Fresh air rushes
in, and you grab hold of Jesus with that wonderful free
will of yours. Well, sure it's free, but only because the
Holy Spirit turned up the heat. That's grace, isn't it?

June 20

Now there are varieties of gifts, but the same Spirit;
and there are varieties of service, but the same Lord;
and there are varieties of activities, but it is the same
God who empowers them all in everyone.

1 Corinthians 12:4–6

God empowers gifts in us as we recognize the headship of Jesus Christ and listen to him as he speaks to us through the Word and the Spirit, teaching us to interpret our lives and circumstances. "All these are the work of one and the same Spirit, and he gives them to each one, just as he determines" (1 Corinthians 12:11 NIV).

The Bible is not about your career or my career, but rather about the acts of the living God—the career of the Holy Spirit. This is so liberating, because if he's the one who's doing it, why worry? It frees you to express the beauty he puts in each of us. This doesn't mean we have no pain as he convicts us and deals with us, but he's primarily leading us into glory, in this world and into the next. This gives us a hunger to rely more on the Holy Spirit. If you're going to be entering into partnership with the Spirit—depending on him in everything and exercising your spiritual gifts with faith and confidence—you're going to have to learn to pray more effectively and more in line with his will.

June 21

"I tell you, though he will not get up and give him
anything because he is his friend, yet because of his
impudence he will rise and give him whatever he needs.
. . . If you then, who are evil, know how to give good gifts
to your children, how much more will the heavenly Father
give the Holy Spirit to those who ask him!" Luke 11:8, 13

Jesus tells a story about a man who didn't want to get out of bed to give bread to his friend. In the Middle East, the whole village would be shamed if you couldn't provide bread for your guest. Therefore, the man's refusal to help his neighbor would bring shame to everyone—his own family included. Clearly, this man doesn't care about anyone. His neighbor persists in knocking on his door, and eventually, to stop the noise, the man gets out of bed and gives his neighbor the bread he wants. Jesus wants to make the point that even someone who doesn't care will give you what you need if you persist in knocking.

Jesus continues by saying that God is not like the uncaring man. He is more like a father who provides food for his children. Earthly parents take care of their children imperfectly, but God, our heavenly Father, knows exactly what we need. He delights to give to us his best gift—his Spirit. The contrast here is between the grudging gift of the neighbor and our heavenly Father who is supremely willing to give. When we ask for help from such a willing God, he will give us bread from heaven—his own Spirit to comfort, protect, and guide.

June 22

"If you then, who are evil, know how to give good gifts
to your children, how much more will your Father
who is in heaven give good things to those who ask
him! So whatever you wish that others would do to you,
do also to them." Matthew 7:11–12

What does God do when we ask, seek, and knock? What does he do when we go to him with empty hands, not knowing what to do next, with a clear view of our need and sinfulness? God gives us good things! One good thing he gives us is a spirit of love for others. Put yourself in another's place, Jesus tells us. Go to God, asking in faith for him to do what you can't in the lives of others, and then go to others with love.

How can you pray effectively unless your prayer is carried to heaven on the two wings of faith and love? I have never seen a bird fly with just one wing, have you? Have you asked the Holy Spirit to give you the wings of faith and love? Ask for a heart surrendered to God, a heart of faith that says, "Your will be done. I want your way. Convict me of sin, and fill me with love." Then you will see clearly how to love others. He will give you the power to love and love and love.

June 23

As a child of God your very nature is to be a peacemaker. A peacemaker is one who brings others together or who comes closer to others in a spirit of reconciliation, willing to risk being hurt in order to be near people. It isn't just staying out of trouble or helping others stay out of trouble. It isn't just about making lines of demarcation to separate opposing sides. Rather, it's an active way of life that, because it is so distinctive, it's very visible in the world. Jesus calls this the blessing of the Christian. The peacemaker works toward peace at home, in the church, with neighbors, and throughout the world.

How does one start to be a peacemaker? Where do you get the attitude, the driving concern, that makes this not a burden that's been dropped on you, but something that is growing from inside you? You get this kind of heart through faith. The heart is cleansed by faith. You have seen what Christ has done on the cross, and having seen that sacrifice for you, you believed it. You were cleansed from your sin; hypocrisy, envy, and selfishness were swept out of you by the blood of the Lamb. Because of this, you see that if Jesus brought *you* to peace, then everyone you meet could be a prospect for his peace program.

June 24

"Blessed are the peacemakers, for they shall be called sons of God." Matthew 5:9

Be a peacemaker in the light of God's love for you and in the power of the gospel. How does God want you to make peace? One way is to keep a tight rein on your tongue; don't repeat negative things about others. God is careful about what he says, and he wants you to be careful, too. Another way to be a peacemaker is by being friendly, kind, and approachable. These are things that draw people to you. As you act by faith, ask God to give you the kind of spirit that enables you to be Jesus to others. A third way to make peace is to ask forgiveness when you have wronged someone. Consider that if you never need to ask forgiveness it might be because you don't let anyone near you. Fourth, like your heavenly Father, do good to your enemies. When you're kind to your enemy, when you reach out to him, pray for him, and try to think of ways to do him good, then you are being like your Father in heaven. Lastly, be a peacemaker by speaking the truth in love, praying for wisdom to know when to speak and what to say.

June 25

"Pray then like this: 'Our Father in heaven,
hallowed be your name.'" Matthew 6:9

The devil likes to sell us on the notion that God doesn't love us. Whatever God is doing, he is an unjust tyrant, and submission to his will is to be robbed, deprived of your dignity and worth, as well as your freedom. But in actuality, these are exactly the things God wants to give you! Made in his image, you were designed to find your freedom in him. If you want to find your way home, you have to go back to God and submit to his will. Christ teaches us about our Father. Of the seventeen recorded prayers of Jesus, sixteen show Jesus addressing God as "Father," and in the last prayer he's quoting the Old Testament.

Jesus taught us that God is Father. So when we talk about God's will, we're not talking about the will of a tyrant but of a loving Father. The picture is that Jesus Christ stepped into history, became a man, lived a perfectly obedient life in which he willed the will of God from the heart, and died on a cross to satisfy that will. If anyone is in Christ, God is for that person. God is not trying to give you suffering for its own sake. He brings suffering into your life to make you like Christ.

June 26

"Out of pity for him, the master of that servant released
him and forgave him the debt. But when that same
servant went out, he found one of his fellow servants
who owed him a hundred denarii, and seizing him,
he began to choke him, saying, 'Pay what you owe.'"
Matthew 18:27–28

Whom are you choking today? Do you struggle to work with certain people? Are there areas of weakness or sin you tolerate in yourself, but cannot tolerate in others? We often assume that the sins of others are much bigger than our own sins. Perhaps you have trouble forgiving habitual sins because the person ought to know better. According to Jesus, the kingdom of heaven has a completely different approach to forgiveness. The sins we have committed against God, far from being minor are, in fact, mountainous.

Whenever we contemplate the sin of another against us, we must see that it is tiny in comparison to our own sin against God. The picture Jesus paints is this: Here is a fellow lifting one hand up pleading for mercy and for forgiveness of a tremendous debt, while at the same time reaching down with the other hand and choking a fellow servant who owes him a pittance. This is the spiritual condition for many of us. You must grasp the fact that if you're reaching out to God for forgiveness, you need both hands. You don't have any hands left with which to choke anyone else.

June 27

Peter . . . said, "Lord, how often will my brother sin
against me, and I forgive him? As many as seven
times?" Jesus said to him, "I do not say to you seven
times, but seventy-seven times." Matthew 18:21–22

As Jesus talks about forgiveness, he's talking about the
kingdom of heaven—a power movement in history
that has come from above, and is so revolutionary that
it has to be from God. A new day is coming when the
law will not be written on stone but on human hearts.
The people of God are going to know him because he
"will forgive their iniquity and . . . remember their sin no
more" (Jeremiah 31:34b). That's what the new covenant
ushered in by the death of Christ is about. The former
covenant exposed sin; the new covenant deals with sin
through the blood of the Lamb of God. It is this new
order of forgiveness brought in by Jesus that now controls history and makes it possible to have the law written
on your heart. Unless you know your sins are forgiven,
how can you know God? The Jesus principle of forgiveness involves the whole person and is essentially unlimited forgiveness that penetrates to your very heart.

Truly the kingdom of heaven brings a revolution—into culture, into history, into families, into
lives—and it produces a sweet peace and harmony that
brings glory to God. You can never be mastered by evil
in any situation if you remember the power to forgive
that comes through the gospel of Jesus Christ.

June 28

"Blessed are the poor in spirit, for theirs is
the kingdom of heaven." Matthew 5:3

Often people want to be filled with the Spirit without being emptied—without repenting. They want to put on all the blessings of Christ without accepting what the Scriptures say about them: about their radical self-centeredness, desire for glory, defensiveness, and all the rest. They are simply looking for an experience, and the result is that the experience eventually runs dry because they have neglected to make room in their hearts for the Spirit.

The deception often takes the form of prayer for the gifts of the Spirit for ministry, which they then receive. But since they never humbled their hearts before God, they respond by being proud and then by taking a great fall. As a result, many others don't believe the gospel works. The truth is that the only reason the gospel doesn't appear to work is that it's never been tried. Grace is for sinners, for the weak. The poor in spirit are blessed because, in their nothingness and their need, they claim Jesus. The barriers are down, and the things that otherwise obscure Christ are gone. They have no record to boast in, no strength, no righteousness. Self has been drained from their hearts, which now can be filled with the Holy Spirit.

June 29

"Behold, I have come; in the scroll of the book it is written of me: I delight to do your will, O my God; your law is within my heart." Psalm 40:7-8

The heart of sin is not loving God with all your heart, soul, mind, and strength; and not loving your neighbor as yourself. No one has ever loved like that, thus we need a savior, a deliverer. Jesus is not like us. He is holy; he never sinned and he delighted to do God's will. Jesus is the only one who ever fully delighted to obey God from the heart. The will of God was his very life; it consumed him and gave him strength (John 4:34). Jesus Christ went to the cross with joy because that is what the law required. It seems strange to us, but that is what God designed people to be like. Jesus is the first normal man in history—the *only* normal man in history. He loves God from the heart, and he loves you from the heart. No wonder he could save his people from their sins. How could the Father have anything against us when this one who died for us did so, not coldly or mechanically, but out of compelling love for the Father's will and for the elect that God had given him? God was delighted that at last someone had appeared in history who loved him totally, and he counted that sacrifice as an atonement for sin. Because of it we are freely forgiven.

June 30

[Jesus] said to them, "Why were you looking for me?
Did you not know that I must be in my Father's house?"
Luke 2:49

The Father's house is no longer in the church building. Jesus is the temple now, and wherever you are he is with you. He reveals the Father to you, and he wants you to meet with the Father. The most startling thing about this statement made when Jesus was a boy of twelve is that he calls God his Father. His aim is to bring us into the same kind of awareness of the Father that he had. In the Old Testament, God is only referred to as father a few times, and then it is meant for the people as a whole, rather than in the personal way Jesus uses it.

What we have here in Luke is the amazing revelation of the very heart of what God is like. The implications of God as our Father are magnificent. As your Father, God knows and loves you personally. He knows about your obsessions, how you wish for a better life, how you want freedom from the things that hinder you. He knows that you want to be a stronger person, to have more freedom, to have more patience, to love others more. He knows that you wonder if people could love you if they really knew you. God really does know you, really does love you, and Jesus introduces you to him.

July 1

Do not use your freedom as an opportunity for the flesh, but through love serve one another. For the whole law is fulfilled in one word: "You shall love your neighbor as yourself." Galatians 5:13-14

Faith, which unites you to Christ, will spontaneously lead to love. No matter how weak you are, how many sins you have, or how low your self-esteem is, faith will work by love. Serving others in love is what discipleship and obedience is all about. You show your obedience to God by your love to others.

Often, the new believer, in hearing about God's love and seeing the smiles on the faces of other Christians, has the impression that the Christian life is an easy one. But before long, reality crashes in giving them the impression that this life doesn't work after all. One way many of us experience this is by constantly trying to perfect one another. We start out to wash someone's feet, but somewhere along the way, we decide to boil the water. We notice others disobeying the Ten Commandments, and in sharply reproving them, we break laws in return. But remember that because we have the Holy Spirit, we have God's law in our hearts (Jeremiah 31:33). What we need to discover is that other people belong to Jesus too. This means that he can disciple them, and you don't have to force your will or your cutting tongue on the other person. Love works *with* Jesus *for* others.

July 2

For the desires of the flesh are against the Spirit, and the desires of the Spirit are against the flesh, for these are opposed to each other, to keep you from doing the things you want to do. But if you are led by the Spirit, you are not under the law. Galatians 5:17–18

In the struggle between the flesh and the Spirit, you can often get immobilized. But here we learn that when you have the Spirit, you're not under condemnation, and you're not powerless. Practically, this is just another way of talking about the gospel. "Not under the law" means to be under the grace of God. It means having the Spirit rule your heart and direct you, and it means being in fellowship with Christ. It also means you can take an honest look at your sin because you no longer see it apart from the cross. You're broken by your failure but not destroyed. Instead, you're driven in your weakness back to Christ. You realize that your efforts to perfect your record and your standing with God and others is causing you to fall flat on your face. You see how strong your flesh is and that you need to take more seriously the power of the sinful nature. In this type of crisis, where you've really blown it, you discover grace you never knew was possible in your perfectionistic efforts.

July 3

It's hard for people to hate you if they feel you really like them. I've met some people who are pretty good haters and who've worked hard to cultivate their anger and bitterness. But if you love them—and not only love them, but *like* them—this can be a new way to reach them for Christ. Ask God to give you a positive image of what that person is going to be as you pray for them and work with them in love as God works with them. Pray to get rid of your negative image of that person as one who can't change. Be as interested in what's happened to them as what's happened to you. Don't simply try to keep from saying bad things, but think through and plan how you can say affirming things. Be appreciative. Get excited about them! The body of Christ is beautiful. Work to bring out that beauty, and it will liberate faith. You might discover that the irresistible power of the kingdom and faith go hand in hand. This is faith working by love, and it is the supernatural activity by which God transforms you, and others, into the image of Jesus.

July 4

Let us not become conceited, provoking one another, envying one another. Galatians 5:26

A negative, destructive conflict will always have conceit in it—someone else's conceit and yours. The red flag that marks conceit is when you think you are better than someone else. Thinking yourself better than others leads to the problem of blindness and presumption, the inability to see yourself as you really are. This leads to a third problem of unkind, damaging words. Destructive conflict leads to wounds and counter-wounds; and it ends with the name of Christ being dishonored. So beware of conceit and the presumption that goes with it. Cry out to God for mercy to identify your own conceit and then to humble yourself and repent of it.

As opposed to destructive conflict, constructive conflict begins with a humbling of faith that recognizes that you didn't earn anything in salvation. It beseeches the Holy Spirit for the power to control your tongue; and, in the midst of the conflict, to begin to affirm, esteem, and appreciate others, no matter how they treat you.

July 5

My son, give me your heart, and let your eyes
observe my ways. Proverbs 23:26

You reach the conscience of another person by first being changed yourself, and out of that change, in love, reaching that other person. Most of the time when we want to see someone else influenced, we look for the best method, how-to, or technique—something we can operate independently of changing ourselves. When we do that, we usually succeed in making the relationship worse. Solomon identifies what we really want in any primary relationship; we really want their heart. It's not wrong to want the heart of another; it is the height of maturity to want that. However, the way we go about trying to get it is often the depths of immaturity.

Perhaps the greatest problem in our close relationships is that we don't like to disturb the usual habits and routines. If we're really going to reach the conscience of another, we have to deal with the question of whether we have first given our hearts to God. It is only as our hearts are open to him that we are able to open them to others. This is where change starts.

July 6

Often we are convinced that we know how to run people's lives better than they do. We act as if it's up to us to be the Holy Spirit for the people around us and try to shape them into our image, without respect for the integrity of the person's own conscience. When you get down to it, the games we play to try to accomplish this can be classified as power struggles. As Christians, we don't like to admit that we engage in these struggles. But you're just lying to yourself if you don't see that you have a problem with this. Often this is what's going on when you're having difficulty in a relationship, and you just want a formula or a technique to fix the problem. But these are not situations where the goal is to find the right combination of words and actions that will get the other person to do what you think is best for them. No, the goal is always to first bring your heart before God so he can root out the selfishness and pride that's getting in the way. Then seek *his* will for the other person and your relationship.

July 7

Put on then, as God's chosen ones, holy and beloved,
compassionate hearts, kindness, humility, meekness,
and patience, bearing with one another and, if one has
a complaint against another, forgiving each other; as
the Lord has forgiven you, so you also must forgive.
Colossians 3:12–13

How many times have you been in a conflict where just the right buttons get pushed and you react? The right words trigger anger, fear, or pride, and you go after the other person in an attempt to regain a sense of power in the relationship. But engaging in a power struggle is not love. Sometimes we fool ourselves into thinking we're being fair and loving by acknowledging the speck in our own eye before yanking the log out of someone else's, but that's not what the Bible teaches. It teaches us to humble ourselves by dealing with our own sin first. If you admit that you constantly need grace from a gracious Lord, he'll help you. You'll be in partnership with him and begin to think differently about your whole way of handling problems with other people. You won't feel so easily defeated, because you'll see those times as opportunities to grow, mature, repent, and change. You can do this because you are confident of your Savior and his love for you. In humility is great power to change you and the nature of your relationships.

July 8

For whoever lacks these qualities is so nearsighted that
he is blind, having forgotten that he was cleansed from
his former sins. 2 Peter 1:9

We love poorly, but either we don't know it, or we are reluctant to admit it. Sin causes blindness. Don't underestimate how much blindness there is in you or in others. Destructive conflicts arise out of blindness, out of failures of spiritual perception. This has been reinforced by the confusion of moralism with obedience to God. Many people think they are obedient to the Word of God when they are simply acting out a superficial conformity to the law or to biblical standards without a heart relationship to the Lord of those standards. Rather than giving your heart to God, delighting in him, and enjoying him as you obey, you go through the motions of doing what you think you're "supposed to do." We need to be moving deeper into biblical patterns of thinking, so that we can see what we have in Christ. Out of that new vision, we can relate to others like Christ did, loving humbly and sacrificially. When we remember God's grace for us in Christ, our defeats become crises that expose our weaknesses, our sins, and our failings and are opportunities for us not to despair but to look to God, the author of all goodness and kindness, who loves us with a father's tender care.

July 9

"If you forgive their trespasses, your heavenly Father will also forgive you, but if you do not forgive others their trespasses, neither will your Father forgive your trespasses." Matthew 6:14–15

Someone has said, "To understand all is to forgive all." That's not been my experience. My experience is that the better people understand each other, the harder it is for them to forgive each another. That's the difficulty in family relationships, friendships, or teamwork. The other side of it is that if you really know *yourself* well, it is hard to accept God's forgiveness for yourself. That's why people resist taking a close look at themselves. But when we avoid facing our own sins, we miss how amazing the offer of God's forgiveness in Christ is for us.

Jesus intensifies the problem by saying, in essence, that the heart of Christian living is forgiving other people. Forgiving others does not justify us before God or take away our sins; however, Jesus makes it clear that a life that is not characterized by forgiveness is evidence of little knowledge about God. Only when you see the depths of God's forgiveness for you, can you begin to accept that you are really and truly forgiven. Change comes as your conscience rests secure in what Christ has done and in the new identity he has given to you. Your experience of God's unconditional love gives you unconditional love for others. As God changes you, you will find deeper joy in forgiving others.

July 10

Christ redeemed us from the curse of the law by
becoming a curse for us . . . so that in Christ Jesus the
blessing of Abraham might come to the Gentiles, so
that we might receive the promised Spirit through faith.
Galatians 3:13–14

The whole point of the gospel is that God put his Son, not simply under the law but under the curse of the law to take away its penalty and provide his righteousness. When you're under that, God never has reservations about you as his child again. His forgiveness is full, complete, and unreserved. Some people see this as an invitation to then go out and do whatever they want, but if you think that, you do not understand it at all. The same faith that brings you to Jesus Christ is the faith that leads you to holiness of life. Neither the person who thinks the gospel is insufficient to overcome sin nor the person who thinks the gospel is simply a temptation to do evil has never really been touched by it. The deeper your knowledge and experience of the unreservedness of God's grace toward you, the fuller will be the manifestation of that grace in you in a life of holy love.

July 11

And because you are sons, God has sent the Spirit
of his Son into our hearts, crying, "Abba! Father!"
Galatians 4:6

Sometimes you are so weak, or your heart is so hurt,
or you're so convicted by your sins, that you can
hardly pray. All you can do is groan and say, "God, be
merciful." According to Paul, even this is powerful.
God sent the Spirit of his Son into our hearts, the Spirit
who cries through us, "Abba, Father." When Jesus made
this cry in the garden of Gethsemane, he had submitted
himself to God completely. Our cry is not like Jesus's
because we are not facing forsakenness. We have been
accepted. We're not going into hell; Jesus went there
on the cross for us. Therefore, when that cry comes
from us, "Abba, Father," it is ultimately a cry of delight.
There may be deep pain in it, but it's also the cry of the
one who delights in the Father. So the call to pray is not
a legalistic one but a call to meet with someone who
wants you there. He has not only provided for your justification, acceptance, and adoption, but has given you
a Spirit who knows how to pray in you and through
you and knows how to delight in God.

July 12

Likewise the Spirit helps us in our weakness.
For we do not know what to pray for as we ought,
but the Spirit himself intercedes for us with groanings
too deep for words. Romans 8:26

Don't think that you can just get up in the morning and pray without doing any thinking. Preach the gospel to yourself, and especially soak yourself in God's promises. Say to yourself, "For God so loved the world," and remember that this verse applies to you and to the people around you. Ask God to take you into that promise of his love for his people, and look at them as those who are redeemed or are being redeemed. God's attitude is one of great love—deep, wide, unsearchable. Ask him to give you that attitude. Then take a good look at the biggest idol of your life, which is self-worship and self-glorying, living for the praise of others, and ask God for grace to hate it. Make it your heart's burden not to spend time trying to inflate and praise yourself or to encourage others in this kind of destructive tendency. Before you ever go to pray, pray. Take the time to center yourself on the grace and glory of God. The best way to begin a time of prayer is to pray for the Holy Spirit to bring you into fellowship with the Father.

July 13

"Whoever believes in me, as the Scripture has said, 'Out of his heart will flow rivers of living water.'" John 7:38

We often pray only as a reaction to trouble. You say to God, "I've got myself into a tangled mess. I blew it with my husband, my wife, my children. I was mean on the phone. My work is falling apart." God rescues you and you thank him for giving you his Holy Spirit. But that is only the beginning, only a trickle. Jesus has promised that rivers of living water would flow from those who come to him. The abundance of water is more than enough to share. Jesus didn't promise the woman at the well a trickle of water, but a "spring of water welling up to eternal life" (John 4:14). When she met Jesus, her mind was filled with her own troubles. But afterwards, her mind filled with Christ, she returned to her village and told everyone about him.

The Spirit shows us the glory of Christ and the wonder of the Father's love, and miraculously fills us with a love for others that has the same intensity as our love for ourselves. The Spirit fills us with God's life, so we can live with a kindness, a tenderness, and a patience that advertises to others that the Spirit is at home in our hearts. As his power fills us, we can live our ordinary lives in a supernatural way.

July 14

"Again I say to you, if two of you agree on earth about anything they ask, it will be done for them by my Father in heaven. For where two or three are gathered in my name, there am I among them." Matthew 18:19–20

Although this verse is often used to bolster morale at a poorly attended prayer meeting, it's not meant to be used that way. Jesus's promise to be present where two or three believers are gathered is set in a disciplinary context where sheep are wandering, and the power of God is needed to bring them back. Jesus is saying that there is additional power conferred on the church when we pray together. Despite our individual inadequacies, he wants us to come together as one body, and as we agree together, he promises his presence and power. "I am among you," he promises. Where the Spirit is, so is Jesus.

God has made each of us a prophet, priest, and king. We bear his authority, and we exercise it collectively, in prayer. Not to come together to pray with other Christians is to stifle and risk the whole ministry of the Spirit in the church and in your own life. The same disciples who fall asleep in the Garden of Gethsemane pray with one mind in Acts and the Spirit is unleashed in the world. The single most important question for you might well be: Will you pray with other believers?

July 15

I have been crucified with Christ. It is no longer I who live, but Christ who lives in me. And the life I now live in the flesh I live by faith in the Son of God, who loved me and gave himself for me. Galatians 2:20

When you come to the end of yourself and stare death in the face—physically, emotionally, or spiritually—the real problem to consider is where your faith is centered. If any problem seems unbeatable, check whether your immobilization is a result of your trusting in the wrong thing. If your faith is centered in yourself, you are trusting in the flesh. Know the power of your Savior and his salvation. The one who lives in you has all power, and he's going to see you through the valley of the shadow of death. As you begin to shift your faith more and more to him, you can say goodbye to the flesh. In fighting against the flesh, you'll find that it has multiple sides to it. Like the water monster Hydra in Greek mythology, when you chop off one head, two more sprout in its place. As you fight your flesh, it will struggle and writhe within you, but it will not have the same power. Develop confidence in the greatness of what you have in Christ. How do you develop this confidence? Begin to ask God for grace; pray that he would change how you think and what you desire.

July 16

Therefore, if anyone is in Christ, he is a new creation.
The old has passed away; behold, the new has come.
2 Corinthians 5:17

One of the devil's suggestions that needs to be dealt with when developing confidence in Christ is that your negative feelings are the real you. That's wrong! The real you is a beautiful new person in Christ. It's true there's a lot of garbage—a lot of sin and selfishness—still inside you, but the real you is the person who's emerging from all that garbage. You must not let the devil cloud your thinking with negative feelings. You must see that's not the real you. Instead, you must begin to act like a child of God no matter how you feel. You don't have to pretend not to have negative feelings, but don't let them inundate you. Begin to develop confidence in what you have in Christ. You are in Christ, and you have the Spirit. That means you can ask God to incinerate the garbage that's inside you and give you life. Ask him for power, love, and joy to be able to walk into the world to serve and help the people around you. You are in Christ and that's his heart. Ask him to make it your heart too.

July 17

So faith comes from hearing, and hearing through
the word of Christ. Romans 10:17

God has really forgiven you. He's not like the person who forgives, but somehow you know you'd better not do it again because they won't forgive you a second time. He doesn't grant you a temporary truce and wait to get you later. God has really accepted you and made you his child. The difficulty in getting on board with it is that you have to take it by faith. You didn't hear the words, "It is finished," or witness the resurrection. All you have is the gospel saying this is so. But as you believe that Word and preach it to yourself, your faith grows. Don't stare at your sin and your problems and then get out your magnifying glass and go looking for your faith. That's a way to get thoroughly depressed. When you hear that Christ was made a curse for you so that you're not cursed anymore, and that God is for you, that builds your faith. Don't resist it. Believe and accept it. Know that the Spirit has been planted inside you and is working to make sure your faith continues to grow. It's not just your work; it's his.

July 18

So you are no longer a slave, but a son, and if a son,
then an heir through God. Galatians 4:7

Have past hurts made you suspicious of people? Let
Jesus speak to you in the midst of that. Maybe you
don't want to listen to him, but there's one word of
Scripture that I hope sticks with you: You are no longer
a slave but a son or daughter. You have the position and
status and love of a child of God. God loves you unconditionally, and God is growing in you the capacity to
love others unconditionally.

This means that you can expect a life that has some
tension in it. Perhaps you've been experiencing the bad
tension that comes from being fixated on an old hurt
or wound inflicted by another. Good tension is when
you begin to learn things about yourself that you don't
like because they're not part of who God has made you
to be. It may even be that the things that are disturbing you are signs of new life, signs that the Holy Spirit
is working in you. Sometimes what looks like a defeat
is only the doorway to a new ministry for you. Where
you hurt most of all, where God meets your need, and
where he brings other people's lives together with yours
may be the springboard for action.

July 19

"Pray then like this: 'Our Father in heaven,
hallowed be your name. Your kingdom come, your will
be done, on earth as it is in heaven.'" Matthew 6:9–10

There is nothing more glorious or effective than prayer. Every time you pray, "your kingdom come," you're asking God to subdue every human agenda, yours included. The Spirit has come to reveal God's power and majesty. He does this especially by forming us into a kingdom of praying people. We taste of the Holy Spirit as we pray. The great hindrance for us in this is that we forget the connectedness between Jesus, the Sovereign One, and the presence of the Spirit. We forget the connectedness between the activation of the Spirit's ministry and group prayer. This in no way slights the tremendous importance of private prayer, but we need to see that when we pray together, the Holy Spirit is present. He comes in greater fullness. Prayer is partnership together and with the Father. It's the most daring thing you can do. The devil wants to convince us that it's boring, routine, and doesn't accomplish much, if anything. This is a lie. Prayer is where we as individuals and especially as a body of believers do battle with sin in our own hearts, call upon God to transform the hearts and lives of those around us, and ask him to reshape the world into what he's designed it to be.

July 20

As we pray most earnestly night and day that
we may see you face to face and supply what is lacking
in your faith. 1 Thessalonians 3:10

An obsession is something that controls you. It has all your time, attention, and interest. For us, obsessions are generally unhealthy and consist of things like sex, food, personal appearance, fears, career, ambitions, revenge, and getting ahead, to name a few. Paul, however, had a magnificent obsession: to present the people of God as utterly beautiful and full of glory when Christ returns to claim them. While most obsessions make one intensely self-focused, Paul's obsession made him—and can make us—aware of Christ's glory, honor, and praise.

Your ministry to others can be filled with the consciousness of Christ as the risen, triumphant Savior who changes lives. If you're like me, you have some repenting to do. There may be times when you have helped people work through their problems and in the process taught them to be *less* dependent on Christ. Sometimes it is better to sacrifice "effectiveness," and instead, to get down on your knees together and ask Jesus for help. It may take longer to work through the problem, but if it's bringing the people to whom you minister into a greater consciousness of Christ, you're on the right road. Everything centers on the glory of a coming Jesus. That is the reality that should guide your life and the lives of those to whom you minister.

July 21

So that he may establish your hearts blameless in holiness before our God and Father, at the coming of our Lord Jesus with all his saints. 1 Thessalonians 3:13

You can't hear the Scripture preached as the Word of God rather than the word of men, unless you see that it is related to Christ, who is the center of the Bible from beginning to end. The whole point of it is that we're headed toward one great event, when we're going to meet the Lord, and we're all going to be on our faces, bowing our knees, bowing our hearts, and acknowledging that Jesus Christ is Lord to the glory of God the Father. Everything you do should flow from an awareness that he is present with you and that he is going to come.

As believers, hearing this is very exciting, but stop and ask yourself whether Christ is present with you now. When you got up this morning, did you give thanks that Jesus is coming? We gather together on the first day of the week because he's alive, and we know that he's returning! The reality is that Jesus Christ is alive, he's going to return, and he's your best friend.

July 22

The only thing that counts is faith expressing itself
through love. Galatians 5:6 NIV

The beautiful thing is that faith has the power to work through love. Our faith is made visible in a life of love. Faith equals God's working by love. This is what will count on Judgment Day. Everything we did by faith through love will shine—it will count with God.

Faith brings us to Christ, and we trust him for our justification. Love does not justify. If love could justify, then you would be justified by good works. Only faith can justify you. But once faith has justified you, then on the Day of Judgment you will not be terrorized, but vindicated. In that vindication, as Christ's righteousness is revealed as the umbrella covering over all your sin, then what will be lifted up is the deeds of love you have done through faith. Paul is saying that you have a special power through faith in Christ. Even through the hardest times, you now have the power of faith to love others. Faith expressing itself in love fulfills the whole law (Galatians 5:14).

July 23

For the whole law is fulfilled in one word: "You shall love your neighbor as yourself." Galatians 5:14

Faith expresses itself in love, and the Spirit produces the fruit of love. The entire law of God is summed up in a single command: love others. But it is faith in Christ through his Spirit that enables us to fulfill the law. Faith does not atone for our sins; rather faith brings us to Christ. Christ justifies us and out of our union with him we love others by faith, and so fulfill the law.

Faith and the Spirit work hand in hand to fulfill the law of love. Our faith unites us to Christ; and the Spirit works in our hearts and unites us with Christ. So the Spirit unites us to Christ through faith. To believe is to be united to Christ, and then through faith, the very qualities that are Christ-like come into your life. When faith unites me to Christ, I have taken hold of the spiritual power source of life, or better yet, it has taken hold of me. When we think about growing in Christ, or when we think about sharing our faith, we always wonder how to do it. The answer is to look to Christ in faith. Does looking at yourself produce fruit? No, but the Spirit has implanted Christ in you, and fruit grows as you focus on him and what he has done.

July 24

And God is able to make all grace abound to you, so
that having all sufficiency in all things at all times, you
may abound in every good work. 2 Corinthians 9:8

Do you know that you have it all! You have a rich
God. You have the grace and love of God in Christ
Jesus, the Spirit of God, the power of God, and the
presence of God. You're a new creature! You've been
brought out of death and made alive. Even though you
know all this, do you still think of yourself as poverty-
stricken? Are you tempted to believe that if you could
have just a little bit of something else, you would be
safe and secure and happy? Are you ruled by anxiety?
Do you think about yourself and your problems a great
deal? God calls us to set that aside, to live by faith, and
to know that we are rich in him. In Christ, you lack
nothing. You need nothing but him.

In giving, we sow seeds that will grow. As Christians
we are not called to be stingy with what we have, but
to give with great joy because we are loved by God. We
are purified and we are one with the Son. Our God is
delighted in us because we are in Christ. It's not surprising then that we would respond to that love by giving. Giving has in it exhilaration, worship, praise, and
freedom.

July 25

And God is able to make all grace abound to you, so
that having all sufficiency in all things at all times, you
may abound in every good work. 2 Corinthians 9:8

Your God is able to make all grace abound to you
so that in all things and at all times—there's no
point at which he won't help you—you will abound in
all good works. The Christian, who is rich already by
faith, is going to get richer. Plan your giving, think it
through, pray about it, but give generously just as your
God is generous to you. God is going to be able to give
you all you need at all times in every way.

Don't think of God as stingy. For those of you
who are worriers, oftentimes anxiety is connected with
a small view of God and his love, grace, and power. If
you were to write a book about your real view of God,
it would say, "My God is stingy. He really doesn't know
how to help me." That's not true! In the surrender of
faith, your God is rich, and you are rich. Do you want
to continue defining yourself as the great worrier, or
are you going to step out in faith today and claim your
identity as a son or daughter of God, made rich in the
Father?

July 26

You will be enriched in every way to be generous
in every way, which through us will produce
thanksgiving to God. 2 Corinthians 9:11

The nature of giving is to sow generously. The attitude of giving is joy and exhilaration. God is able. God has strength to meet your needs. If you're going to learn how to give, become full of faith. To become full of faith, read the Word and ask God to show himself to you. Anything that threatens you, anything that you're afraid of, take that to God and get to know him better. Then in every situation, see what opportunity is available for doing good and giving of yourself.

If you are a worrier, do you believe that there might be things there for you to repent from? Much of worry consists of us trying to play God and be in control of our lives. You can repent of that. You have the Spirit; you have faith; you know Christ. Thank him for making you rich. Ask him to teach you how to handle material things. Ask him to make you generous and not afraid.

July 27

Know this, my beloved brothers: let every person
be quick to hear, slow to speak, slow to anger;
for the anger of man does not produce
the righteousness of God. James 1:19–20

Often when I write letters and have to say something I don't think the person will like, I say "my
dear brother" or "my dear sister." I think that's what
James is doing here when he addresses his readers as
"my beloved brothers." Before he says the hard thing,
he wants them to know that he loves them and is concerned about them. What follows is the climax of what
he's been writing. The call he issues to be "quick to hear,
slow to speak, slow to anger" is nearly the exact opposite of what we normally do. It certainly is for me!

Notice that James sets things up in the previous
verse: "He brought us forth by the word of truth, that
we should be a kind of firstfruits of his creatures." So as
you hear this call remember that Christ, through the
preaching of the gospel, has changed you and made you
a new creation. And because you're a new creation, my
dear brothers and sisters, you can hear what is hard to
hear and begin to change. You have the Spirit, you have
the Word, you have the prayers of God's people, and it
is possible for you to be "quick to hear, slow to speak,
slow to anger" because of God's grace to you in Christ.

July 28

Know this, my beloved brothers: let every person
be quick to hear, slow to speak, slow to anger;
for the anger of man does not produce
the righteousness of God. James 1:19–20

A renewed awareness of the Holy Spirit's work could
well begin by admitting that we are slow to hear,
quick to speak, and quick to get angry. What kind of
hearing is James writing about here? Most of us, when
we read this passage, feel we are better listeners than we
actually are. Personally, I find it very easy to listen when
I'm being told something I want to hear. This is not the
kind of listening James is writing about. Neither is he
writing about half-listening while we think of a response
to rebut or counterattack what's being said. The kind
of listening James is talking about means going deep
enough to hear God teach us through another person,
even if we're hearing something we don't want to hear.

How do you measure up to this standard of listening? Do you believe you have something to learn
from everyone, even if they're criticizing you? We need
to have a more realistic view of ourselves and cry out to
God for grace to be different. We're all in the same boat,
and we all need to learn what it is to pray from the heart
for something to happen *in us* first and foremost. That
is where revival begins.

July 29

When I get angry I often feel entitled to my righteous indignation. How about you? When you get angry, do you feel entitled to your anger? Do you find yourself saying that all you really want is justice? Usually when I hear someone demand justice, I step far away from them and watch for lightning bolts. If you and I were really to get justice, where would we be? We all constantly wrong others in many, many ways. If we treated others the way God intended us to, affirming them, being kind to them, loving them, we wouldn't have anything to worry about. But we don't do that, so what we actually deserve is what Jesus received on the cross—the wrath of God. The obedient one, the one who listened to God, who delighted in his will, who was committed to it, that one was bruised for our iniquities. The fact is that I have been forgiven through Christ's atonement—his substitutionary death on my behalf. I have been forgiven through faith in him. Therefore, I ought to be forgiving others, and I ought to be going oh-so-easy on my own rights.

July 30

Therefore, get rid of all moral filth and the evil that is so prevalent and humbly accept the word planted in you, which can save you. James 1:21 NIV

Many times when we are led to a deeper understanding of Christ and his gospel, we begin to feel badly about the mess we've made of our lives and think we need to sit around for years and look it. We define our lives by the losses of the past and fail to see that God's plan of redemption is good. No matter what has happened, the plan is good. And if you humble your heart and bow down, grace will be with you (James 4:6). God will love you, and you will taste of his love. Don't condemn yourself anymore, and don't condemn other people either!

Here's one application for this: When someone comes to you with criticism that seems to you like an attack, listen carefully and apologize wherever you honestly can without defending yourself. Don't sit there planning your counterattack while you half-listen. You can do these things when you know you've already been forgiven for all your sins. You can listen to criticism when you know your sin and your mistakes do not define you, but instead the love of Christ and his work on the cross defines you.

July 31

Not to us, O LORD, not to us, but to your name
give glory, for the sake of your steadfast love
and your faithfulness! Psalm 115:1

One of our foundational problems as Christians is
trusting in and making idols of good things. In
our time, many people can admit to making idols out
of their own comfort or pleasures, but family itself has
become a kind of idol too. We start to live for our family in the ways we are meant to live for God, and then
we're surprised by how anxious and fearful we become.

The reason families often fracture and shatter
is that family members are looking for power in the
wrong place. This is the crisis for us, and we won't get
deep change until we see where the deep sins lie. When
the psalmist says, "Not to us, O LORD . . . but to your
name give glory," we have to put our families in there
and say, "Not to me, not to my family as an exten-
sion of my own ego, but to Jesus Christ give glory."
Humble yourselves as a family. One of the signs we're
not doing this is the high level of anxiety in families
now. Consider this: if your home is revolutionized by
your family members living for the praise of God, if
you stop glorifying yourself and instead humble yourself and live for the glory of God, you will so enjoy
Christ that you will be a threat to the world and to the
kingdom of darkness.

August 1

But we will bless the LORD from this time forth and forevermore. Praise the LORD! Psalm 115:18

By the end of this psalm, the writer is captivated and thrilled with the vision of God. He has forgotten about himself and is enjoying a real sense of being partners with God. What a shock it is to the world when happiness is rooted in God.

Let me put it another way. The first question in the "Westminster Shorter Catechism" concerns our primary purpose in life: "What is the chief end of man?" The answer is, "to glorify God and enjoy him forever." It's not to glorify God and be miserable forever. The point is that where you have God, you have delight. You can't enter into God's glory without giving up your own. As you enjoy him, as you are with him, you start to reflect his radiance, which is brighter than anything you could have on your own. You cannot know God as he is without having joy. To know God is to be fully alive! If you want to know God better, draw near to him and he will draw near to you.

August 2

Not to us, O Lᴏʀᴅ, not to us, but to your name
give glory, for the sake of your steadfast love
and your faithfulness! Psalm 115:1

There will be no power in your life if you're living
for your own glory. I've experienced this myself. I
thought I had faith, understood repentance, and knew
the gospel, but the glory of God had never come to me.
I'd never been empowered by falling on my face broken before the Lord and giving up my own ambition,
honor, and glory. When I finally did fall on my face, I
said, "I give myself to your glory." I had never imagined
the wonder and joy of tasting God's glory. I was filled
with joy and peace.

Have you surrendered your life to the glory of
God? Have you said, "Here am I, Lord, send me. I will
go where you want me to go. Not my will but yours be
done. I will delight in your will"? Surrender yourself
and let God deal with the evil in your heart. Then be
dangerous and go to battle against Satan and the evil in
the rest of the world. Jesus died to cleanse us and make
us glory people. Delight in him and delight in his will.

August 3

Always in every prayer of mine for you all making my prayer with joy, because of your partnership in the gospel from the first day until now. Philippians 1:4–5

You can only pray with joy when you know Christ and make yourself his servant, and understand that others belong to him too. Unless you have this sense of oneness, you'll have trouble praying for others. We have prejudices against others, and we tend to like people who are like us. In his letter to the Philippians, Paul prays for *all* the "saints"—all the other believers— with joy because he's had these barriers broken down.

If you pray for others with joy, your life begins to be freed of the anxiety that plagues it. I don't know if you worry about anything, but I've found that I can worry about most things. Just let your imagination run wild, and you'll find you have an anxiety factory in your heart that can produce all sorts of things for you to worry about. But if you turn your heart toward prayer for others with the joy of knowing how Jesus can work in their lives, all that worry and anxiety starts to melt away. And all the hatred and mistrust and prejudice that you've built up in your heart toward other people starts to melt away, too. When you see this happen in your own heart, you are seeing the gospel at work, and others will begin to see it as well.

August 4

"Truly, I say to you, unless you turn and become like children, you will never enter the kingdom of heaven."
Matthew 18:3

Jesus is a strange teacher. When he says something strange, most of us have the habit of turning him off. He's always a bit too much, goes too far, and seems too extreme. But Jesus didn't just give us a body of writings with authority; he is a life-giving Spirit. He is actively seeking to put his words into our hearts, to cause us to live out these unexpected things that show God has intruded from the outside. He is continually working to get us to see this world and our lives through his eyes. The strangeness has a wonderful sanity to it that makes life bearable, livable, and enjoyable.

Here, he is calling us to the lowly position of children. We instinctively want control, but a little child is never the one in control. You will never have any part in Jesus if you think you can be saved up on your adult throne. We want God to save us, but we don't want to leave our throne. Faith, however, is about claiming Christ in humility. It is about seeing your own insufficiency, your own need, and crying out for help. The problem is never with the inadequacy of God, his salvation, or his Christ, but rather that the heart is still on the throne and must come down in order to meet Jesus.

August 5

After this he went out and saw a tax collector
named Levi, sitting at the tax booth. And he said
to him, "Follow me." And leaving everything, he rose
and followed him. Luke 5:27–28

What stands out in Jesus's calling of Levi (Matthew) is that there's no persuasion and no explanation. There's just the unvarnished invitation of Jesus, "Follow me." The text emphasizes that when Jesus speaks to him, Matthew hears internally and obeys. Jesus said, "Follow me," and Matthew got up, dropped everything—his business included—and followed him. When Jesus calls, you follow. Matthew knew that Jesus was worth following.

The same goes for you: you aren't going to follow Jesus unless you think he is worth following. If you don't know that he is the Son of God with power to forgive your sins, give you a new life, love you, solve your deepest problems, comfort you, give you security, and fulfill you, you're not going to come. You're going to be searching for your answers elsewhere. But Christ speaks to your heart. He is so authoritative, so powerful, and so attractive that you can't say no. His love draws you, and you put your trust completely in him. He's the one who does it. He's the one who draws you to see how valuable he is.

August 6

[Jesus] said, "Those who are well have no need of a physician, but those who are sick. Go and learn what this means, 'I desire mercy, and not sacrifice.' For I came not to call the righteous, but sinners."
Matthew 9:12–13

The religious leaders and Pharisees felt very superior to other people because of their scrupulous obedience to their laws. What they failed to see was that their superiority was thinly veiled hypocrisy. When we come to Christ, it is because he has shown us our sin and our need for a Savior. But then we gradually make progress in the Christian life. As we make some progress, we begin to notice that others haven't made as much progress as we have. The tendency for the Pharisees and for us is to separate ourselves from sinners in the wrong way. We sit at the table of the separated ones, instead of at the table of the repentant ones.

That's why Jesus cautions, "Beware of the leaven of the Pharisees, which is hypocrisy" (Luke 12:1). The kingdom comes when people repent. I've never met anyone who likes to repent because it means giving up your insanity. The insanity that we share with the Pharisees is the feeling that we are better than other people. But if you've ever glimpsed an iota of God's holiness, you couldn't be anywhere but on your face.

August 7

And when Jesus saw their faith, he said to the
paralytic, "Take heart, my son; your sins are forgiven."
Matthew 9:2

Only Christ can lift our burden of sin. He lifts the
burden of our external sins, and of the deeper
ones too—our hypocrisy, lack of love, and betrayals in
relationships. He lifts the burden of our sin of being
committed to going our own way, and ignoring God's
purposes for us. Jesus bore the penalty that we deserved
for our sin, as he hung on the cross under God's wrath
for us. But when he rose from the dead, his resurrection
was the sign and seal that Christ's sacrifice was satisfac-
tory to the Father. On the cross of Christ, the human
problem of sin was solved for all who believe once and
for all. This is why we wait for him with an eager eye—
the one we love!—because he lifted the burden. All the
rot in our lives, our troubled conscience, the oppres-
sion, the scorn of others is all gone. We are free. Take
heart. Your sins are forgiven.

August 8

For I desire steadfast love and not sacrifice, the
knowledge of God rather than burnt offerings.
Hosea 6:6

It's easy to externalize our religion. We go to church
regularly, we pray, we fast, we tithe, we do everything
that is required of the religious person, and as a result
we congratulate ourselves. But the very heart of the law
is a call for us to be merciful. Do you love others? Do
you love God? Have you missed that what God desires
is that in all your relationships you be touched by a
spirit of compassion, that you be merciful in your basic
approach to people? Jesus is gently calling those of us
who think we are better than others. You're not going to
honor someone if you don't love them.

Begin to recognize where you overestimate the sins
of others and underestimate your own. Often we don't
show mercy because we think others have it coming.
But that's not love. Under God's direction from Jesus,
we learn that the heart of obedience is to love others.
This enables you, in freedom, to admit the bitterness
and resentment you're harboring against other people.
You can love, and out of that love you can show respect
to others. You can be this way because Jesus has called
you and he is your partner in it. When you know that
Jesus loved you so much that he died to break sin's
power over you, you can't help but leave behind your
harsh attitude of superiority toward others.

August 9

Continue steadfastly in prayer, being watchful in it with thanksgiving. Colossians 4:2

The kingdom of Satan is a self-centered kingdom. This means that in order to combat it, we must deal radically with self-love in ourselves first, before the kingdom of God can begin to touch others. As the kingdom of self is broken down in us, then we are qualified by the Spirit to begin breaking it down in others. Don't underestimate the power of the Word of God in the lives and hearts of people who are proclaiming it to others.

This is a call to prayer, which is the kingdom's supreme weapon. When two or three are gathered together to pray, there the King is present. When the new covenant comes, prayer—corporate and individual—is the dominant theme (Acts 1:13–14). Prayer is the very heart of discipling the nations. To pray in a kingdom manner, pray as a son or daughter of the King. Even though you may feel that you belong in the kingdom of self, remember that in reality you belong to the kingdom of love, the kingdom of God. It means you ask for the Spirit's help to live out of your new identity and to call others into the kingdom as well.

August 10

If we say we have fellowship with him while we walk in
darkness, we lie and do not practice the truth.
1 John 1:6

As you pray, the one thing you want to remember
is that you are made for fellowship with God, and
you want to get into fellowship with him right away. In
other words, pray until you're in fellowship with God,
until you have a sense of God's presence. Now, don't get
discouraged if it doesn't happen, and don't stop praying altogether. There will be times when you pray for a
sense of God's presence and all you get is the sound of
your own words. Nevertheless, aim to pray until you're
in contact with God because prayer is an expression of
our relationship with God as our Father.

Confession of sin is one way to get into contact
with God because it removes the barriers between you.
But, because sin means to center everything on your
own will and thoughts, praise can also be a way of getting rid of sin and drawing close to God. The hardest
sin to recognize and repent of is the sin of being self-
centered. Praise is God-centered adoration. To praise
God means to focus on him and, thus, to repent of
self-centeredness.

August 11

Moreover, as for me, far be it from me that I should sin against the LORD by ceasing to pray for you, and I will instruct you in the good and right way. 1 Samuel 12:23

It's hard to be in fellowship with God if your life is filled with anxiety. How can you deal with anxiety? Start by recognizing that you're a partner with God in his kingdom work. Take the matters that cause you anxiety or fear and pray that each situation will be changed. Pray confidently and don't doubt that God will work. When you find yourself doubting that change is possible, repent and pray again with confidence.

The way to have success isn't always by changing the other person or situation. In fact, often your attempts to change things freeze others into their position or make the entire situation worse. The kingdom of self is always raging in you and in the people around you, so praying for success is really struggling against evil—against an unholy kingdom, a kingdom of wrath, fear, and lust. What you're really struggling for in prayer is to love others as God loves them and to seek to bring yourself in line with what he is doing, both in your life and the lives of the people around you.

August 12

Praying at all times in the Spirit, with all prayer
and supplication. To that end keep alert with all
perseverance, making supplication for all the saints.
Ephesians 6:18

The reason people don't pray much is because ultimately they don't feel it's very important. People are
bored by prayer because how they do it is boring. There
is no kingdom purpose in it, so why bother God with
all those words? The point is to pray for grace, so you
can begin to act in love toward others. If you're like me,
you spend most of your time thinking about what you'd
like other people to do for you, including God. So your
prayer time ends up being mostly about yourself, and
you don't see much progress because God doesn't seem
to be answering your prayers. And the times you do
pray for others, you're still praying for what you want
for them or from them.

But what would happen if in your prayer time, you
resolve to find ways to serve others by love. Pray for the
grace and love of the Spirit to take over, so that you can
be part of God's kingdom purposes for them. Think
about how they might be suffering or discouraged, or
struggling with sin or facing temptation. Start to do
battle for them in prayer. When you begin to do this,
prayer will be anything but boring.

August 13

Brothers, if anyone is caught in any transgression, you
who are spiritual should restore him
in a spirit of gentleness. Keep watch on yourself,
lest you too be tempted. Galatians 6:1

The more effective, successful, and fruit-bearing you
become in ministry in God's kingdom, the more
you'll find yourself engaged in conflicts with evil—evil
in yourself, and evil in others. You'll go through agony
as you discover there are evil things that you really love.
You'll be appalled by the discovery of how much you
love certain evils and their benefits, but you'll also discover that your Father is in partnership with you. So he
will send things into your life to teach you to hate evil.

What's more, if you really love people, you have a
duty to resist their evil, to stand up against it and say no
when everyone else says yes. This means you might have
to say no when it means experiencing the disapproval of
others, to say no when it costs you a friendship, to say
no when it means death to your pride. In a sense, you
must be willing to risk everything in order to do right.

August 14

But if you have bitter jealousy and selfish ambition
in your hearts, do not boast and be false to the truth.
This is not the wisdom that comes down from above,
but is earthly, unspiritual, demonic. For where jealousy
and selfish ambition exist, there will be disorder
and every vile practice. James 3:14–16

Over the years, I've heard a lot of people confess their sins, but I can only remember a couple people who confessed the sin of jealousy. And yet, Scripture seems to indicate that jealousy is a problem that's common to *all* people. If you don't think you have a problem with jealousy and yet you find your spiritual life stagnant, it may be worth examining whether you do indeed have this problem. The first thing to look at is how you react when your gifts and talents look like they're second to someone else's. How do you feel when someone is praised for doing something you think you did better? What about when no one remembers to thank you? You did all these good things for someone, and they never even seemed to appreciate it! Is this starting to hit closer to home? Jealousy is selfish coveting, a burning desire to have what someone else has. At its core, it's a rejection of God's plan for your life. You're really saying that what God has given you isn't sufficient and what he's doing is not good.

August 15

It has become known throughout
the whole imperial guard and to all the rest that
my imprisonment is for Christ. Philippians 1:13

The Greek here actually says, "I am in chains *in* Christ." That may mean the same as being in chains *for* Christ, but it also means a lot more. It means your whole life's plan is being fulfilled by that chain around your wrist because that's Christ's chain. You're not just here *for* Christ, but being *in* Christ, you have been brought to this place of weakness for a particular purpose. Your identity as a Christian is that you have believed Christ and now belong to him. Paul's view of his chains is this: every problem can become an opportunity because it's a problem *in Christ*. When Paul looks at his particular problem, he says it's really served to advance the gospel. His situation is happening in the plan of God, so God's glory can be advanced. If you think everything is happening to you by chance, that this universe is a total orphanage and you are the most lost orphan in it, you will react with bitterness and jealousy toward others who seem to get a better deal. You have the best deal God could give you. Christ is in you, Christ is for you, and you are not an orphan. Everything that happens to you *must* be turned for your good and God's glory.

August 16

The former proclaim Christ out of selfish ambition, not
sincerely but thinking to afflict me in my imprisonment.
What then? Only that in every way, whether in pretense
or in truth, Christ is proclaimed, and in that I rejoice.
Philippians 1:17–18

Often, we want the approval of others, so we'll
know who we are. If people thank us, appreciate
us, and tell us we're doing well, then we feel we mean
something. Some of that is natural and good, but if
that's where you are searching for your identity, you will
always strive, struggle, and be in turmoil because you
will never find it that way. Instead you'll be jealous and
envious of those who seem to be the frontrunners, and
that will lead you to be discouraged. But we don't get
our identity from other people; we get it from Christ.
Jesus paid for our sins—even our sins of jealousy and
resentment—and he has made us God's own children!
He has given us all the rights and privileges of sons and
daughters, and therefore we have no reason to be envious of anyone else because we've been given so much.
Say again and again, "I'm a child of the King." There's
no cause to be jealous of others or to have an identity
crisis. Christ has given you worth and dignity. Take joy
in the life he's given you.

August 17

And most of the brothers, having become confident in the Lord by my imprisonment, are much more bold to speak the word without fear. Philippians 1:14

Courage can be natural or spiritual. We saw what happened to natural courage when Peter cut the ear off the high priest's servant, then didn't know what to do when Jesus told him to put away the sword. Several hours later, Peter denies Jesus three times. Many of us, in the heat of the moment, have similar nerve, and we also have that kind of collapse when we don't know what to do.

Spiritual courage, however, is different. It comes as a gift of the King to the church experiencing persecution and suffering. It's the kind of courage Paul shows during his imprisonment for preaching the gospel that allows him to use it as an opportunity to share Christ with his jailors. And it's the kind of courage he says his brothers in the Lord are displaying in the face of his imprisonment. They see Paul, who is faithful even in chains, and decide to be faithful where they are to preach the gospel. The Word went out in all different directions, as Christ's followers began to show spiritual courage. We have been given the same Spirit that was in Paul and in those people, and we too can preach the gospel with courage.

August 18

But God shows his love for us in that while we were still
sinners, Christ died for us. Since, therefore, we have
now been justified by his blood, much more shall we be
saved by him from wrath of God. Romans 5:8-9

As you go through the process of suffering and learn
endurance, your character improves and strength-
ens before God. When you endure suffering, when you
rejoice and boast in it, you get a stronger hope and
greater assurance of God's love and grace for you. The
more you struggle with sin and Satan and grow in faithful obedience, the more you are liberated in your inner
life. You grasp in a deeper way that when you were
helpless, when you had no strength, when you were
ungodly—when you were a rebel who despised him and
organized your life around something else—you were
saved by grace. More and more you see the cross, you
see your unworthiness, and you see the glory of God.
The conflict is no longer between you and God. You
have assurance that you will be saved by this Christ who
has kept you and preserved you by his life; that he even
now intercedes for you and stands between you and a
broken law. This living Christ, who lives *in* you, lives
for you moment by moment, and there is no wrath left
for you.

August 19

I write these things to you who believe
in the name of the Son of God that you may know
that you have eternal life. 1 John 5:13

Many people say they believe, but it's rather like a person who says they're married but live in a different house from their spouse. The whole idea of faith is that it brings you into a spiritual union with Jesus Christ. If you're not living with him, you don't have his righteousness covering you. In one sense, it's a lot like getting married. Vows are one thing, but at some point, you have to surrender yourself to the other person. Faith has in it that same element of surrender. You surrender to a righteousness outside yourself—to the obedience of Christ and the person of Christ. By this surrender, you say, "Jesus, I give myself to you." Anything less than that is not faith at all, but only an opinion of salvation that is not rooted in reality. If you're really saved you have eternal life, and you begin to know it. I want you to be confident that you've placed your faith in Christ. When you're confident of that, you can also be confident that God hears you.

August 20

And this is the confidence we have toward him, that if
we ask anything according to his will he hears us.
1 John 5:14

The confidence we have because we're in Christ is that of a member of a family. Think about children. When they come and ask for something, do they not expect it? If they're like my children, they will wheedle, persuade, hint, suggest, or sometimes even cry when they want something. But our Father in heaven doesn't need to be persuaded like that because he already knows our needs and is most willing to help us!

There is, however, some "fine print" that is pretty basic to prayer. On the one hand, there's the promise that God hears you and you can be confident of that. But on the other hand there's the clarification, if you ask "according to his will." This implies that the very center of your prayer life—and your life in general—is seeking the will of God. This is easy to forget. The natural thing to do is to take your anxieties and doubts with you into prayer in such a way that you are more anxious when you finished than when you started because you would not surrender them to God. You can't pray effectively, boldly, and daringly unless you're renouncing your own way and trying to find God's way. Let me assure you, God is not reluctant to show it to you if you will surrender.

August 21

By this we know that we love the children of God, when we love God and obey his commandments. For this is the love of God, that we keep his commandments. And his commandments are not burdensome. 1 John 5:2-3

When you surrender to God's will, you can have peace amidst circumstances that have caused you much anxiety. Despite what you may think, God's will is not for you to worry about everything. The Holy Spirit wants to put to death your worry and anxiety. He may even want you to begin to enjoy life.

So, what is the will of God? One of the things that God wants for you is to internalize his law. As John expresses it, he wants us to be people of love, aggressive in love. Or to put it a different way, he wants to make us look like Jesus Christ. The theme of 1 John is that God wants to fill us with faith that lays hold of Christ and that leads to love and obedience. Obedience is just an aggressive form of love. It means that we can forgive our enemies. We can bless them, and we can be kind to them. In fact, we might even be able to work up enough of this love for our friends. Sometimes it's easier to forgive our enemies than our friends because at least we know we are supposed to forgive our enemies! But forgiveness for both enemies and friends is what it looks like to live a life of love for God.

August 22

We know that everyone who has born of God does not keep on sinning, but he who was born of God protects him, and the evil one does not touch him. 1 John 5:18

We have not yet tapped the resources that are in God when it comes to prayer. If we prayed more, we might find it isn't quite as easy to worry. Jesus keeps us safe from the touch of the Evil One. If you have dark thoughts—defeatist, destructive thoughts—recognize and acknowledge that those did not all come from you. Many of them came from the devil, and you do not have to adopt his view of yourself or of reality. You can walk in hope. It doesn't mean you won't have to fight and struggle; that's what John means when he writes, "keep yourselves from idols" (1 John 5:21). But the victory is yours. He's saying don't go back and trust in your own works and your own righteousness. Don't think that Jesus is weak and powerless. Don't think the devil is sovereign. Don't think that your sin is so powerful, that Jesus can't deal with it. Rather, believe that God loves you and that Christ died for you; and because of that, you can stand against unbelief, sin, and weakness. You can grow, and you can be happy. With everything that you've been given in Christ, you have every reason to be happy, so let it creep in. God wants that for you.

August 23

Indeed, I count everything as loss because of the
surpassing worth of knowing Christ Jesus my Lord.
For his sake I have suffered the loss of all things and
count them as rubbish, in order that I may gain Christ.
Philippians 3:8

Paul is saying that Jesus's blood and righteousness are his only hope, not only in the past, but in the present and future as well. In other words, he doesn't trust in Christ for his salvation and then keep moving forward by the strength of his own power with the law to guide him. Justification by faith is not something you leave behind; it is the permanent foundation of your life. It comes when Christ died for you, atoned for your sin, and made you a child of God; but Paul is reminding you that this is also your chief goal. Make it your whole purpose never to build a righteousness outside of Christ or to depend on any record of righteousness other than Jesus's. Like Paul, consider all the outward displays of your personal righteousness a loss that you may have this one goal of knowing Jesus Christ, who emptied himself to establish this free forgiveness for you. Christ did not consider his heavenly honors worth holding on to, but gave them up to save you. Seeing Christ this way should prompt you to give up trusting in anything but Christ. Make him and his sacrifice the basis of your life, your goal, and your supreme value.

August 24

For his sake I have suffered the loss of all things and count them as rubbish, in order that I may gain Christ and be found in him, not having a righteousness of my own that comes from the law, but that which comes through faith in Christ. Philippians 3:8b-9

When you achieve success, be careful not to fall into the trap of thinking that all is well because of what you have done. Always remember that grace is not for achievers; it's for the bankrupt. "Blessed are the poor in spirit" (Matthew 5:3). Blessed are they who have nothing, who need all things, who only know how to beg. The line of reasoning that Jesus uses is that your values based on your own righteousness are inconsistent with his righteousness. When you ignore your union with Christ and begin to think of yourself as an independent religious achiever, you end up living like an orphan. This is why Paul not only wants to "gain Christ," but also to "be found in him." Christ himself is where you are, and where you're heading. You maintain your union with Christ, you run after it, and you do it by shedding your own values. You are always trying to get a clearer understanding of what Christ did for you in taking away the penalty of sin and making you acceptable to God. It is not that grace justifies and the law sanctifies; it is all of grace.

August 25

That I may know him and the power of his resurrection, and may share his sufferings, becoming like him in his death, that by any means possible I may attain the resurrection from the dead. Philippians 3:10-11

It's easy to develop an attitude where we are confident that we can handle things on our own. But one use of the law is to expose our sin and show us ever more fully our need of Jesus and his righteousness. You're never able to handle the law. You're never able to grab it and run with it because it packs a wallop. You can only depend on Christ as the one who grabbed it and ran with it. Because you're in Christ, your redemption is secure and you can move on to the next stage. But always you have two goals: faith seeking only Christ's righteousness, and love seeking fellowship with Christ. Wanting to know Christ—the power of his resurrection and sharing in his sufferings—is just another way of saying that love has the goal of fellowship with Jesus. Rather than being confident in yourself, place your confidence in the resurrected Christ. He sits at the Father's right hand interceding for you. You've been shown your terrible sin. The law exposed you, the cross completed it, and now you see it settled. Yes, you are a sinner, but you have found a full grace. You can love others, and you can love Jesus.

August 26

And the peace of God, which surpasses all
understanding, will guard your hearts and your minds
in Christ Jesus. Philippians 4:7

What is Christ's secret for true happiness, or better yet, his secret for true peace? In Philippians 4:4–6 Paul gives us three commands from Christ: first, rejoice in the Lord at all times; second, be visibly gentle, be so gentle that others notice it (Philippians 4:5 NIV); and, third, don't worry but pray. By now you're thinking, *Good night! Who can do all that?* These commands may seem pretty far from where you live, but the result of practicing them is that the peace of God enters your life—not simply peace of mind, but full peace that comes only from God.

Whether we like it or not, we tend to idealize what we're doing. You pour your heart into the perfect marriage, the most effective ministry, the most meaningful work, or the closest relationships. Pretty soon, you're so identified with the work that you no longer have any vision of Christ. Your personality is so tied up in it that if something goes wrong—which it will—you are crushed. Paul's message, though, is that we rejoice because Christ is in control. We are gentle because Christ is in control. We pray because Christ is in control. And when Christ is in control, you can experience true peace.

August 27

Rejoice in the Lord always; again I will say, rejoice.
Philippians 4:4

When Paul says to rejoice always, a striking thing about it is that it means you keep rejoicing. Rejoice in the present moment, and as you move into the future, keep rejoicing. Paul doesn't say to rejoice sometimes or only when things are going well, but always, in all circumstances, no matter what's happening. This rejoicing may seem impossible, but remember, belief and joy go together. As Peter says, "Though you have not seen him, you love him; and even though you do not see him now, you believe in him and are filled with an inexpressible and glorious joy" (1 Peter 1:8). It's against this backdrop that Paul sets his command to rejoice *in the Lord*. You can only rejoice if it's in the Lord, and faith puts you in the Lord. It's in union with Christ that we are righteous, that we stand together for the gospel, that we maintain our unity.

When Paul says to rejoice always, another striking thing about it is that we are called to rejoice not just individually but *together*. The whole context is our unity with Christ and our rejoicing as a body. If I do not rejoice, I'm pulling the body down. If I do rejoice, I'm pulling the body together and moving it forward. You won't get the depth of the command until you see that it's something that happens together.

August 28

Let your gentleness be evident to all. The Lord is near.
Do not be anxious about anything, but in everything,
by prayer and petition, with thanksgiving, present your
requests to God. Philippians 4:5-6 NIV

It's hard to be gentle if you are not rejoicing. If you're not rejoicing, but wallowing in frustration and anxieties, and somebody crosses you, you want to strangle him. But if you're rejoicing, knowing that you're part of God's plan, there's a resurrection ahead for you, and you're in the Lord, you can afford to be gentle. Gentle means the opposite of contentious and self-seeking. The basic idea is bigheartedness and tenderheartedness because you know that Jesus is coming back and he is bringing a glorious resurrection!

A life of prayer is the capstone of it all. We are told not to worry, but to pray. Prayer includes a reverent attitude, and the recognition of God as sovereign, in control, and working all things together for my good. Christ is interested in what you pray and wants to bring you near to God. For that reason, you can put aside worry and pray. Prayer is a privilege and a duty, but it's also a condition. You're not going to be fulfilled as a Christian unless you realize that prayer is the condition of all that happens in the kingdom. The kingdom moves not by human power but by prayer.

August 29

Do not be anxious about anything, but in everything by prayer and supplication with thanksgiving let your requests be made known to God. And the peace of God, which surpasses all understanding, will guard your hearts and your minds in Christ Jesus. Philippians 4:6–7

Paul is giving us a vision of how things work and how they don't. They do not work by worry and strife or personal ambition. They don't work by being right and judging other people. Rather, they work by praying. We are part of a kingdom of grace. If you don't pray, you don't understand how grace works and you don't understand how the kingdom works. Prayer is how you breathe. In prayer, we claim the promises of God; the central promise is the gift of the Spirit who brings life to the church.

Often, our prayers are too general and we never see the answers we desire. Bring to God as specific requests the things you worry about. Draw near to God with reverence and awe, and out of that ask him for particular things that will contribute to your holiness, to the holiness of the church, and the salvation of others. And then thank God for answers. When you remember all the things you have to give thanks to God for and you give thanks to him, your fears and anxieties tend to drop away. In thanksgiving, you deal with the reality of the kingdom, and the result of that is the gift of peace.

August 30

Then Jesus calling out with a loud voice, said, "Father, into your hands I commit my spirit!" And having said this he breathed his last. Luke 23:46

This is not a prayer of the dying; it's a quote from Psalm 31:5. It's a prayer in the face of death, but it's a prayer of life. Jesus is saying here, with authority, "Father, I trust you. I am headed for life. I'm not headed for death." Now, although he was going to die physically, he was not going to die as a defeated victim. He gave up his spirit with authority, and even with a great cry of power. With this cry, the veil in the temple was torn from top to bottom. The voice of Jesus in his weakness tore that veil in two. An earthquake followed in which the very earth itself was torn in two. The graves of the saints were opened up, resurrections followed, and people went into the city to talk to their friends and relatives (Matthew 27:51–53). What an afternoon that must have been for some people! Can you imagine? We make this so sentimental, but it is throbbing with realism, throbbing with life. And that's what Jesus was doing on the cross. The prince of life was defeating death, not being defeated by it. This is the Jesus that we know. Have you missed his greatness?

August 31

When Jesus had received the sour wine, he said, "It is
finished," and he bowed his head and gave up his spirit.
John 19:30

Many people approach the cross without asking this question, "What was finished?" The answer to that question is simple, yet profound. On the cross, Jesus finished the work of redeeming us from the power of sin—from all the things we do that hurt each other, from all the things that shame and disgrace us, from everything that is broken in this world. You and I cannot hope to enter into what Jesus suffered in his soul when he was on the cross. Can you imagine someone who is completely holy and pure and good suddenly being exposed to all the guilt and all the evil that people like you and me have done through the ages and receiving all the punishment for that?

On the cross, Jesus Christ was made our substitute, and faith claims this Jesus as our savior. Because of this, we know our sins are paid for. To put it another way, what God did that day in human history was to conduct the last judgment ahead of time. He passed judgment on his Son and condemned him in order that we may be declared "not guilty," forgiven, and accepted through this substitute, the Holy One who died in our place. It is finished.

September 1

Not many of you should become teachers . . . because
you know that we who teach will be judged more
strictly. We all stumble in many ways. Anyone who is
never at fault in what they say is perfect, able to keep
their whole body in check. James 3:1–2

Usually, we think of ourselves as mature if we have a
position of authority and can correct others. Also,
we instinctively think that being an effective leader is
getting everyone to do what we want. But the fact is, we
are mature when we're able to correct our *own* tongues.
James's instruction in how to lead is very different from
what we might think. His conclusion is not that you
shouldn't lead. In fact, the counsel is to do some vigor-
ous leading. But when you get to the end of his letter,
you'll be surprised at how he tells you to lead. When
you have been humbled and your pride broken, when
you have drawn near to God, when you have stopped
presuming you can control the future, when you have
stopped judging people, then you will be ready to lead.
Humble yourself so that when you speak the truth to
someone, you will have taken the log out of your own
eye before you look for the speck in the other person's.
God wants to make you into a person who is filled with
grace and who knows how to use your tongue for the
benefit of others and to draw them to Christ.

September 2

"When the Egyptians see you, they will say, 'This is his wife.' Then they will kill me, but will let you live. Say you are my sister, that it may go well with me because of you, and that my life may be spared for your sake."

Genesis 12:12–13

Faith doesn't exist in a vacuum. If I asked you how strong your faith was, you might examine your heart and pray and meditate about it, but the more you looked for your faith, the harder it would be to find. This is because faith is based on knowledge and trust. You either trust a person or you don't.

In Egypt, when Abraham told Sarah to pretend to be his sister, he forgot about God's promises and focused on himself and his circumstances. Having looked away from God, he fell into fear and deception. When you panic in the face of a difficult situation, you often find yourself trying to trick your way out of it. The fact that your deception works sometimes, makes you inclined to do it again. But eventually, it catches up with you like it did with Abraham. Then you discover that the point all along was not for you just to escape the situation, but for you to grow in faith in the midst of it. When fear replaces faith, you will fail the test. That's why, whatever the circumstance, it is so important to remind yourself over and over again of who God is and to trust him to carry you through. And he'll do it!

September 3

Then I said, "I will appeal to this, to the years of the
right hand of the Most High." I will remember the deeds
of the LORD; yes, I will remember your wonders of old.
Psalm 77:10–11

If you're going to hire someone and you want to know
if he's reliable, you read his résumé and check his references. The more evidence you have about his reliability,
the more confident you'll be when you employ him.
The same thing is true about God. You can't trust God
until you believe that he has committed himself to you
and that he's going to be faithful. If you don't believe
God is for you, you won't have much faith. How can
you have faith if you believe God is dreaming up some
new trick or trap to push you into? When it comes
down to it, many believe that whatever God is doing is
going to be horrible. No wonder we have trouble drawing close to God when we're convinced he has it in for
us! But God's promise is that he has bound himself to
you in love. You have to learn that you have no faith
and no power apart from this promise. You will never
have strong faith unless you cultivate a knowledge of
God's character, not only by studying the Bible, but
also by looking back over your life and reinterpreting it
as evidence of God's purpose to bring you closer to him.

September 4

The Lord your God is in your midst, a mighty one who will save; he will rejoice over you with gladness; he will quiet you by his love. Zephaniah 3:17

God wants you to learn to trust both in his love and in his power. If God does not have control over the situations you face, you have every reason to panic because your only option then is to believe that it's up to frail, flawed people—namely, you—to control the situation. But once you realize that doubting God is a strategy of the devil's, and abandon it, then your faith can grow. Then you can say no to temptation when people play on your fears to get you to do something wrong. You don't have to lie or cheat to get ahead out of fear that you won't be taken care of or won't have what you need. You cannot mature, unless you believe in the power of God. If he cannot do it, then what is the meaning of love? You can say that God is love all you want, but unless he controls every part of your life—unless he's personally involved with you as your teacher, your Lord, your master, and your friend—you aren't going to grow in righteousness. You will only grow in fear, trickery, and deception.

September 5

"You will call upon me and come and pray to me, and I will hear you. You will seek me and find me, when you seek me with all your heart." Jeremiah 29:12–13

Do you sometimes have trouble reading the Bible—so much trouble that you feel like quitting trying to read altogether? If this happens often enough, you can start to approach the Bible—and God too—with fear. You become reluctant to read the Bible or pray out of fear that you won't get anything from it. When this happens, you are starving faith and feeding unbelief.

Know that God loves you and has proven his love by sending Jesus to die for your sins. In every circumstance—Scripture reading included—regardless of how it feels, God is with you, ready to help and teach you. Pray for God to show himself to you. Don't worry about making long, complicated prayers, just say the words, "Lord, show yourself to me." If you can pray that, God hears you. How he loves his children who believe! God has power to help you, to change you, to make you look like Jesus. He fills you with faith and gives you courage, so that when the next challenge comes, you can take your stand and see God work. You come to know God through faith. This God is yours and he lives.

September 6

But he said to me, "My grace is sufficient for you, for my power is made perfect in weakness." Therefore I will boast all the more gladly about my weaknesses, so that Christ's power may rest on me. 2 Corinthians 12:9

In our hearts, we really don't think of ourselves as poor and weak. We're always saying we'll work on getting close to God when we get stronger and have more knowledge. But what really matters is your coming to God on the basis of his promises, and saying, "Help, I have nothing." That's what grace is all about. Grace means you have nothing—you have no resources and you're a sinner—and that, unless Jesus had died and rose from the dead for you, you would be condemned forever. Grace means that if God had not given you his Spirit, you would never have believed. Grace means you bring nothing to God, who makes you into something and gives you everything. That is the heart of grace. Many times, we don't think bringing nothing is good enough; we want to do something that sounds more active—we want to be told what to do, what steps to take. But the biggest change that can have the biggest impact happens on the inside. Come empty-handed to God; he will give you everything; he will give you himself.

September 7

The Spirit of the Lord GOD is upon me, because the
LORD has anointed me to bring good news to the
poor; he has sent me to bind up the brokenhearted, to
proclaim liberty to the captives, and the opening of the
prison to those who are bound. Isaiah 61:1

When it comes to heroes, we prefer someone like Superman with his ability to fight off bullies. By comparison, Jesus doesn't look like a hero. He's crucified on a cross and looks helpless and weak. Even as adults, we give our hearts and our worship to Superman in the sense that we try to be super-people who find our strength in ourselves. But there is one thing Superman can't do: he can't change anybody. We're no better; we can't even really change ourselves! Jesus, on the other hand, has come *specifically* to change people. This is the substance of the good news. No matter who you are or what you've done, Jesus has a salvation to give you that will change you at the deepest level. In making himself helpless and dying in our place, taking our punishment, Jesus saves us in a way that we never could ourselves. Through his sacrifice, we are given the Spirit of God who begins to transform our hearts. He changes us from primarily loving and serving ourselves to loving God and serving others. The result is that instead of destroying our enemies, we can love them and offer them the same message that they too can be changed.

September 8

And Jesus returned in the power of the Spirit to Galilee, and a report about him went out through all the surrounding country. And he taught in their synagogues, being glorified by all. Luke 4:14-15

A seminary professor once challenged me by saying that I had never learned to depend on the Holy Spirit for ministry. I tried to go to the Scriptures to investigate more carefully, but I thought my interpretation might be off theologically and I might get the wrong view. So I turned to the writings of John Owen, who said basically the same thing as my professor: you can't do anything without the Holy Spirit. Still doubting, I thought, *Well, that's John Owen. Puritans can be wrong.* Then I decided to read Calvin's commentary on John 1. He said the same thing! He said you're as dry as dust if you don't have the Spirit come into you through faith in Jesus. He also said that you have to keep getting grace from Jesus all the time. Finally, I heard another professor speak on Luke 11:1–13 about the call to ask, seek, and knock. He said we were asking, seeking, and knocking for the Holy Spirit. I realized that I had never done that in my ministry! Surprised, I thought, *You know, the Bible is right. I guess I can trust it!* From that point on, I decided I was going to ask and ask and ask. Will you do the same?

September 9

*Jesus stood up and cried out, "If anyone thirsts,
let him come to me and drink. Whoever believes in
me, as the Scripture has said, 'Out of his heart will flow
rivers of living water.'" John 7:37–38*

Did you know that you must receive Christ daily?
Daily you have to see the glory of Christ. Daily
you have to let the cross grip you right where you are as
a sinner. Because where you are defeated is where other
people are defeated too. When you go to Christ daily
you are liberated, then you will know where others need
liberation and the river of living water will flow from
you to others. On the cross, Jesus gave himself for his
people. Jesus died with a holy passion for you, for me,
and for all his people. God loves the world so much
that "he gave his only Son that whoever believes in him
should not perish but have eternal life" (John 3:16).

God takes hell seriously. He says that people are
perishing. Modern men and women create their hells
on earth and say that there are none to come. But they
are so mistaken. There is a holocaust ahead unlike anything that has ever happened before. Do you see others
in the light of eternity? If you see people as lost, if you
know that without Christ you are lost as well, then you
will be ready to tell others the good news about Jesus
Christ who saves sinners.

September 10

"But you will receive power when the Holy Spirit has
come upon you, and you will be my witnesses
in Jerusalem and in all Judea and Samaria,
and to the end of the earth." Acts 1:8

A witness is one who has the Spirit. The Spirit is a reality in you because you have gone to Christ in repentance and faith. So why is this last command from Jesus so hard for us to live out? Often it's because we are blind to the needs of others. We are swept along by the current and pace of modern life and we just don't share Christ. Are you ready to take Christ's challenge and look through the outer shell of people and see them as needy? Or, when you look at people have you already written them off as unreachable?

Instead of deciding whether or not God will save someone, start by praying that the Holy Spirit will make your heart tender like Jesus. Are you tender toward people? Do you touch them with love? Are you gripped by what Christ can do for them? Pray, asking for living water for yourself, but then don't just sit there. Make a list of five people you think are never going to get saved, and then start praying that the Father will seek them and make them true worshipers (John 4:23). As you pray, the Spirit will open doors of sharing that will be remarkably simple—maybe as simple as "Jesus loves me and he loves you too."

September 11

Thus it is written, that the Christ should suffer and on the third day rise from the dead, and that repentance and forgiveness of sins should be proclaimed in his name to all nations, beginning from Jerusalem.

Luke 24:46–47

Our faith becomes anemic when we live as though Jesus were still in the tomb. Jesus wants to take us deeper, so he explains the *reason* for his resurrection. The resurrection is not a freak event or a random act of chance. Rather, it is part of God's purpose, and the whole of the Old Testament converges on that empty tomb and on Jesus risen from the dead. The theme of the gospel is that Jesus came to "seek and to save the lost" (Luke 19:10). What did he have to do as this seeking savior? He went around forgiving people their sins. If he had done this for no reason, he would have been a fool. When Jesus died on the cross, he drank the cup of our punishment. His resurrection from the dead certified that God accepted his payment, and he was "raised for our justification" (Romans 4:25). The great question is this: do we see the reason for the resurrection? If you live as though your sins have not and cannot be forgiven, you are living as though Jesus were still in the tomb. He is not! He lives so that you may be justified before God. And that is too wonderful a truth to ignore.

September 12

"Whoever is not with me is against me, and whoever
does not gather with me scatters." Matthew 12:30

You cannot be neutral with respect to Jesus. You are
either for him or against him—on one side or the
other. He doesn't primarily look at what you do but at
the state of your mind and ultimately your heart. You
may feel superior to other people. You may even be rela-
tively better than other people, but Jesus asks the question, "Are you for me or against me?" Are you building
his kingdom, or are you tearing it down? In simplest
terms, either you love him or you don't. Either you
follow him or you don't. Either you trust him as your
Lord or you don't. You cannot be in the middle. Ask
yourself this: Have I ever done a single thing because I
love Jesus? Or reverse it: Have I ever stopped doing a
single thing because I love Jesus? This is what the Lord
is concerned about—the state of your mind, the state
of your heart. As he speaks to us, then, we need to take
him seriously. Our worst sin is that we think we're neutral when we're not.

September 13

But God shows his love for us in that while we were still
sinners, Christ died for us. Romans 5:8

Jesus says that if someone hits you on one cheek, you should turn to him the other (Matthew 5:39). But what's our natural response to being struck? We hit the guy on both cheeks! I can remember actually doing this once when I was a teenager. When a fellow hit me on one cheek, I quickly hit him on both. I was convinced that was the right way to do it, to teach the guy respect for humanity . . . especially for me! Our natural instincts lead us to work against Jesus, to sin. But sin is not just about being selfish; it's not just about doing bad things. Sin is against the person of God. We have all fallen short of the design and the plan of God for our dignity. We were created in God's image, made to be filled with his glory. We were made for peace, love, friendship, and joy. He put his glory in us, and we were to center everything on him with thanksgiving, service, and obedience. When we sin, we're really attacking God.

And yet, while we were sinners, Christ died for us. Let those words ring in your ears and bring faith to your heart! You can obey God and love others, not simply because Jesus has shown you how, but because Jesus's sacrificial love has changed you into someone who loves as he loves.

September 14

The beginning of the gospel of Jesus Christ,
the Son of God. Mark 1:1

Jesus is the heart of the gospel; he is the good news. What you get here at the beginning of Mark's gospel is a picture of Jesus as the compassionate servant. But the One who is compassionate also has power. Your faith will be weak if you think that Jesus has mercy for you, but no power; or if you think he's powerful, but doesn't really love you. Or perhaps you are pretending to be indifferent to Jesus, but deep down you've given up—you don't think you can be forgiven, your sins are too bad; and you don't think you can change, your efforts to improve have always failed. But Jesus has the power to cleanse those who don't think they can be cleansed. He's the Savior, and he can make you free. He loves you. He's not ashamed of you.

It can be hard to hold onto the truth about Jesus when you go out and face your problems again, when you experience shame and think that no one loves you and that you're alone. You have to cultivate a deep, personal knowledge of him and refuse to listen to other voices that draw your heart away from him. If you see that he is Jesus Christ, the Son of God, compassionate King, and omnipotent Savior, that's enough to get you excited and to keep you moving toward him in faith.

September 15

And Jesus said to them, "Follow me, and I will make you become fishers of men." Mark 1:17

The heart of the Gospel of Mark is that Jesus is the suffering servant. He's the majestic one, but he's the majestic one who suffers on a cross. This has a tremendous effect on our prayer life and on how we follow Jesus. If you've made up your mind that you are going to avoid suffering, the gospel is not going to reach very deep into you. It's hard to pray when this is the case because you're afraid of getting hurt. When you have reservations about your whole relationship with God, you do not pray boldly. People tend to think of bold prayers as ones asking God for miracles, fire from heaven and all that. But the real miracles today are shown in hearts that love others. The kingdom you're praying to see is the kingdom of love. It's not a wishy-washy kind of love; it's a love that has fire in it and righteousness in it. It is love that holds on and forgives. This kind of love will cost you something. It will cause you to suffer, just as it caused Christ to suffer. But this is the path of the gospel. This is how we pray, and this is how we follow Jesus.

September 16

"The time is fulfilled, and the kingdom of God is at hand; repent and believe in the gospel." Mark 1:15

Jesus wants to make you into someone like him, someone who seeks out and fights for those who are lost. To be like this you have to become a little more reckless and a little more foolhardy.

Imagine that you have an acquaintance with whom you've built a relationship and won their friendship. Would you be willing to share with them how you needed God's help to change something about yourself? Would you tell them about how you repented and experienced God's forgiveness and mercy? Would you ask them whether they've ever experienced repentance? If you pointed your finger at your friend and told them to repent, they'd probably be scared to death. But if you embodied repentance in front of them, that's where they'd see the power of Jesus. That's the kingdom; that's the power! That's revival. Are you willing to fight for it where you are?

September 17

"One thing I do know, that though I was blind,
now I see." . . . He said, "Lord, I believe,"
and he worshiped him. John 9:25, 38

After Jesus heals him, the blind man immediately begins to act differently from when he was a beggar. The Pharisees, looking for evidence that Jesus healed on the Sabbath, interrogate the healed man concerning the details of his healing. As they keep pressing, he comes back at them saying, "I have told you already, and you would not listen. Why do you want to hear it again? Do you also want to become his disciples?" (John 9:27). At this point, the healed man is excommunicated. But Jesus finds him, and the healed man worships the one who healed him. The blind beggar has found a new identity in Jesus Christ.

When Jesus speaks, people are changed. This man, once a blind beggar steeped in shame, boldly stands up to the religious leaders, shaming them with his simple wisdom and faith. He is humble; he knows how to get to the heart of things; he is fearless. What we see most prominently here, though, is Jesus's power to build out of nothing a new body of people who are being freed from their oppressive bonds and from shepherds who do not really love or care for them. Jesus is the true Good Shepherd who leads his sheep with love.

September 18

[Moses] called the name of the place Massah and
Meribah, because of the quarreling of the people of
Israel, and because they tested the LORD by saying, "Is
the LORD among us or not?" Exodus 17:7

In *testing* God, literally *blaspheming* him, the Israelites were saying that God was not among them and couldn't help them. They denied his power, presence, authority, and ability to redeem and help. When they quarreled, the people brought a judgment against God, denying that he was fair and just, and believing that he had mistreated them and deserved condemnation. God had rescued them from the Egyptians to be his people, yet their praise turned to grumbling in the face of difficulty. You would expect God to respond with a crushing blow, a bolt of lightning perhaps, but instead, God tells Moses to strike a rock to supply the water Israel needs.

A careful look will reveal how similar this story is to yours. How do you quarrel and test God? How are you dissatisfied with him? Don't you expect him to strike back at you for grumbling against him? And yet the blow does not fall on you, just as it didn't fall on Israel. That blow falls on God himself. "He was pierced for our transgressions, he was crushed for our iniquities; the punishment that brought us peace was upon him, and by his wounds we are healed" (Isaiah 53:5 NIV). Have you been captured by the extent and depth of Jesus's love?

September 19

"Whoever believes in me, as the Scripture has said, 'Out of his heart will flow rivers of living water.'" John 7:38

Do fears and anxieties lead you to grumble and complain? Do you worry about the future? Are you troubled by sins of the past? Or have you grabbed hold of the glory and the power of the mighty salvation that is yours in Christ? Because of it, you are not bound to what you've always been. Change is possible when you go to where the waters of grace flow. Jesus says there will be in you a "spring of water welling up to eternal life" (John 4:14)—not only enough to satisfy you, but an overflow to others. He calls you to stoop down in humility, and drink and live.

By nature, we look to other sources for water, or we hope life will be easy for us so we won't need anything. But living water is for those in the desert, and it comes only through the blood of Jesus Christ. This water goes inside you and accompanies you through all of life. When you're down and you feel your thirst building, don't give in to despair but ask Jesus to show you the cross and his glory. Ask him to carry you through the temptation and to help you praise him as you go. Find another person to walk with you; someone who can encourage you to praise God and tell others about the great joy that is found in Christ.

September 20

The angel of the LORD came back a second time and touched him and said, "Get up and eat, for the journey is too much for you." 1 Kings 19:7

Elijah had been very zealous for the Lord to no avail. His pleas to Israel had fallen on deaf ears; the people had rejected God, destroying his altars and murdering his prophets. Elijah is the only one left, and he is running for his life from wicked Jezebel. Angry, self-righteous, and filled with self-pity, he wants God's justice for the evil in the land.

Have you ever felt like this? You look at the world and it all seems hopeless; or maybe there's someone you're trying to help who refuses to change. Elijah almost seems to have developed a heart that judges God. Our inclination is to think he needs an attitude adjustment; maybe a face-to-face confrontation with God would straighten him out. But this is not how God comes to him. Instead, God sends an angel who cooks Elijah a meal. God is very tender. He wants to reach Elijah's conscience, his heart; so instead of turning up the heat or freezing him out, he offers encouragement. God wants the person before he wants the person to straighten up. How many times do we fail to reach someone because we're trying to get them to do what we want before we get close to them? We'd be far better off remembering how God comes to us.

September 21

Hear now, O Joshua the high priest . . . behold, I will
bring my servant the Branch. . . . and I will remove the
iniquity of this land in a single day. Zechariah 3:8-9

Jesus is the high priest who is greater than Joshua.
He lived a perfect life and died on the cross for the
sins of his people. He rose again and ever lives to be our
priest, to stand before God and represent us to him.
Every one of your prayers offered in Jesus's name go
straight to heaven, not because you pray so well but
because Jesus does.

Like Joshua, Jesus was not only a priest, but a king
(Zechariah 6:11). He doesn't just pray for you; he helps
you in ways you will never believe possible. He uses
his awesome power for your ultimate good. Power and
compassion are brought together in one ruler, who is
also your advocate. Unlike the priests and kings who
came before, Jesus will never be replaced because his
work is finished. He *sits* at the right hand of God
(Hebrews 10:12), resting in his victory and his rule. He
is the conqueror who has defeated death, the devil, and
sin. This seated high priest is waiting for the day when
everyone is fully under his authority. You have a part
in that great work. You have been freed from sin and
death and given new life. Go, then, and bring to others
the good news about this wonderful priest, so that all
can know his forgiveness, his freedom from guilt, and
his peace.

September 22

And the angel of the LORD solemnly assured
Joshua, "Thus says the LORD of hosts: If you will walk
in my ways and keep my charge, then you shall rule
my house and have charge of my courts,
and I will give you the right of access among those
who are standing here." Zechariah 3:6–7

We're not called to defend ourselves in the court of God, but to throw ourselves on the mercy of the court. We *are* guilty. But Jesus died—the innocent for the guilty—so that God might forgive you. Faith, simply wanting Jesus, takes on an enormous significance. Faith means taking Jesus as your righteousness since you have none of your own. It is giving up building your own record. It is abandoning even your favorite lusts. It means trusting Jesus and giving your life to him. Faith means you no longer have to worry about God's judgment because of the blood and righteousness of Christ. What assurance! And what a missionary consciousness that builds. Forgiven in order to forgive. Forgiven in order to take the message of forgiveness to your neighbor. Forgiven in order to be free. Justified to go, but not nervously in your own self-effort. Recognize where you're holding back from something God is calling you to that is beyond what you can see as your ability. He wants you to be a fuller, richer Christian, and he may want you to expand your life and ministry in a new way. Jesus does the impossible, and he can do it in and through you.

September 23

"If you then, who are evil, know how to give good gifts
to your children, how much more will the heavenly
Father give the Holy Spirit to those who ask him!"
Luke 11:13

Have you ever prayed for something with no idea how to proceed or how God would answer? You'll be encouraged to know that helplessness means you are on the right track. You begin to pray when you say *I don't know how*. The first thing you need is the Holy Spirit. The last thing you need is the Holy Spirit. And the thing you need in the middle is the Holy Spirit. When you're discouraged and down and don't know what to pray, ask God to send the Spirit to control you, to convict you, to cleanse you, and to be the bread to revitalize you. In the position of humility you can receive the Holy Spirit in power.

You cannot pray for someone effectively unless that prayer is carried on two wings, faith and love. When you pray with faith and love, you move beyond simply asking for what you want. You begin to pray with an eye toward submission to the Holy Spirit's control in your life and in the life of the other person. This is what ultimately brings real hope and real joy, both in your life and in the lives of the people for whom you pray.

September 24

When they saw the star, they rejoiced exceedingly with great joy. And going into the house they saw the child with his mother Mary his mother, and they fell down and worshiped him. Matthew 2:10–11a

The most difficult thing to do in life is to draw near to God without any reservation. To say you have nothing that is yours; it's all his. To say you will follow his star, his glory, and not your own. We have all kinds of fine print we want to put in the contract, so he doesn't "put one over" on us. We hedge our bets, so we can escape if things get rough. But God doesn't permit that. What the wise men did is a stirring example of what God wants us to do. Through their astronomical study, the God who became the baby in the manger guided them to worship him. This Lord is one who built in them that single-minded desire to come. And their coming to the king of grace ushers in a new age. It is God's turning point, an age of grace. Do you want a completed life? You can't get it by taking things for yourself. These men had extraordinary joy because they saw the divine glory in Jesus Christ, and they gave everything for it. When the heart has seen the king, nothing really matters but the glory of the king. Then your life is fulfilled.

September 25

Finally, brothers, pray for us, that the word
of the Lord may speed ahead and be honored,
as happened among you. 2 Thessalonians 3:1

God is not running a social security program; he's running a beautification program. He's turning those who are depressed, discouraged, and overwhelmed with the ugliness of their own existence and who do not know they're headed for hell, into beautiful vessels filled with joy, with a song in their hearts and on their lips. He brings glory to his name by going into situations where people are hopeless and helpless and changing them!

God wants us to pray that we might have the courage to live before him in ways that are not natural to us. There is nothing else that will make us able to do our work, to see the power in the gospel, and to get away from our deadness than to pray. To breathe, for us, is to pray. Pray at all times. Who are the people that you have trouble loving? Pray that God would give you opportunities to show kindness and love to them. Pray for your city or town that you might see Christ breaking in and bringing about his change. Pray that your heart may be captured by the glory of seeing Christ made known to all people.

September 26

For in him all the fullness of God was pleased
to dwell, and through him to reconcile to himself all
things, whether on earth or in heaven, making peace by
the blood of his cross. Colossians 1:19-20

God gave his whole being, as it were, in the person of his Son. The incarnation was a mighty event. The fullness of deity, the fullness of God, lived in Christ; this accounts for the work of God in history. God takes sinners and brings them to himself through the sacrifice of his Son on a cross. Through this we are not only reconciled to God, but also to each other! We are no longer the enemies of God and no longer the enemies of each other. Maybe this seems like old news to you. You've heard it before and it's helped you in the past, but somehow it never gets very deep into your life. I want to emphasize right now, how full this forgiveness and reconciliation is for you. The One who suffered in his humanity was also the awesome Son of God—deity unabbreviated. If you have a problem believing your sins are forgiven, you probably have a low view of Jesus. It is grace that shows us the wonder and worth of Jesus's sacrifice and righteousness. How liberating to believe that Jesus died for sinners, lives for sinners, and now intercedes for sinners! This is amazing grace, an encouraging salvation, and a mighty forgiveness.

September 27

You then, my child, be strengthened by the grace that is in Christ Jesus. 2 Timothy 2:1

The fullness of God's work is the holy, sanctifying Christ working in history. When Jesus died on the cross as God, he rose as God, and having won the victory, he received and shed forth the Holy Spirit. His Spirit makes it possible for us to be sanctified—one mighty work following another. So often we don't see that the glory of Christ dwells in us! The challenge from Jesus is not to underestimate the power and vastness of his forgiveness. It is rooted in the very character of what deity has done in Christ. The Holy Spirit conquers you, lifts you up, works in you where you are, changes you, and gives you a life centered on a holy love for others. You do not have a small God or a small salvation. The message we need today is that we are weak. This awareness is good if it drives us to God's strength. It is there that we find grace, and once we find it, we are called to surrender to it, to cooperate with it, and to let it flow through us.

September 28

Take care, brothers, lest there be in any of you an evil, unbelieving heart, leading you to fall away from the living God. But exhort one another every day, as long as it is called "today," that none of you may be hardened by the deceitfulness of sin. Hebrews 3:12-13

The danger in sin is that it is not a neutral power. It comes with seduction, the heart of which is to make you believe that it's a good thing. When it comes with its greatest power, it doesn't come in a way you'd expect. Often it comes cloaked in our own righteousness and wisdom. The greatest seduction of sin is when you're right. This is when the Bible tells us to beware. Our souls become so filled with our own righteousness and the love of our own praise that we are blinded to the love of God and the righteousness of Christ through faith. The symptoms of this are complaining, harshness in judging others, and being unmoved by the great works of God right in front of you. If you do not walk in love, you are being deceived by sin. How can a warning like this be positive? God's call is not to draw back, but to draw near to God and draw together. Pray for others, rather than judging them. If you have something against another person, talk to them about it instead of sitting there holding a hammer over their heads waiting to clobber them. And if you're struggling, come out of hiding and ask for help from your brothers and sisters in Christ. Only together can we "hold firmly to our confidence and the hope in which we glory" (Hebrews 3:6b NIV).

September 29

> But she came and knelt before him, saying, "Lord,
> help me." And he answered, "It is not right to take the
> children's bread and throw it to the dogs." She said,
> "Yes, Lord, yet even the dogs eat the crumbs that fall
> from their masters' table." Matthew 15:25-27

Jesus is not indifferent to us. He's not walking the
other way; he's not on vacation having forgotten
about us. God himself has been revealed in Christ, and
therefore the gospel itself is a promise, the gospel itself
is bread, the gospel itself is the very fullness of God in
our midst.

The Canaanite woman received one tiny word from
Jesus that gave her an opening into the promise; in that
crumb, she found great spiritual power. How is it, then,
that we often have a whole bakery filled with bread that
we ignore? The promises have come and been fulfilled.
There's plenty of life for us. Why, then, do we come up
short of that life with no ability to do what we want to
do? We find ourselves leaving a worship service hungry.
We pray and are hungry. What is lacking? What this
woman had that we often lack was a deep need that she
knew no one could meet except Jesus. Her need is what
drove her shameless persistence. Like her, you must be a
real person, coming to a real God, with your real needs,
and expecting real answers and a real transformation.
You don't hold back until you see those answers, you persist and persist and persist until you see the favor of God.

September 30

Then Jesus answered her, "O woman, great is your
faith! Be it done for you as you desire." And her
daughter was healed instantly. Matthew 15:28

Often, when we pray, what we're after is a spiritual
security that guarantees that nothing will ever
knock us off our feet again. We organize our lives and
plan our futures, and what lurks deep in our hearts is a
desire for security to replace our need for Jesus. All we
want is to avoid having to ask God for mercy. We wonder why we have no satisfaction, no power, no strength,
and no life.

Most of us are dissatisfied with our prayer life, but
what we don't see is that God also is dissatisfied with it.
God wants to teach us how to pray, and he sends into our
lives those things necessary to teach us to be shamelessly
persistent, so we will grow, be fulfilled, and live out our
identity and calling. God may not want us to continue
to pray with the same old dullness and routine. When
God shows you your weakness and you think he has
forgotten you, you get broken at the wrong place. God
wants to break us at the point of our pride, and we let
ourselves get broken at the point of our trust. The whole
point of a promise is to be strengthened as you claim,
out of your weakness, what you do not have. There has
to be something shameless about prayer. Your comfort is
that God loves you. He doesn't offer you indifference or
turn his back, but gives you everything you need.

October 1

May the Lord direct your hearts to the love of God and
to the steadfastness of Christ. 2 Thessalonians 3:5

Paul's prayer for the Thessalonians is for the love of God and the steadfastness of Christ to go deep into their hearts. What does this entail? You may think that if you study the Bible enough, all your problems will be solved. But after you try that for a while, you realize that what all your study is producing is a mental agreement to truth that doesn't go very deep. Other times, you might think that going deep into the heart must certainly mean feeling something deeply. But before you know it, the feelings fade, and you're back at square one feeling as if everything you learned is lost.

So, Paul's prayer can't be simply about the mind or the feelings. Instead we need the involvement of the whole heart. We need the Spirit to direct our *whole being* into the love of God and the steadfastness of Christ. Paul is dealing here not with what we want, but with what we need. We're not often very wholehearted beyond a few fitful impulses, and our great *need* is to be led by the Holy Spirit wholeheartedly into the love of God and into the steadfast endurance of Jesus Christ.

October 2

May the Lord direct your hearts to the love of God and
to the steadfastness of Christ. 2 Thessalonians 3:5

In the early years of our marriage, I was very much in love with my wife. She had no faults and I didn't either. Five years went by, and I discovered she had a few faults. Ten years went by, and she discovered I had a few. Twenty years went by, and we discovered we both had many faults! It wasn't that time was making us less perfect; we'd always had faults. But as we went along, what was deep in our hearts rose to the surface and had to be dealt with.

Maybe in some of your relationships, you're discovering that your love has been very much on the surface. It's now almost impossible to endure some of the faults of the other person. Our weariness in well-doing is a result of our inability to be wholehearted. We prefer to stick to the surface in relationships. The Holy Spirit, however, gives us two great motives for working wholeheartedly: the love of God and the steadfastness of Christ. The root of the word *motive* is the same as for the word *motor*—God gives a sort of motor power to continue the wholehearted work of love. Because God loves us and because Jesus endured all sorts of hardships for us, even to the point of death; we have the resources we need to love others wholeheartedly.

October 3

May the Lord direct your hearts to the love of God and to the steadfastness of Christ. 2 Thessalonians 3:5

Often we begin enthusiastically to follow and obey God; however, our enthusiasm fades away because we are not wholehearted. We love ourselves, we're weary and easily bored, and we quickly quit. So often our real goal is to please people, and our real concern is to make a good impression. As long as we're trying to please other people, our efforts will continually fade out. However, if we persevere with a motive to glorify God and do it wholeheartedly, God accepts that.

We need inward power, we need wholeheartedness, we need to persevere, we need to be filled with love, and it must be the Lord Jesus who is our teacher, our pilot. Jesus, Savior, pilot me—not simply over tempestuous seas, but right squarely into the love of God and the steadfast endurance of Jesus Christ. We don't just need the power to be in our hearts; we also need Jesus to put it there. We often look for other pilots, other teachers, but there is no one else who can pilot us into the love of God.

October 4

We have confidence in the Lord about you, that you are doing and will do the things that we command. May the Lord direct your hearts to the love of God and to the steadfastness of Christ. 2 Thessalonians 3:4-5

When we come to Jesus, he doesn't start out by saying, "I want you to know what you have to do." Rather, he says, "I want to cover your unrighteousness with my righteousness."

Jesus is the one who walked in the love of God. On the cross, he died to blot out our sin. He doesn't call us to go somewhere that he hasn't been himself. He walked into the love of God—to the very end of it—and he paid for our sin so that God no longer sees it. Having covered it over, he then invites you to come and believe in him. Repent of your sin, of your self-centered ways, your tendency not to follow through, your half-heartedness, your weariness, and all the rest of what you are, and his righteousness will cover you. His righteousness is placed to your account by faith, and your sin is placed to his account by faith. Legally, you are accepted by God, and he puts his Spirit in your heart. Then the love of God is directed into your soul, and the steadfastness of Christ becomes your own.

October 5

Now we command you, brothers, in the name of our
Lord Jesus Christ, that you keep away from any brother
who is walking in idleness and not in accord with the
tradition that you received from us. 2 Thessalonians 3:6

God wants to direct your heart by his Spirit "to the
love of God and to the steadfastness of Christ"
(2 Thessalonians 3:5), and he places great emphasis on
the way you relate to people and your work. Most of us
don't feel that laziness is all that bad, but Paul writes,
"If anyone is not willing to work, let him not eat"
(2 Thessalonians 3:10). That's pretty serious!

There is a lot of sin in the lives of Christians
because they're lazy. They don't want to do the hard
work of repenting and growing, so their sins multiply.
They are sluggish and bored because they are too lazy
to change anything. We hesitate to say anything to others, because we too are lazy. This is where we need the
wholeheartedness that comes from the steadfastness of
Christ. Often, laziness is how the fear of being wholehearted is manifested. We are afraid of trying and failing, of being rejected, of being required to give more
than we have or more than we want to give. The way
to stop being lazy in the way you live and the way you
work is give yourself to it wholeheartedly and trust the
love of God and the steadfastness of Christ to provide
what you need.

October 6

As for you, brothers, do not grow weary in doing good.
2 Thessalonians 3:13

Do we have gifts that are moldering because we've been too lazy to develop them? We need to be directed into the love of God so that we might get up off our couches and do some work! What's the biggest reason that you and I do so little in the kingdom? Mostly, it's because we're lazy and feel sorry for ourselves. We feel that God should have given us different, better gifts, and we complain about what we could have been or could have done if we'd just had something different.

Do not be weary in doing good. Everything that you think is a burden is an opportunity if you're walking in step with the Spirit. If you're really seeing what Christ did at the cross and his love has penetrated your heart, you're going to want to move, but you have to do some practical things. One of those things is to turn from any tendency to feel sorry for yourself and whine. Don't say you're going to look at the cross and then lie down and go to sleep. Look at the cross, and think about Jesus and how he endured to the end. Think of him going to the depths for you, loving you, bearing your burdens, understanding you, and caring for you. Let that draw you into the love of God, and instead of complaining, begin to praise God as you work.

October 7

For you were called to freedom, brothers. Only do not
use your freedom as an opportunity for the flesh, but
through love serve one another. Galatians 5:13

The idea in Galatians is that the faith that unites
you to Christ spontaneously leads to love. Often,
methods of following Christ are taught that come with
a bunch of new laws to follow—it almost becomes a
new Mount Sinai. It's a great mercy to meditate on a
passage like Galatians 5:13—6:10. The Holy Spirit will
use these verses to show you how your life can be a life
of love; he can give you the confidence to believe that
you already have this love through faith.

Once you are convinced of these things, you can
do almost anything. But if you aren't convinced of the
power and wonder of Jesus's love for you, of your free
justification and that you are God's dearly loved son or
daughter, and that his love is unconditional, it's very
hard to love others. Faith leads to love. It doesn't matter
how weak you are, how many sins you've committed,
or what kind of self-image you have. Following Christ
is about serving others in love, and we have the power
do it because Christ is in us. That's how he lived his life,
and it's how he's empowering us to live ours.

October 8

All things are full of weariness;
a man cannot utter it; the eye is not satisfied
with seeing, nor the ear filled with hearing.
Ecclesiastes 1:8

The story of life is that you do the same things over and over and over again. You wash the dishes and mop the floor, and the next day you have to do it all over again. You work hard at your job, and every day there's more work to be done. Or maybe you have a relationship with a person, and the better you get to know each other the less you like each other. The routine of life lacks excitement and is downright boring; it seems to just keep going round and round. What will satisfy the heart yearning for meaning?

If you're trying to make this world your home with all its unfinished circles of time, you're attempting the impossible. You're living in a dream—better yet, a nightmare! You need to see that all of life, even at its most routine, is filled with glory because and only because the glory of the eternal God dwells within you because of what Christ did on the cross. It was there that his work was finished. Existence doesn't keep going round and round without end. Jesus accomplished redemption, fully and completely, and purchased for us a life abundantly full of purpose and meaning.

October 9

He has made everything beautiful in its time.
Also, he has put eternity into man's heart, yet so that he
cannot find out what God has done from the beginning
to the end. Ecclesiastes 3:11

You cannot be happy if all you live for is this world. Suppose it were possible to be happy without knowing how to love people and knowing how to love God. Would this be true happiness? Of course not! Certainly not in terms of the kind of joy God wants you to have. God made you for himself, and he made a hunger in your heart for eternity. If you're trying to make your home in this world at this time, you're being shortsighted. Instead, you need to keep in mind that your ultimate destination is at home with the eternal God. You need to know about heaven, about God's love and his glory. You need to cultivate your identity as a child of God.

The living God says, "Wake up!" The answer to how you come awake is found in the death and resurrection of Jesus. When you are united with Jesus, you are made alive in the fullest sense. This means that not only are you now able to truly love others and love God, but you are now capable of experiencing true happiness and true joy.

October 10

I perceived that whatever God does endures forever;
nothing can be added to it, nor anything taken from
it. God has done it, so that people fear before him.
Ecclesiastes 3:14

When God comes into history and does something, it's something big. When Adam and Eve sinned, a revolution occurred. Because of sin, sickness came, work became a toilsome burden, and the end of the road was death—ashes to ashes, dust to dust. We humans were tasked with subduing the earth, but the earth ends up subduing us and plowing us under. From our perspective, nothing endures except the earth.

But God sent his Son into history to do what Adam couldn't do, and what nobody else could do either. God himself stepped into history and died to take away sin, guilt, death, and bring eternity into time. What happened when Christ died on the cross and said, "It is finished," was what he'd been teaching all along. He told his disciples, "My food . . . is to do the will of him who sent me and to finish his work" (John 4:34 NIV). Jesus is the only man who ever lived who delighted in God from the heart, and the one man you could never point a finger at and say he wasn't perfect. This is the one who died for us with infinite compassion. The great result of Christ's death was an exchange: he took our sin on himself and gave us his righteousness. He placed us forever under God's favor.

October 11

And going a little farther he fell on his face and prayed,
saying, "My Father, if it be possible, let this cup pass
from me; nevertheless not as I will, but as you will."
Matthew 26:39

In the garden of Gethsemane, Jesus prayed, "Not my will but yours be done." And then on the cross Jesus drank to the last drop the cup of God's wrath that we deserved. All of God's wrath and anger at our evil was poured out on Christ. Though we are still sinners, by grace we are under the umbrella of Christ's payment for our sin. We have a guaranteed future in heaven because we've received this Jesus. He's become ours through faith that is a gift of grace from the Holy Spirit.

Are you convinced of the truth of this? Although you are a Christian, are you living like you still have to pay for your own sin? The work of Christ has broken into time. The eternal God now lives in us. And when we die, we're simply going through a door into our eternal home. Therefore, don't set your heart on how your bank account is doing. Be ready to throw it all away. Be more ready to give because it's been given to you and more willing to forgive because you've been forgiven. In love, put yourself in other people's places, just as Jesus on the cross put himself in your place. Never glory in anything else.

October 12

The Lord answered her, "Martha, Martha, you are
anxious and troubled about many things, but one thing
is necessary. Mary has chosen the good portion, which
will not be taken away from her." Luke 10:41–42

Both Martha and Mary are believers and both are zealous; but in this case, one is wrong and one is right. The difference between these two women is this: Martha is characterized by action based on human wisdom and understanding; Mary is characterized by action based on meditation and prayer. Martha has accepted many responsibilities, but finds herself completely overwhelmed. Although Martha has a strong personality, she has a weak center—she depends on her own abilities rather than on God's strength. As Martha sees it, she is overwhelmed because Mary, her sister, is sitting at Jesus's feet instead of helping her.

Martha is doing something dangerous, all her activities and ministries are shifting her away from Christ. She thinks that she and Jesus are a kind of team. She works with him for a while, but then she criticizes him. She's burnt out because Mary is sitting at Jesus's feet not helping her. The point is that Jesus, in permitting Mary to sit at his feet, is really the one to blame for Martha's exhaustion and frustration. Depending on her own abilities rather than on God, Martha drifts onto the road of depending on her own works to gain acceptance with God. She is trying to earn her salvation. Mary, on the other hand, is doing what is needful—receiving Christ and resting in him.

October 13

[Mary] came with an alabaster flask of ointment of pure
nard, very costly, and she broke the flask and poured it
over his head. . . . And they scolded her. But Jesus said,
"Leave her alone. Why do you trouble her? She has
done a beautiful thing to me." Mark 14:3, 5-6

What drives you: emptiness or the fullness of Christ? Meditation is the act of coming into fellowship with the Father through Jesus Christ. God's will is that we adopt a lifestyle that's controlled not by drift, dreaming, or dozing, but by a consciousness of God. Action comes not out of our emptiness and drivenness but out of fellowship with Christ.

Mary's zeal is concentrated on Jesus. God's will for us is that like Mary we see all things in relationship to Jesus Christ. His love is the heart of the covenant life that streams down from Jesus. Waiting on the Lord is the one thing needed. This waiting builds faith in Jesus Christ. Concentrating on the love of Christ fills you with his love. Thus your assurance grows and grows. This is what meditation is all about. But, as you meditate, you need to depend on other Christians. You need to be accountable to another Christian who will encourage you and pray for you. Because the Holy Spirit loves humility, he will bless the relationship of accountability. Be honest with God and tell him how hard it is to pray. As you mature, try to make the whole day a time of meditation and prayer so that you see everything through God's eyes.

October 14

That which we have seen and heard we proclaim also
to you, so that you too may have fellowship with us;
and indeed our fellowship is with the Father and with
his Son Jesus Christ. 1 John 1:3

The beginning of John's first epistle (1 John 1—2:10) is sweet to my soul because it tells us the basis of our assurance of faith. It tells us that we have very real proof from the apostolic message that Jesus Christ is the personal Light who came into this world and who now lives. John talks about what he and the other apostles had seen firsthand. They had seen Jesus live in this world, as a man. They saw him crucified and raised from the dead. Because they were there, they know that Jesus is the Word of life springing forth on that third day with all reality and power. What was inconceivable actually happened: they heard, touched, saw, and beheld, the risen Christ!

The personal Word, Jesus, is a living reality. He is seated with the Father in heaven and there he intercedes for us as our advocate. This is the one who is reported authoritatively by the apostles. This is the heart of our connection. We know whom we have believed. We have a mighty salvation because we have a mighty Savior.

October 15

But if we walk in the light, as he is in the light, we have fellowship with one another, and the blood of Jesus his Son cleanses us from all sin. 1 John 1:7

There's a lot of evil and darkness in this world, but there is no darkness in God. God sent Jesus to introduce us into his light. God's light illuminates our minds; it is true and pure and drives darkness out of the hearts of people. Jesus is the holy light of God, the very Word of God present, revealing him. Wherever Jesus is and wherever his message is preached, there is life and light. People are changed. There is communion and fellowship. If you have experienced his mighty salvation, there is more and more light in you and less and less darkness.

The basis of this mighty salvation is the blood of Christ. It is the blood of Christ that enables us to acknowledge the truth, that there is darkness and evil in us. It is the blood of Christ that cleanses us from sin. It is the blood of Christ that gives us the freedom to expose ourselves to the light and experience his forgiveness. And it is the blood of Christ that allows us to have genuine fellowship with one another. This message was designed to be shared. It's a mighty salvation, and we wouldn't feel complete if we didn't share it with others, that they too may have fellowship with the Father, with the Son, and with us!

October 16

Before this faith came, we were held prisoners by the
law, locked up until faith should be revealed. . . . You
are all sons of God through faith in Christ Jesus, for
all of you who were baptized into Christ have clothed
yourselves with Christ. Galatians 3:23, 26–27 NIV

Before faith came we were held prisoners by the law,
but the law leads us to Christ. Now we are sons and
daughters of God through faith in Christ. Now we are
clothed with Christ, born again, baptized by the Spirit.
The reason the law couldn't help you is that the law
points you to you. The gospel, however, points you to
Christ.

How does this apply to your spiritual growth? It's
by faith in Christ that your life is filled with the power
of the Spirit to love others and to go with the gospel to
the world. Why does Paul defend justification by faith
so vigorously? Because it is the spiritual power that
moves the church of God. The reason he defends justification by faith, sonship, and adoption so forcefully
is that only those who are in Christ—who have placed
their faith in Christ alone, who know they are adopted
sons and daughters—have spiritual power. In the midst
of their own weakness, they have tremendous power
from God. Knowing you are God's child through faith
fills you with joy. You don't have to take yourself so
seriously. Use your gifts without fear, because now you
are liberated.

October 17

For all who rely on works of the law are under a curse;
for it is written, "Cursed be everyone who does not
abide by all things written in the Book of the Law,
and do them." Now it is evident that no one is justified
before God by the law, for "The righteous
shall live by faith." Galatians 3:10–11

Paul wants to drive home the point that if you are going to be accepted by God on the basis of law-keeping and your own righteousness, then you have to do it all. And if you don't do it all you are under a curse. The law is not based on faith. It requires perfect obedience. Only those who obey God's commands perfectly will live. If Adam, our representative, had obeyed perfectly, then we would have lived through him. But he wasn't perfectly obedient, so he died.

What a great contrast: the righteous will live by faith! Abraham believed and it was counted to him as righteousness (Genesis 15:6). We can be right with God through faith in Christ. Christ's righteousness is ours as a free gift through faith. Christ redeemed us from the curse of the law by becoming a curse for us. The penalty for the broken law fell on Christ. Now we no longer look to our record in observing the law, we look in faith to what Christ has done for us. You are justified, made alive through faith in Christ. Claim Christ and live.

October 18

I have been crucified with Christ and I no longer live,
but Christ lives in me. The life I live in the body, I live
by faith in the Son of God, who loved me and gave
himself for me. I do not set aside the grace of God, for
if righteousness could be gained through the law, Christ
died for nothing! Galatians 2:20-21 NIV

Often we forget to live by faith in the Son of God who loved us and gave himself for us. We are prone to lose the knowledge of the holiness of God revealed in his law and forget how deceitful our own hearts are. We feel like we are probably okay, and we wonder why others can't get it together as well. But when the foundation of justification by faith in Christ fades, soon we are living in a bottomless pit of guilt and obligation. We are right back under the law!

Our pride drives us to try to sanctify ourselves. But when we are broken and realize we have nothing, we are driven to Christ. Justification by faith always points you away from yourself and says that Christ alone is your righteousness. No matter how feeble you are, if you understand that your foundation is all of Christ, there is a total humbling that brings the power of Christ into your life. When you know that, you are willing to take the risks that go with moving out with the gospel.

October 19

"See that you do not despise one of these little ones.
For I tell you that in heaven their angels always see the
face of my Father who is in heaven." Matthew 18:10

The "little ones" that Jesus speaks of are the children who believe in him. They are dependent and humble. Our temptation is to despise the little ones; but if we despise others, if we are irritated by those who seem "little" to us, we will have trouble controlling our tongues. Let the Holy Spirit show you that you yourself are a little one, weak, vulnerable, and easily led astray. Jesus exposes our weakness, lack of faith, stubborn hearts, and rebelliousness. When you recognize the depths of your own self-centeredness, then you will be able to esteem others as better than yourself. Jesus brings home the truth that we who are irritated by others are, in fact, irritating also. In addition, we are irritable and easily stirred up in our passions to judge others.

Once I was convicted that I had to confront a brother. I prayed and prayed that the brother would know Jesus in a real way, and that God would penetrate his cold heart. I went on and on praying for him. But in the middle of the prayer I felt someone staring at me. With a start, I realized I was staring at myself. I was broken in the dust. God convicted me that my sin was much worse than this other brother's.

October 20

"What do you think? If a man has a hundred sheep, and one of them has gone astray, does he not leave the ninety-nine on the mountains and go in search of the one that went astray?" Matthew 18:12

The Father is pictured as the happy shepherd who is happier about finding the one lost sheep than about all the other sheep that didn't wander off. God doesn't become irritated with our irritating ways. He goes after us, and after us, and after us. He carries you back to safety in his loving arms. God is not willing that any of these "little ones"—no matter how stubborn and irritating and provoking—be lost. God wants us to value others the way he does, embracing them and taking them to our heart.

Think of the fatherly gentleness of God; this is how gentle and tender you should be toward people who provoke and irritate you. Quickly repent of being provoked and then say, "Father, take me into your love. Show me what you did on the cross for this person—and for me. Show me that, really, I am worse than that 'irritating' person." Submit to be corrected by God. Tell God that you don't want to gossip and complain. Ask God to show you that Jesus isn't only a teacher; he's a lover who can come near to you and give you grace just like he did on the cross. Move with the great river of God's divine love conquering this world for Jesus.

October 21

To the praise of his glorious grace, with which he has
blessed us in the Beloved. . . . In him we have obtained
an inheritance, having been predestined according to
the purpose of him who works all things according to
the counsel of his will, so that we who were the first
to hope in Christ might be to the praise of his glory.

Ephesians 1:6, 11–12

What can you say about a plan that includes the God of the universe sending his only Son to die for those who hate him? And what's more, adopts those same enemies into his family as dearly loved children, all with the rights and privileges of the firstborn heir? Paul says that the only response is praise for his glorious grace!

How different from us is the way the Father deals with his enemies. I don't want to sacrifice for my enemies; I want to go after them, to set them straight, to prove they are wrong, to vindicate myself. When we look at the cross and see the love of the Father that sent the Son, and the love of the Son who endured the wrath of God for us, we are in touch with something that is completely foreign to our natural way of thinking. It is utterly humbling to know that I have been saved from the pit by such great love. I'm stricken by the wonder of it, but I'm also overflowing with joy "to the praise of his glorious grace."

October 22

[God's purpose is] to unite all things in [Christ], things
in heaven and things on earth. In him we have obtained
an inheritance, having been predestined according to
the purpose of him who works all things according to
the counsel of his will. Ephesians 1:10–11

The master purpose over all of life is to cooperate and surrender to this God who is gathering all things together in Christ. A sure sign that we are not surrendering and trusting in God and his plans, is when we are impatient. What are you impatient about? Is God's program going to fail? No, it will not. Are you going to be lost? No, you are not. Is the kingdom going to keep moving? Yes, it will. Will people be brought in? Yes, they will.

So why are we impatient? Because we're trying to be the lords of the plan; we are not submitting to our heavenly Father. Do you know that every step you take is part of a bigger thing that God is doing? As you are faithful in small things, bigger things will follow. That's the heart of patience. If you want to have sanity and stability, submit daily to God as sovereign. But don't let that make you passive; if God is for you, you can't lose. Whatever you do, do it with your whole heart and then it will have a radiance to it. And don't be afraid of people when you share Christ. Forget about yourself and remember how big your God is.

October 23

But whatever gain I had, I counted as loss
for the sake of Christ. Philippians 3:7

Once I preached at a church that was full of bitterness. My sermon was about having Jesus as your
goal in life. At the end of the service when I gave an
invitation for anyone who didn't truly have a relationship with Christ to come forward, one of the elders, a
leader of the church, stood up and said, "I don't have
anything to say about Jesus as my goal because I haven't
been born again." He turned his life over to Christ there
and then.

Later, in conversation, some of the congregation told me that they had been taught that the Ten
Commandments are like a ladder you climb to get to
heaven. Obeying them, they were taught, made one
right with God. The problem was that they were trusting in their own efforts for salvation.

The elder who stood up in the service may have
made a complete fool of himself, but he did what was
right. You have to leave behind your own righteousness,
your own virtues, and turn to Christ. If you believe in
your own righteousness, it's very difficult not to be bitter against people who wrong you. If you have a bitter
spirit, ask what there is about you that you think is so
great. Come down off the throne; find Jesus and his
righteousness.

October 24

I press on toward the goal for the prize of the upward
call of God in Christ Jesus. Philippians 3:14

Our goal is to obtain Christ in all his fullness. But how do we do that? As you look at Philippians as a whole, you can see that Paul urges full, uncompromising, unquestioning obedience to Christ. Jesus tells his disciples, "You are my friends if you do what I command you" (John 15:14).

We are to come to Jesus as obedient, humble servants. He purchased our salvation, we belong to him, and therefore we give up the things we find glory in and strain to become fully obedient to him. That's how we pursue the upward call. In ancient Rome, the winner of the race was called up onto a platform to receive the prize. For believers the prize is Christ, but the upward call is ultimately being with him in the new heavens and new earth. If you set your heart on living for what's in front of you and if your concern is only for yourself, you will never discover the exhilaration of pursuing Christ.

October 25

*Brothers, join in imitating me, and keep your eyes
on those who walk according to the example
you have in us. For many, of whom I have often told you
and now tell you even with tears, walk as enemies
of the cross of Christ. Philippians 3:17–18*

Many times we act as though we are mere spectators at the race. We cheer on those Christians who are in the race, but we ourselves sit on the sidelines and watch. But Paul is telling us that we've been justified, we've been pardoned, and we've been made sons and daughters *that we might run!* If you're mature, you must think of yourself as a runner, not a spectator. When it comes to knowing God in Jesus Christ, there is no such thing as a spectator sport. We are not justified to sit; we are justified to run.

This means we need to be obedient in every part of our lives. Many times we think, whether consciously or unconsciously, that we can go on vacation from God. What's really happening then is that we think of God as the enemy of our happiness, and we go our own way. But God is not our enemy. He's our friend, and he wants to make us happy and free. That's why he gives us his Spirit to keep us running the race. He also gives us each other, and Paul encourages us to join together to help each other along the way.

October 26

"She has done what she could; she has anointed my
body beforehand for burial." Mark 14:8

Jesus's view of Mary's gift to him is that "she did
what she could." Jesus is telling his disciples and
us that if you give what you can; if you serve with all
your heart, then that's all you need to do. Martha was
chasing many things. She put on quite a banquet all
by herself (Luke 10:38–42). But that's not what Jesus
is asking us to do. When you are in Christ, you simply
use what you have and are for God's glory. You do what
you can. That's very freeing, isn't it? Implicit in Jesus's
words is the idea of total giving. There wasn't anymore
that could be done.

We constantly want to protect ourselves, so we
fear that if we give too much, we will lose it. But what
is given to Christ is never wasted or lost. Parents, are
you doing what you can? Are you bringing your child
to Christ in prayer? Are you sharing with them your
weaknesses? If I could go back again, I would have done
so much more to open up and show my children how
Christ helped me with my weakness. Do what you can.
Don't try to cover up. Be vulnerable. Accept criticism.
Let your life be like a broken perfume jar.

October 27

"She has done what she could; she has anointed my body beforehand for burial." Mark 14:8

As the shadow of the cross hung over him, Jesus was anointed by Mary. Today the cross is no longer a shadow; it is our reality. Jesus was crucified, buried, and rose from the dead; and he is now my life, my all. Because this is so, I am secure in him. I serve; I do; I give; and I go—all out of that knowledge. As I go, I know that Jesus is with me all the way.

I often want life to be more like a canal than the river it is. If you too feel that you deserve smooth sailing straight to the sea with no rough water and no twists and turns, then you are probably looking for a canal too. The river of life is, however, full of bends and rapids. Are you fighting with God because he hasn't given you a canal-like life? Were you expecting something much smoother than it has been? Instead, look to Jesus. When you give everything to Jesus, he gives himself to you. Trust that he can lead you through your river-life. You are loved by him, and you can give to others out of that security. Don't waste time on regrets about the past or fears about the future. If you do well, don't gloat. If you make a mistake, don't give up. With Jesus you can navigate this river with joy, and see it all as a grand adventure.

October 28

"Truly, truly, I say to you, whoever believes in me will also do the works that I do; and greater works than these will he do, because I am going to the Father."
John 14:12

Spurgeon once told a group of pastors, who all wanted to be successful like him, that as long as they were full of the gospel and the Holy Spirit, they could do works greater than anything he had done. They didn't quite believe him, but he was just repeating Jesus's words to his disciples. It really is that simple. In Uganda, a man from the mountains became a Christian. He got married, built a hut, planted a garden, and soon he had twenty people studying the Bible with him. What qualifications did he have? Only the gospel and the Spirit—that was more than enough.

Don't complicate things. If you have your heart right with God, his Spirit and his gospel will begin to influence people through you just by your example. Making and growing disciples for Jesus is caught before it is taught. If you get a hold of the love of God in Jesus Christ for you and daily walk in that love, then you are going to find that the Christian life is actually enjoyable. It's not a trap or a prison, but a life filled with confidence and joy—something to invite others to and something others will be attracted to!

October 29

And so we know and rely on the love God has for us.
1 John 4:16 NIV

Pride can take many different forms. You can look spiritual to others, while underneath, pride is at work, trying to take over God's work in the kingdom. Trying to own your work for God, being controlling, and wanting to impose your own will on others are all ways we express pride.

Why am I proud? Why am I defensive? It's because I don't trust the love and power of God working in this world and others. I don't believe that God is in the business of changing people and situations. I have made up my mind out of a combination of pride and insecurity, which often go hand in hand, that I must be in control. If you have a problem with patience, that's a manifestation of pride. You haven't let the Holy Spirit and the Word search out your heart. The key is turning from your self-will and self-love and letting the love of God take over in your life. Instead of making sure that others really love and respect you, know and rely on the love that God has for you.

October 30

But he gives more grace. Therefore it says, "God opposes the proud, but gives grace to the humble."

James 4:6

When I first became a Christian at nineteen, I was full of joy. I was so broken by my sin and so amazed at the love of God in Christ that I couldn't wait to tell others. I went to our local church, asked if I could preach, and then told everyone that to live for the glory of God was joy inexpressible (1 Peter 1:8). Then I started going door-to-door to share my faith. Soon I had a group around me studying the Bible. Out of my weakness, I began to memorize Scripture. The church began to notice and because they thought I was a "strong" Christian they hired me to do evangelism. But gradually I lost my connection with joy inexpressible and began to confuse intelligence and knowledge with faith and grace. In my pride, I thought that if you had enough Christian education, Bible knowledge, and theology, God would be with you. But the truth is that "God opposes the proud." Grace is for the humble. Without the grace of God at work, no matter what your theology or how much knowledge you have, your life will lose the power and the presence of God.

October 31

But he gives more grace. Therefore it says, "God
opposes the proud, but gives grace to the humble."
James 4:6

The heart of growing as a Christian and helping others to grow is discovering that the fight with our sin is not just hard or difficult, but impossible. We can't solve the simplest problem without grace. If you go into battle without Jesus, you will fail. I learned this when I first became a pastor. I thought I could lead a church because I had been successful in ministry in other churches, but it didn't work. I knew I was powerless, but didn't know why. No one came to pray, and no one really came to hear me preach.

The problem was my pride. I didn't know much about grace or about relying on Jesus for daily help, so I didn't share grace with others. I wanted a well-organized church, and it was—as well organized as the local cemetery and just as dead. In my life and in my preaching there was no touch of the love of God, no grace. When we come to the impossible and are broken again and again, that's when we cry out to Jesus for grace. That's what changes yourself and others. That's the heart of growing to be like Christ.

November 1

Let us then with confidence draw near to the throne of grace, that we may receive mercy and find grace to help in time of need. Hebrews 4:16

How does the grace of God work in our lives? Martin Luther said that to understand God's grace you should picture yourself as a caterpillar that's trying to crawl out from a ring of fire. Grace is when someone picks you up and carries you over the fire. You can't save yourself. Your only hope is help from above. To get grace, you have to start by admitting you are caught in a ring of fire with no hope of saving yourself. You have to know that you have a desperate need, and that only Jesus Christ has the power to pick you up and save you. That is what prayer is all about. In prayer we say, "I have nothing—no strength, no wisdom, no righteousness. But I have a God who has given me the gospel, and in that gospel he promises it all for the asking." Draw near to Jesus with boldness. Become a beggar and approach the throne of grace to receive grace and find mercy to help you in your time of need. As you do that, he will make your life a daily miracle of grace.

November 2

He said, "I am the voice of one crying out in the
wilderness, 'Make straight the way of the Lord,' as the
prophet Isaiah said." John 1:23

John the Baptist never seems to have an identity problem. He knows who he is. He's the voice. His task is to be a light showing people in their darkness what Christ is all about. The religious leaders, who come not to be baptized but to interview him, find him disturbing. They are offended by his baptism. They do not identify themselves as sinners, therefore they do not need to repent—they do not need to be baptized.

The religious leaders refuse to acknowledge themselves as needy sinners. They think of sin as something the unwashed people do—the guys who frequent bars and brothels, the tax collectors who cheat people out of their money, the prostitutes. But sin goes deeper than they think. At its core, sin is about living, not for God's glory, but for the praise of others. John gives them an opportunity to turn things around by pointing out Jesus to them. But still they refuse to repent. How often do we do this too? We don't think of ourselves as sinners and miss the call to repentance. Often we look way too much like the religious leaders of John's day.

November 3

The next day he saw Jesus coming toward him, and
said, "Behold, the Lamb of God, who takes away the sin
of the world!" John 1:29

John the Baptist made himself unpopular with the religious leaders of his day by baptizing Jews and by implication saying that they needed to be cleansed too. But what he said about Jesus made him even more offensive to them. He didn't call him the one who takes away the sin of Israel, but the one who takes away the sin of the world. John says that the whole point of the Word becoming flesh is so that God's love can reach the world—not just the Jews, but God's lost sheep throughout the whole world.

John the Baptist, the last prophet of the old covenant, identifies Jesus as the last lamb to be sacrificed. Prior to this there had been tens of thousands of sacrifices made in the temple, but now we see that all the animals supplied by men are to be replaced by this new Lamb that God is providing. After this Lamb, there will be no other sacrifice. There is no other lamb that can take away the sin of the world—that can take away your sin and mine.

November 4

"Truly, truly, I say to you, unless one is born of water
and the Spirit, he cannot enter the kingdom of God."
John 3:5

In a physical birth, the baby doesn't really do anything on its own to come into the world, but receives life as a free gift. Spiritually, when Jesus says that you can't see the kingdom of God unless you are born again, he's saying that God must give you the new birth. It's not something you create by religious activity, moral change, baptism, or anything else. It must be a work of God. New life comes to you through Christ's touching you by the finger of the Spirit.

The new birth is a gift, a cleansing gift and comes with some pain. Sometimes the new birth comes to one like a bolt of lightning, but that's not really the normal pattern. What you need to see is that there must be a cleansing, washing action in the heart. All Jesus's language about being born of water and the Spirit has in it the idea of something holy happening inside you—even if you don't feel holy.

Not only is there a purifying, cleansing effect, but there's also life in the new birth. Some people think that after they die they'll have eternal life. But if you don't have it now, you won't have it then. When you believe in Jesus and depend only on him, you have eternal life, which you begin to experience right now.

November 5

"The wind blows where it wishes,
and you hear its sound, but you do not know where
it comes from or where it goes. So it is with everyone
who is born of the Spirit." John 3:8

When Jesus talks to Nicodemus about being born again of the Spirit, he uses the wind to illustrate the mystery of the new birth. You can see the effects of the wind, but the wind itself is invisible. The "wind" of the Spirit comes and descends on a person's heart. The dead are made alive. The Spirit comes as a regenerating, renewing power.

Jesus explains to Nicodemus that this was part of God's plan from the beginning, that "as Moses lifted up the serpent in the wilderness, so must the Son of Man be lifted up, that whoever believes in him may have eternal life" (John 3:14–15). Here he's showing himself to be the fulfillment of Old Testament redemption, and he's calling Nicodemus—and you and I—to look to him and be saved.

This is power. The curse is replaced with joy. Where once there was sin, condemnation, and death, now Jesus stands as mediator offering forgiveness, pardon, love, and acceptance. We who believe are justified and given life and peace with God through faith.

November 6

"But that you may know that the Son of Man
has authority on earth to forgive sins"—he said
to the paralytic—"I say to you, rise, pick up your bed,
and go home." Mark 2:10-11

What if, the first time I met you, I said to you, "Your sins are forgiven"? You would think me a very odd person indeed! The people in Capernaum also were taken aback by what Jesus said to the paralyzed man. But then the paralyzed man takes up his mat and walks out! For some, the wonder of the miracle overshadowed the authority Jesus claimed for himself. When Jesus called himself the Son of Man, his listeners would have known that he was referring to a vision that Daniel had of one who is both human and divine: "Behold, with the clouds of heaven there came one like a son of man, and he came to the Ancient of Days and was presented before him" (Daniel 7:13).

Do you see what's going on here? The eternal, unchangeable, sovereign God, ready to act, moves into history. The plan is that Jesus, the Son of God, would take to himself a human nature and redeem us. The Ancient of Days said to the Son, "Go to earth, be with sinners, represent them, and die for them, that they might be set free." Some were only excited by Jesus's miracles and missed the deeper healing. Let's not miss the deeper healing of sins forgiven and our future assured.

November 7

When Jesus saw their faith, he said to the paralytic,
"Son, your sins are forgiven. . . . But that you may know
that the Son of Man has authority on earth
to forgive sins . . . I say to you, rise, pick up your bed,
and go home." Mark 2:5, 10–11

Imagine the scene in Capernaum: Everyone is crowding around Jesus. Everyone wants to be healed. There is a group of men who have a friend. They don't know everything about Jesus, but they have put their faith in him. They know enough about Jesus to go straight to him and not let an obstacle like a crowded room get in their way. As they lower their friend into the room, Jesus looks at them, sees their faith, and says to the paralyzed man, "Your sins are forgiven."

They came to Christ, so now he is teaching them who he really is and what he really came to do for broken people. He is God's answer to their deepest need, not just for physical healing, but for the deeper healing of forgiveness of sins. Jesus came to reconcile us to God, to make us friends with God through faith, and to transform us. He takes that which is broken, beaten, and useless, and makes it live and move. Have you heard Jesus say, "Get up and live"? Only Jesus can transform your life and make you a new person through faith in him.

November 8

Now some of the scribes were sitting there, questioning in their hearts, "Why does this man speak like that? He is blaspheming! Who can forgive sins but God alone?"
Mark 2:6–7

The scribes who were listening to Jesus had a problem. In rabbinical teaching it was held that only God could forgive sins and that this would only happen on the day of judgment. You couldn't know ahead of time that your sins were forgiven. Now Jesus—Son of Man and Son of God—breaks into the world and says, "Friend, your sins are forgiven and not just at the day of judgment, but forever."

Jesus can say this because he truly is God and Judgment Day fell on him at the cross. Your sin was judged on the cross. That doesn't mean Judgment Day is cancelled, but now, for those who put their faith in the Son of Man, it's Vindication Day. You will sail through with flying colors. There is not a great big "Maybe" over your life; there is God's great big "Yes." Your sins are forgiven. Write that over your life. You will be accused—by your conscience, by other people, by the devil. But Jesus did not come into the world to condemn the world. He is not here to accuse, but to bring forgiveness, to be a bridge between God and the sinner (John 1:51). Come to Jesus by faith; ask for forgiveness, and you will have a living relationship with God that lasts for eternity.

November 9

What do you do when you notice (yet again) that you are a sinner? Paul calls us to a "godly grief" that brings life instead of despair. Good grief loosens us from all that we center our lives on (our idols) and turns us to Christ. In good grieving when you confess your sins, you turn from them in distaste. Your grieving is over the fact that they have grieved God. Often when we confess our sins, our confession is self-centered. We want to get rid of the sin because it embarrasses, disappoints, and shames us. And so it sticks around—the guilt doesn't go and the shame hangs on. But good grief is like a knife; it cuts so deeply into the heart that it heals, cleanses, and brings a new freedom.

Paul puts it powerfully, when he says that good grief has no regrets. This is astonishing because the one thing that seems to go with grieving over our sins is regret. But here is a grief so powerful, so life-changing, that it has no regrets. Only Jesus could do this work. No mere human could do this for you. You can't read a book and learn repentance; you need Jesus to teach you. Pray today that Jesus will speak into your life and give you the empowerment that comes from a healing, healthy, sorrowing over our sins and the broken world sin has produced.

November 10

Hope does not disappoint us because God has poured out his love into our hearts by the Holy Spirit whom he has given us. Romans 5:5 NIV

As a nine-year-old, I went on a tour through the Oregon caves. The guide said that if you put your hand on a rock and made a wish, it would surely come true. So I wished my brother would come home from the war. He didn't come home then or ever, and I was devastated. We all have disappointments—unfulfilled wishes and hopes. Our disappointments collect in our hearts and can add up to a life characterized by hopelessness and grief. Yes, life under the sun is disappointing (Ecclesiastes 1:14). We grieve because nothing in this world gives us what we want or need.

But then we read that we have a hope that does not disappoint us, because God has given us the Holy Spirit. God had an appointment in history—the great work of his Son in dying on the cross, rising again, ruling the world, and coming again. God's appointment leads us out of disappointment and fills us with the Spirit. Because we have the Spirit of Christ, we see the world from the standpoint of Christ, with resurrection hope and resurrection power. If you are in Christ, you are a son or daughter of God. And no matter what happens, he is working to release his own powerful Spirit, to conquer your heart and the whole world with his love and hope.

November 11

Not only that, but we rejoice in our sufferings, knowing
that suffering produces endurance, and endurance
produces character, and character produces hope.
Romans 5:3–4

When I found out that I had cancer, I grieved as
I felt the loss of all my hopes and dreams for
the future. What helped me in my grief? A good grief
over my sins. The knowledge that I had peace with God
(Romans 5:1). I said to God, "Forgive me, Lord, for
being Jack Miller, a man of too many words and not
very much love. Forgive, forgive, Father." Knowing
God's forgiveness in Christ, knowing I had peace with
God became the anchor for my soul.

How do you know that you believe in Jesus? How
do you know your sins are forgiven? Maybe you just
believe that you believe. But the certainty of God's love
for you and your faith in him grows as you endure grief
and suffering. Your very character changes when you
don't give up your faith, and when you keep on going
to Jesus asking for forgiveness and help in the midst of
grief. That endurance breeds hope—a hope that doesn't
disappoint. This hope becomes an anchor for your soul
because God has poured out his love into your heart
through the Holy Spirit he has given you.

November 12

You see, at just the right time, when we were still powerless, Christ died for the ungodly. Romans 5:6

After I was diagnosed with cancer, I felt like all of the forces of hell were let loose in my life. The devil really wanted to get my faith. I thought that even if I recovered physically, I would never minister again because I was so shattered emotionally and spiritually. But God brought me to this verse, "Christ died for the ungodly." The word translated *ungodly* is a powerful one. It is so powerful that the Hebrew equivalent in Deuteronomy 25:1 says that no judge shall ever acquit the guilty. When I thought about how "ungodly" described my natural state and remembered what Christ had done for me, what a comfort it was! God, the righteous Judge of the universe, justifies the ungodly because he gave his Son. He took upon himself the grief of griefs—even my ungodliness and yours. My grieving was caught up in the glory of the love of God on the cross for the ungodly. Caught up in that, my grieving became rejoicing in my reconciliation with God.

Don't turn your back on this love. Grieve over your ungodliness, but then let your grief open your eyes. With the tear in the eye of faith you see the glory of the cross, the glory of the new body, the glory of the resurrection, and your glorious place in Christ.

November 13

If anyone is caught in any transgression, you who are
spiritual should restore him in a spirit of gentleness.
Keep watch on yourself, lest you too be tempted. Bear
one another's burdens, and so fulfill the law of Christ.
Galatians 6:1–2

Our natural tendency is to judge and condemn others. But here we find that, because of the cross we've been freed from God's curse and liberated as sons and daughters. We are now free to humble ourselves and walk along with someone who is erring, even if they've sinned in a way that may be very terrible.

When you bear each other's burdens, what you are carrying is the burden of the other person's sin. What motivates you is your compassion. You come alongside the sinner, not trying to crush them, but putting your arm around him or her as much as you can, as if to say, "Jesus loves you, so do I, and we want you to know this." In this way, Paul continues, you "fulfill the law of Christ." Having said earlier that you can't be justified by the law, he's not now advocating taking up a new law by which to be justified. Rather what he's talking about is how the power of the cross and a crucified Lord produce a life of love. The law of Christ here is a life of love that comes out of the cross.

November 14

Grace to you and peace from God our Father and
the Lord Jesus Christ, who gave himself for our sins
to deliver us from the present evil age, according to
the will of our God and Father, to whom be the glory
forever and ever. Amen. Galatians 1:3–5

Jesus Christ "gave himself for our sins to deliver us from the present evil age." Catch along with Paul the biblical point of view that the present evil age is fleeting and temporary. Paul wants to rescue us not only *from* this "present evil age," but *for* a future age of glory. That's what Jesus did when he gave himself for us by dying on the cross. He gave himself for our sins, and that sacrifice had the power to rescue us from all the evil of these crooked days. There is, then, in the cross and in the preaching of the cross the power for you and for me to be delivered from all the evils of our time.

Once we have seen that we have been rescued, we begin to see persecution as an opportunity to show that we do not belong to this present age. We can say, "I will not fight their evil with evil as though I were part of this age. If they curse me, I will bless them. If they hurt me, I will pray for them." We have been rescued, and we are being rescued.

November 15

Those who belong to Christ Jesus have crucified the
flesh with its passions and desires. Galatians 5:24

When we have disappointed expectations, we are often tempted to become hopeless about life and view God as very far off. But this is when you can learn much about the power and grace of God. In this hour, God's love can be fulfilled in you. You can bless where you're cursed; you can forgive; and you can give. That's what it means to fight in the Spirit.

Only by going through the agony of that soul struggle can you discover the strength of your flesh and the strength your faith. As long as the sailing is smooth and there are no leaks in the boat, you won't see this. But when the storm comes and fear sets in, and you see nothing but weakness in yourself, and you just want to jump overboard to save yourself, that is when God's Spirit reminds you that you're a child of God. Then you realize the power of faith to weather storms that unbelief cannot. To have Christ redeem you, to take away the penalty of your sin, and then to begin to break the power of it, he has to break you with it. That's how faith grows. I don't expect you to say "Amen" to that, but that's where the reality is and that's where the power lies. Praise God that he's able to do that.

November 16

But the fruit of the Spirit is love, joy, peace, patience,
kindness, goodness, faithfulness, gentleness, self-
control; against such things there is no law.
Galatians 5:22–23

If you want to be winning in the fight, if you want to
be growing, if you want the Spirit's fruit produced in
you, you have to obey. That's the whole point of *walking* by the Spirit. You have to obey and keep on obeying, whether you feel like it or not. But the source and
life of this obedience is not the law, but the cross and
the faith that claims Jesus. That faith works by love, and
it can't work any other way. Faith must work by love
because faith receives Christ. Because it overflows from
Christ, love follows.

Love is not what justifies us, but it is always there
when we have been justified by faith. The Father is a
welcoming God. He doesn't condemn you; he calls you
out of your sin. He doesn't want you to "play church."
He wants you to live and be discipled. In all this, he
gives the Spirit. Repudiate what is not yours—the works
of the flesh—and let love flow. Love is the fruit from
which the others grow—joy, peace, patience, kindness,
goodness, faithfulness, gentleness, and self-control. All
these flow out of faith working by love.

November 17

"Blessed are the merciful, for they shall receive mercy."
Matthew 5:7

If we could see ourselves as God sees us, we would be broken in a thousand pieces. When we were outside of Christ, we were wretched and miserable. God wants us to be broken by knowing the depths of his pity and love for us, and then to share his mercy and kindness with others.

Think about it this way: Suppose you have shown a lot of mercy to someone. But they haven't ever thanked you or acknowledged what you have done. When that happens to me, my instinct is to want to choke that person. But when you know God's mercy to you in Christ, when you know the forgiveness of sins, your hands are so full of God's good gifts of mercy and grace that you don't have a hand free to choke anyone. What could someone possibly do to you that would compare with what you have done to God? This perspective frees you from being a prisoner of someone else's bad behavior. When your hands are full of God's mercy, that mercy will overflow to others.

November 18

"But love your enemies, and do good, and lend, expecting nothing in return, and your reward will be great, and you will be sons of the Most High, for he is kind to the ungrateful and the evil. Be merciful, even as your Father is merciful." Luke 6:35–36

Mercy starts as an attitude of grace toward others, but it doesn't end there. It reveals itself in merciful actions that persist and persevere. The idea is that the person needing mercy is very weak, not able to return any favors, and probably at least partly responsible for the mess they are in. Anyone who wants to help him or her has to go a long way down, and they have to do it again and again.

So this passage challenges us: Are we going to do what's natural and give to those who thank us? Who are able to give something back? Will we welcome to our table only those who can welcome us back? Or will we be merciful as our Father in heaven is merciful to us? Without the Spirit this mercy would be impossible. But a new age has come, the Holy Spirit has entered the world, and he has the power to enable you to do these things. By his power you keep on moving toward others with God's merciful kindness. Jesus is in the business of building a church full of people who persevere in sharing God's mercy by treating the undeserving with compassion, tenderness, and forgiveness.

November 19

"And as you wish that others would do to you, do so to them." Luke 6:31

When Jesus talks about mercy, he clears up any confusion we might have by giving us a simple rule to follow: whatever you wish others to do for you, do so to them. We are to ask ourselves: If I were in that person's position, what would I want done for me? Jesus is not telling us to give in to someone's feelings or demands, but to think seriously and clearly about what would be best for the other person.

Putting ourselves in another's place goes against what we naturally want—for others to put themselves in our place. We reverse Jesus's rule of mercy. But Jesus says if you are really merciful, you will put yourself in the other person's position. And you will do it with such a tender heart that the person you extend mercy to will see Jesus in the compassion and kindness you share.

How can this happen? Ask Jesus to have mercy on you, to give you a practical Christianity that gets right down to the way you live with your spouse, your children, at work, when you are under authority, and with those you have authority over. Ask the Spirit to give you a deep understanding and compassion for others. Tell the Lord that you can't do this yourself and ask him to do it in you.

November 20

> I tell you, though he will not get up and give him
> the bread because he is his friend, yet because of
> the man's boldness, he will get up and give him
> as much as he needs. Luke 11:8 NIV

What is prayer? Prayer is talking to God about your needs on the basis of Jesus's name. Often we have a vague, guilty feeling that we should pray, but we don't have much motivation. But, like the man who at midnight kept pounding on his neighbor's door asking for bread, effective prayer comes out of need. It's our need—a health crisis, a bad habit, deliverance from temptation—that drives us to ask God for specific help.

When I was fourteen, I was a young atheist. One day the doctor said my sister was going to die. How would an atheist respond? I prayed, "God, I don't know whether you exist, but if you do and you heal my sister, I will try to be better." My sister did live. I didn't start acting any better, but I wasn't quite an atheist anymore. For the first time I realized I was not complete in myself. My human adequacy failed when I was faced with death. I had nothing in myself to meet the need of the moment. When we realize that is true every day, our need drives us to everyday prayer.

November 21

Which of you who has a friend will go to him at
midnight and say to him, "Friend, lend me three
loaves, for a friend of mine has arrived on a journey,
and I have nothing to set before him"? Luke 11:5–6

Effective prayer starts with knowing you have nothing. In Luke 11, knowing his need, the man keeps
knocking until he gets an answer. The opposite is also
true: if you have a strong sense of your own compe-
tence, then there isn't much reason to pray.

I learned this when my wife, Rose Marie, was pregnant with our first child. I had been getting up every
morning to pray from six to seven, and I went around
telling everyone that they too should get up and pray
from six to seven. Then Rose Marie was pregnant and
sick. So I spent the morning bringing her tea and toast
and feeling like I was losing my prayer life. But eventually it dawned on me that it isn't the hour from six to
seven that teaches you to pray; it's knowing your need.
It's the morning sickness that teaches you to pray. It's
the wife you don't know how to help and love that
teaches you to pray. It's the husband you can't cope with
that teaches you to pray. Prayer becomes effective when
you don't have any clue how to make life work and yet
you believe that God sees your struggle and helps you
as you ask and keep on asking.

November 22

"What father among you, if his son asks for a fish, will instead of a fish give him a serpent; or if he asks for an egg, will give him a scorpion? If you then, who are evil, know how to give good gifts to your children, how much more will the heavenly Father give the Holy Spirit to those who ask him!" Luke 11:11–13

Does God exaggerate sometimes? Do you have to cut his promises down to size? No! Jesus really promises that God gives the Holy Spirit to those who are needy, to those who keep on asking, seeking, and knocking.

In Luke 11, Jesus has already talked about the food—the bread, eggs, and fish—that sustain our physical life. In verse 13, he goes on to talk about what sustains our spiritual life. He promises that when you ask for the Spirit—for spiritual sustenance—your heavenly Father who delights to give good gifts will give you his Spirit. When was the last time you asked for the Holy Spirit? Do you think that God couldn't love you so much that he, who gave his one and only Son for you and the Holy Spirit to you at your conversion, would not also give you what you need to sustain your spiritual life? Of course he will. He is your good, heavenly Father. As you ask, every day he will give you more of his strength, more of his wisdom, more of his joy, more of his power, more of his peace. All you have to do is ask and keep on asking.

November 23

"And I tell you, ask, and it will be given to you; seek,
and you will find; knock, and it will be opened to you."
Luke 11:9

There are three things you should ask for regularly when you pray. First, ask for fellowship. Ask God to make the idea of partnership between you and him a reality. Second, ask God to move you from fear to faith. With all the people and situations that cause you fear, boldly ask the Father to give you what you need to not live out of fear in the face of them. When you go into those situations or face those people, pray for faith and trust that God will provide. Third, ask for forgiveness for yourself and for your sins, but also ask for forgiveness that you can offer to others. Many times, when you fear people, you need to forgive them for something. There's something in them that's intimidating or that you don't like. Rather than lashing out at them or running away in fear or suppressing your feelings, take your emotions to God. When you do this, you're learning to be honest with God. You're able to tell him the whole truth about yourself. But you're not leaving it there; you're moving from fear to faith; you're moving into forgiveness; and you're asking him to give you a spirit of love in every situation.

November 24

Claiming to be wise, they became fools, and exchanged
the glory of the immortal God for images resembling
mortal man and birds and animals and creeping things.
Romans 1:22-23

Often, we're more interested in particular *sins* than we are in *sin*. Now, this doesn't mean that you shouldn't fight your sins, but you need to be thinking about the bigger problem, which is the strength of the flesh. God is concerned about a more total program, a life of faith, at the center of which is his glory and praise.

We often don't place unthankfulness high on the scale of our serious sins. But we often fail to give God the glory for what he's done. Instead we give credit and look to created things for success and happiness; we look to ourselves, other people, money, and possessions. This, we learn in Romans, quickly spirals into self-focused lusts and desires that lead to all kinds of sins. Remember that, while our sins grieve our Father, he never views us as outcasts. He always views us as wandering sheep, as little ones who are precious to him. What he wants us to do is move into the center of his will, and we can begin by giving him thanks for all he has done.

November 25

"If you then, who are evil, know how to give good gifts
to your children, how much more will the heavenly
Father give the Holy Spirit to those who ask him!"
Luke 11:13

Have you ever prayed for something and not gotten an answer? Perhaps you prayed for your wife, your husband, or your child to change and still they haven't changed. Maybe things have even gotten worse. When you don't get what you ask God for, the questions come. What is going on when God seems to not hear our prayers? Doesn't Jesus say that we can ask, seek, knock, and receive? What kind of God is this who doesn't seem to know how to help? Maybe you even feel that today.

But Jesus says that the Father's best gift—what we need for every part of life—is the Holy Spirit. The first thing we need is the Holy Spirit, the last thing we need is the Holy Spirit, and what we need in the middle is the Holy Spirit. As you ask God to send the Spirit to control you, to cleanse you, to convict you, to be the bread that revitalizes you, to make you alive when you are discouraged, to give you words when you don't know what to say and what to pray, then you will notice that he has filled you with a spirit of love that begins to change your whole life.

November 26

When Jesus taught his disciples to pray this, he was teaching them (and us) to ask God not only for our daily physical needs, but also for our daily spiritual needs. He is teaching us to pray, "Give us the bread of life today." Every day we are to ask our heavenly Father to give us life, to give us something that makes life worth living, to give us bread from heaven.

In the Middle East, bread is everything—it's the spoon and it's also the food. Jesus says that when we pray, we need to ask for what feeds our soul. We are to ask for the bread of life. Later in the chapter, Jesus connects this to the gift of the Holy Spirit. In Luke 11:13, we expect Jesus to talk again about food. He has already mentioned bread, eggs, and fish, but now he goes on to talk about what sustains our spiritual life—the Holy Spirit. Jesus is still talking about essentials, but now he has moved from what we need to sustain us physically to what we need spiritually. For our daily spiritual life, we need the Holy Spirit. We are to ask for the Spirit and keep on asking. That's how we receive the bread from heaven that sustains our soul.

November 27

"When you pray, say: 'Father, hallowed be your name.
Your kingdom come.'" Luke 11:2

When we pray, "hallowed be your name, your kingdom come," we are praying that this world will be made holy, like heaven. We are praying that every power not of God will be turned over and every human empire destroyed. Read the news and you will see that God is turning over empires right now. God will have only one kingdom. Jesus alerts us to the signs that his kingdom is coming: earthquakes, wars and rumors of war, hearts growing cold. Right now he is getting ready for his final kingdom.

God has equipped us well to live in this world. We are a holy temple. Christ dwells in us by the Holy Spirit. The Spirit teaches us the meaning of the cross. He convicts the world of sin and unbelief. When people know they are sinners and know they need a Savior, then the door is open for the kingdom of God to come in and change everything. Keep on asking for the Spirit—for yourself and for the world.

November 28

To each is given the manifestation of the Spirit
for the common good. 1 Corinthians 12:7

When I was small, I had two well-defined character traits: I whined a lot, and I bragged a lot. The root of it was that I was always comparing myself with other people. If I didn't measure up, I whined. And if I did measure up, I wanted everyone to know about it. We all want to feel superior to someone, don't we? But if we're going to minister out of the Holy Spirit, the Bible has a different message for us: "For who sees anything different in you? What do you have that you did not receive? If then you received it, why do you boast as if you did not receive it?" (1 Corinthians 4:7).

Gifts become dangerous or crippled or both if we are boasters, whiners, and complainers who are trying to use them in a competitive, jealous way. This doesn't only happen when you feel *superior* to others; it can also happen when you feel *inferior*. Maybe you've set impossibly high standards for yourself and when you fail to reach them you go around despising and condemning yourself. Ask the Holy Spirit to cleanse you of competitiveness, comparing yourself to others, self-exalting bragging, and self-condemning whining, and you will discover gifts that you never dreamed you had.

November 29

So now faith, hope, and love abide, these three;
but the greatest of these is love. 1 Corinthians 13:13

How do we learn to love? In describing the way of love, 1 Corinthians 13 begins with patience and ends with perseverance, as if to say, "Don't quit in-between." In that in-between, as you persevere, you begin to understand that love is a gift that you have to seek day in and day out. As you persevere in asking for this love, the Holy Spirit reveals himself to you. He takes the gifts Paul wrote about in chapter 12, sifts them, and uses them for his glory.

Depend on the Holy Spirit. He is the sovereign one. If you want to know how to exercise your gifts with love, ask the Father to give you the Spirit with his control, presence, and guidance. Ask him to humble your heart, to make you depend on him, to help you to listen to him with sensitivity, and to give you an obedient heart. It is often the case that we don't listen to the Spirit because we've made up our minds that we already *know* what we should do. What he calls us to then is radical submission and teachability that doesn't destroy our personalities, but rather brings them into fullness and fulfillment in Christ.

November 30

I do not cease to give thanks for you, remembering you
in my prayers, that the God of our Lord Jesus Christ,
the Father of glory, may give you the Spirit of wisdom
and of revelation in the knowledge of him, having the
eyes of your hearts enlightened, that you may know
what is the hope to which he has called you.
Ephesians 1:16–18

We need the eyes of our heart opened if we are to understand what the Father of glory is doing. The news doesn't paint a picture of a world filled with God's glory. Haven't there been recent events that don't seem to have been part of God's plan? Things that didn't bring much glory to him?

But we are being called to believe what we can't see with our physical eyes. Only with eyes opened by the Spirit, can we see that Jesus Christ has been raised to the throne of the universe and is bringing everything under submission to the Father. With our spiritual eyes wide open, we believe that everything is part of his great and glorious plan, including everything that happens to you and me. With the eyes of faith, we step into a new way of living that brings God glory. We grow in patience, kindness, forgiveness, and love, despite inglorious circumstances. The whole world is beginning to sparkle with people who live for the praise of his glory (Ephesians 1:12).

December 1

"Behold, I stand at the door and knock. If anyone hears
my voice and opens the door, I will come in to him and
eat with him, and he with me." Revelation 3:20

Jesus comes to each of us and says, "Today I want to meet you right where you are. I want to reveal the Father. I want you to know my heart of love and my power. I am the one who is able." Jesus is the only one who is able to make you like himself. He wants to fill you with his Spirit. And he changes us, not so we can boast, but so we can laugh a bit at ourselves. Because we know God's grace is for sinners, we don't have to take ourselves so seriously!

Jesus gives us his Spirit to remake us. He wants to break us in order to free us for sane, healthy living. He wants to free us to learn about the love of God and how to love others. He wants to make our lives a daily miracle of grace. That will include some really hard things. You can't grow unless you are fighting the world, the flesh, and the devil. But if you are willing to let the Lord do those things through you, you will have joy inexpressible. Won't you meet with Jesus today?

December 2

But he gives more grace. Therefore it says, "God
opposes the proud, but gives grace to the humble."
James 4:6

Years ago I quit preaching and teaching seminary in the same week because I thought others were full of pride. It turned out that I was better at detecting pride in others, than in myself. But God, in his mercy, showed me that I was proud and unwilling to humble myself before others. Just like when I was first saved, I was overcome by my sin and by God's great love for me. When I humbled myself before God, I was amazed at how quickly I learned to love people. I always thought that love was something that some people had and others didn't. I thought that being able to love well goes with your personality; it was genetic and I didn't have that gene. But being humbled before God and studying the good news of God's love in the gospel, convicted and changed me. As the Spirit revealed my desire to control, dominate, and impose my own will, God began to replace those things with love for others. In the two years following this humbling, I saw more people radically changed by Christ then in the previous two decades. In my own strength my ministry was dead, but with the power of God at work, people were changed. He gives grace to humble us, and then gives the humble grace.

December 3

Jesus answered her, "If you knew the gift of God,
and who it is that is saying to you, 'Give me a drink,'
you would have asked him, and he would have given
you living water." John 4:10

The gift of God that Jesus is offering to the woman at the well is the Holy Spirit. He is promising that the water he gives, which is the Spirit, will become a spring of water—enough for her and for someone else. So her encounter with Jesus, with living water, leads to her remarkable, simple testimony, "Come see a man who told me all that I ever did. Could this be the Christ?" (John 4:29). What a beautiful way to share one's faith! Pentecost hadn't come yet, but still there was a flowing of the Spirit taking place. Living water flows from Jesus to the woman and through her to her friends, neighbors, and family.

What does it mean to be a witness? For the woman, it started with finding out who she herself was ("he told me all I ever did") and who Jesus is ("could this be the Christ?"). She then immediately shares with those who also need living water. We too need to see that the people with whom we live and work, need living water desperately. Only in Christ is found the life-giving power of the gospel. Have you met Jesus? Has he told you about yourself and filled you with the living water of the Spirit? If he has, go and tell someone else.

December 4

"Come see a man who told me all that I ever did. Could this be the Christ?" John 4:29

Sometimes we make sharing our faith too complicated and think of all the reasons why being a witness won't work in whatever relationship or situation we are in. Or we share our faith as a duty, trying to impose our will on others, and then we wonder why they don't respond. But meditate on this passage and see the beautiful simplicity of the women's testimony. Her encounter with Christ shows her that she is needy—that she thirsts for living water. The idea of thirst is that you have a need you can't fill in yourself. Christ meets her need, and so she naturally shares what he has done for her.

When I don't share my faith, the issue always is that I have grown cold to my need for Christ. I have forgotten that I am a sinner who needs cleansing. I need the gospel. I need the righteousness of Christ. Jesus died to cleanse me by his blood, and that blood has the power to cleanse others too. On that same cross, Christ bought for me the gift of the Holy Spirit, the gift that satisfies and makes life meaningful not just for me, but for others too. When I remember all that Jesus did for me, then I share my faith with everyone I can. I want everyone to know about the man who meets my need.

December 5

Jesus stood up and cried out, "If anyone thirsts, let him come to me and drink. Whoever believes in me, as the Scripture has said, 'Out of his heart will flow rivers of living water.'" Now this he said about the Spirit.

John 7:37–39

I met a woman in London who lived in one of the worst areas of the city and worked among the gangs there. As she shared her faith with them, the gangs in that part of the city disappeared. The police even took notice. When I asked her what she had done, she explained, "It all started when I read the gospel of John. Jesus went into the world. He went down, so I did too. I went out and met people, listened, and told them about Christ." Her method wasn't very complicated, was it? But it all flowed from her relationship with Christ. If you heard her pray, you would know that she was drinking of Christ.

Do you know how to pray? In John 7, Jesus is talking about the flow of life. This life flows to us through the Word—through meditating on the promises of God as we claim them for ourselves and others in prayer. The life God wants to give us, comes to us as we ask for the Spirit. And when we are filled with the Spirit, rivers of living water will flow from us to others. This is a life that overflows to others. As you pray, are you claiming that kind of life for yourself?

December 6

Don't lie to God about how you're struggling. If you struggle with lust, tell him. If you're harsh and judge people quickly, if you're cold to God, tell him the truth. Grace always runs with power where the truth is told. It's the ministry of the Spirit that in the moment you admit your weakness, already he is making you strong. You may not feel strong, but you will be. It's a mysterious paradox that we have to relearn every day, sometimes every hour. The sweet teaching ministry of Jesus draws you back to the foot of the cross and reminds you that your sins are forgiven. Jesus is for you. The Spirit is in you, and he's going to lead you through this. Your very weakness becomes a stepping-stone for you to serve him. Where you are vulnerable is where you learn to cry out, to be poor in spirit, and to find grace in your time of need. The mystery of grace—the mystery of God himself—is that he will not stoop to your lying, but he will stoop to your confession. You cannot have grace if you defend yourself before God, but you can have grace if you lay down your weapons and let Jesus be your advocate.

December 7

John the Baptist had prepared the way for Jesus by preaching that every person needed to be washed: Jew as well as Gentile, religious leader as well as tax collector and prostitute. The Jewish religious leaders hated John for calling them hypocrites, and they hated Jesus even more when he came along.

When Jesus began talking about God's grace and love, he did it from the angle that no one is pure and holy. Jesus preached that everyone needs to be cleansed by God. Everyone is a prisoner; everyone is blind; everyone is oppressed. Our hearts are in rebellion against the living God, and we need to be changed. Jesus points out that in the Old Testament when Israel rejected the prophets, God sent them to Gentiles who received God's grace instead. Jesus boldly warned the Jews that the same would happen to them. After this the religious leaders wanted to kill him. Instead of being convicted of their sin and repenting, they tried to get rid of him. We face the same choice today: be cleansed from our sin through Christ or hold onto our pride and self-righteousness. Which will you choose?

December 8

I pray also that the eyes of your heart may be
enlightened, in order that you may know the hope
to which he has called you, the riches of his glorious
inheritance in the saints. Ephesians 1:18 NIV

Paul prays that the eyes of our hearts would be enlightened that we might be flooded with the light of the gospel, that we might know we are sons and daughters of God and not orphans, and that we might know that we are headed for glory and right now have a taste of it. Then, no matter what happens to us, no matter what we discover about ourselves or others, we still glory in Christ. In the midst of hard circumstances, weakness, and sin, we can still see that God is for us, that everything is part of his glorious plan, and that we are going to grow and mature. This is our marvelous hope.

With this hope, we pray differently for people. We become more realistic. We realize that other people aren't floating on clouds of holiness either; they are like you and me. So we pray that we will experience Christ's power and glory. We pray that God will open eyes, and give new strength and power. If we agree in prayer about these things, then revival will come, starting with your heart and mine.

December 9

I pray also that the eyes of your heart may be
enlightened in order that you may know the hope
to which he has called you, the riches of his glorious
inheritance in the saints, and his incomparably great
power for us who believe. Ephesians 1:18–19 NIV

Paul wrote this from a first-century Roman prison, knowing that the likely end to his imprisonment would be death. But he wasn't afraid because Christ had already captured him. He had met Jesus and staked his life on the good news that Jesus died for his sins and rose again. Paul believed the gospel, and it changed him. He knew his sins were forgiven and he would not perish but live forever, and that filled him with hope. His soul was filled with an inward force that could not be taken away, placed there by the Spirit. Hard circumstances only served to strengthen his hope.

Recall a time in your own life when something was terribly hard and almost unendurable. If you are a believer, hard circumstances, as painful as they are, strengthen your faith and confidence in Christ. That's the resurrection power of Christ at work. In the darkest moment, when you can't see anything, you look up and see the bright stars of God's promises. Christ is with you now. Christ will one day raise your body in glory and you will see him face-to-face. That was Paul's hope. There was nothing that could shake Paul; he was a prisoner of hope.

December 10

I pray also that the eyes of your heart may be
enlightened in order that you may know the hope
to which he has called you, the riches of his glorious
inheritance in the saints, and his incomparably great
power for us who believe. Ephesians 1:18–19 NIV

Many things we count on in life we don't get. Even a human inheritance can be taken away at the last moment. But the inheritance Paul talks about here is special. It's God himself. Why does Paul pray with such fervor that the eyes of our hearts will be opened? It's so we can comprehend the riches of our inheritance—a relationship with God that lasts forever.

I was visiting a dying woman who said that she didn't want to leave this world and go to heaven, because heaven sounded boring. I asked her to recall the happiest time in her life. She said that times with her family had been the happiest. I agreed that the best thing in the world is being with someone who loves you and whom you love. Then I told her that that's what heaven is like. Throughout eternity Christ will be giving himself to us, so we might know the Father better and be filled with inexpressible joy. God will look us in the face and say, "I love you." The Father will put his warm arms and heart around us. That's our God, that's his radiant love, and that's our inheritance forever.

December 11

Jesus spoke to them in parables, saying, "The kingdom
of heaven may be compared to a king who gave a
wedding feast for his son, and sent his servants to call
those who were invited to the wedding feast, but they
would not come." Matthew 22:1–3

When we read this parable, we notice right away that Jesus is talking about a happy event. A king has prepared a wedding banquet for his son, and the wedding hall is filled with guests (Matthew 22:10). But who are the guests? The welcome goes out first to the insiders—the religious, the moral. But they ignore the king's invitation. It is always foolhardy to ignore a king's invitation. Jesus is using this story to say, "Wake up! Don't take the king's invitation lightly; your life will be forfeit."

When I was in Ireland, we shared the gospel with a group of Travellers (Irish gypsies). We were telling a man about Jesus, and his wife told us to leave. She saw herself as an insider. She was sure that she was good enough—she and her family didn't need Jesus. She didn't want anyone to pull her where she didn't want to go. You can be an insider without even being religious. But will you be saved? You have to come to the banquet to be saved. And to come, you have to know that you need saving. I'm a poor sinner. Are there any others around?

December 12

"Then he said to his servants, 'The wedding feast is ready, but those invited were not worthy. Go therefore to the main roads and invite to the wedding feast as many as you find.' And those servants went out into the roads and gathered all whom they found, both bad and good. So the wedding hall was filled with guests."
Matthew 22:8–10

The first set of invited guests—the insiders, the self-satisfied, the self-righteous—have rejected the king and his invitation. So now the king's servants go out into the streets and gather whomever they can find, "both bad and good." All are invited. Likewise, the invitation goes out from our great King Jesus: "Come to me. No matter where you have been or what your sins are. Come and welcome. I am the bread of life. I died for sinners. Won't you come and live?"

How easy it is to forget the invitation and invite to the banquet only those we think God can save. We decide that the elect can only be the elite. And we begin to judge others by saying, "God can't reach that person." But listen to the voice of Jesus saying, "Go to the street corners, invite anyone you find." For our God does wonders for the high, the low, the good, and the bad. The invitation is for all to come and feed on his Son.

December 13

> When the king came in to look at the guests, he saw there a man who had no wedding garment. And he said to him, "Friend, how did you get in here without a wedding garment?" And he was speechless. Then the king said to the attendants, "Bind him hand and foot and cast him into the outer darkness." Matthew 22:11–13

Into this happy scene, Jesus introduces tragedy. A guest without the proper garment is ejected from the banquet. This garment represents the righteousness of Christ—the free grace of sins covered over by the blood of Christ. The fact that the guest was without the proper garment was a picture of his presumption. He didn't have a repentant heart; instead he was full of self.

This seems harsh, doesn't it? But Jesus wants to deal with our presumption. Presumption looks like faith, but at the heart it's a confidence in yourself, not in Jesus and what he has done for you. What is your confidence in? A religious experience? A decision for Christ? Going to the right church? Having the right theology? None of it is a substitute for a personal relationship with Jesus and being clothed with his righteousness. If you fear that you are unrepentantly self-indulgent and only live for your own comfort, go to Jesus and ask, "Is it I, Lord?" (Matthew 26:22). Consider whether you are wearing the wedding garment provided by the King.

December 14

"For many are called, but few are chosen."
Matthew 22:14

Why does Jesus have to bring election into this parable? He does it to remind tough sinners like you and me that Jesus's irresistible call to us is our only hope. Election isn't for the elite. It's for those who know they have nothing to bring. It's the other side of free justification by faith. Jesus says as an absolute decree, "I justify sinners freely, once and for all, and forever."

As a sinner, I don't need a small God who can only forgive me if I turn toward him. I need a God who can draw me to himself. How did I ever come to surrender to God's love in Christ? Because I first chose him? No, because he chose me and behind that choice is an absolute decree in eternity, where the Father set his love on his elect and drew them to himself. Election does not mean that God pushes sinners away, but that God brings dead sinners to life in himself. God does for us what we cannot do for ourselves. It can't be that he saves you halfway and you do the rest. He saves you all the way. Do you want such a Savior? Come to Jesus.

December 15

Jesus said to Simon Peter, "Simon, son of John, do you
love me more than these?" He said to him, "Yes, Lord;
you know that I love you." John 21:15

How do people change and become fit to live
with? Habits are really hard to change. At least
I've noticed that my wife's are. And she has probably
noticed the same thing about me! Only God's love for
us and our love for God brings deep down change. So
Jesus's questions are emphasizing what he really wants
from Peter—his love. He is asking him: Do you truly
love me? And is your love for me changing you at the
deepest level? Does it cause you to pray? Does it help
you say no to your desires? Is it teaching you patience?

Peter had been boastful in promising Jesus he
would lay down his life for him. He had also been fearful when he denied knowing Jesus. Jesus wants Peter to
see that these struggles, at their heart, are about whom
he loves. When you give your heart to Jesus, to him who
laid down his life for you, you will change. The love of
Christ will control your mind, your will, your choices,
and your words. It's going to get right down to the way
you live, the way you are when you get up in the morning, even before you have coffee. Jesus is asking you
today, "Do you love me?" How will you answer?

December 16

He said to him the third time, "Simon, son of John,
do you love me?" Peter was grieved because he said to
him the third time, "Do you love me?" and he said
to him, "Lord, you know everything; you know that
I love you." John 21:17

Peter is in transition. He is on his way to becoming the powerful preacher that we see in the second chapter of Acts. But first he must be restored after denying Jesus. So Jesus presses home to Peter's conscience his great need to love Christ and be loved by him. And finally Peter says humbly to Jesus, the Sovereign, omniscient, God-man, "Lord, you know all things, you know that I love you."

Knowing the love of God in Christ is the only thing that brings stability to Peter's life—and to ours. What do you do when you have failed? When you are outcast and forgotten? When you encounter difficult circumstances? You have to choose. Do you love Jesus? Do you know that Jesus loves you? Do you find your stability in God's love for you? That's what happened to Peter, and God made him into a man of power. That's what knowing the love of God does through the Holy Spirit. It changes weak, fearful people into those controlled by the love of God.

December 17

Jesus said to Simon Peter, "Simon, son of John, do you love me more than these?" . . . "Feed my lambs." . . . "Tend my sheep." . . . "Feed my sheep." John 21:15–17

Like the rising of the sun brings light to the world, love for Jesus always results in love and care for others. You can't have one without the other. After Jesus questions Peter, he gives him a command—get to work caring for others. He doesn't say, "Take some time to repent further." He calls Peter to the great work of feeding his lambs, the weak ones, and caring for and protecting his sheep.

Have you made the connection between loving Jesus and loving his sheep? Sometimes love corrects. But correction should come from a loving, tender, patient heart that wants to protect from danger. You can only keep shepherding stubborn sheep as you learn about the love of Jesus. As Jesus's love shapes you, his love will be made visible to those you live and work with. What you are in your God-ward relationship will define who you are and how you treat those around you. That's what life is all about—Jesus's love for you and entering into his love by having a love for him and a love for others.

December 18

"Truly, truly, I say to you, when you were young, you used to dress yourself and walk wherever you wanted, but when you are old, you will stretch out your hands, and another will dress you and carry you where you do not want to go." (This he said to show by what kind of death he was to glorify God.) John 21:18–19

How do we develop character in ourselves and others? We can't teach character unless we have it, and that's a problem because the church often lacks character. We can only get it as we learn about Jesus's holy, powerful, transforming love. But we want so many other things besides the love of Christ: an easy life, popularity, acceptance, good principles, and even sound theology. But without love to Christ forming the character, all of it is only self-will. And without the love of Christ shaping our will and character, even good things become demonic, divisive, and cruel.

So Jesus ends his message to Peter by saying, "Follow me. Follow me to your death and you will glorify God. Follow me and I will make you great." Peter desired to be great and God is going to do that through his death. The heart of love for God is surrendering our will to him. Peter surrendered to Christ and became great. As we surrender to God's love, our character is formed like Christ, and we also become great in God's kingdom.

December 19

"For the Son of Man came to seek and to save the lost."
Luke 19:10

In Gold Beach, Oregon, the small town where I grew up, dogs were considered part of the family. But we had a garbage man with a short fuse who carried a hunting rifle. And if a dog came out barking and threatening him while he was collecting garbage, he would shoot the dog. Of course he was a hated outcast. No one would have ever invited him for dinner or gone to his house. That's probably how people in Jericho felt about Zacchaeus.

But the Son of Man came to seek and to save the lost. He heals the blind, touches the leper, and invites himself to the sinner's house. Jesus came not to call the righteous and respectable, he came for sinners. Jesus is saying that we are inwardly what the poor and the outcast are outwardly. Unless we understand this we will not be saved, for how can you be saved if you don't think you need saving?

In our town, a couple of Christians went to the garbage man and told him that Jesus loved him. It was good news to him, and he gave his life to Jesus. He stopped shooting dogs and started going to church. Jesus came to Gold Beach and saved the garbage man. He came to Jericho and saved Zacchaeus. Do you know what you are? Do you know that Jesus came to save you?

December 20

And when Jesus came to the place, he looked up and
said to him, "Zacchaeus, hurry and come down, for I
must stay at your house today." Luke 19:5

Imagine Zacchaeus's surprise when Jesus called him by
name. Jesus knew him! When Jesus stops and calls his
name, Zacchaeus realizes that Jesus is seeking and saving him. Jesus's love is a splendid love. You can never
contain it. It always catches us by surprise.

Like Zacchaeus, we go about our lives, thinking
that we are unseen. But Jesus stops, looks right at us,
and says, "Come down." Do you know that Jesus is
speaking to you right now? He is looking at you; he
loves you. And although your heart has been so hard
and you wanted to go your own way, not Jesus's way,
still he calls you by name and says, "I love you." That's
the kind of Savior God sent into the world. The One
who looks with love; the One who doesn't merely pass
by, but the One who can sovereignly look into your
heart and cause you to respond to his love. He can put
love where before there was sin and rebellion. Now you
know the love of God, you know you are lost, and that
Jesus came to seek and save the lost. Hurry, come down,
Jesus must stay at your house today.

December 21

And when Jesus came to the place, he looked up and said to him, "Zacchaeus, hurry and come down, for I must stay at your house today." Luke 19:5

Jesus doesn't just knock on the door of our hearts; he moves in with us! Jesus doesn't wait for sinners to invite him in. He knocks and invites himself in. When we hear Jesus knocking, some of us bar the door. Jesus then sets a fire in the basement to get our attention. Then we have to open the door to escape the heat, fire, and smoke.

The truth is that if Jesus didn't do the saving, you and I would never get saved. Who really wants to admit that they are a sinner in rebellion against God? The fire might be a bad habit we can't break, a husband or wife who is more than we can handle, a child who breaks our heart—whatever it is, Jesus knows how to use it, so we, in desperation, open the door and let him enter. Then you discover that what you resisted is the most amazing gift in the world. Salvation has come to your house—as it did to Zacchaeus's. When Jesus went home with him, Zacchaeus was filled with joy. Jesus proved his love by dying on the cross for you, not as a good person, but as a sinner. Will you welcome him into your heart today?

December 22

In the same region there were shepherds out in the field, keeping watch over their flock by night. Luke 2:8

The shepherds on Christmas cards are clean, well-dressed, and tending white sheep. Those scenes seem far removed from our real world of problems, fears, and sorrows. But the truth is that the shepherds stood on the lowest rung of society. I found out why when I worked with sheep shearers. My job was to tie up the sheared wool and put it in a sack. The wool was dirty, greasy, and smelly. At the end of the day, I smelled so bad that my family would back away from me.

So why would God announce the Savior of the world to shepherds? Because God always comes to the humble, to those who have nothing to brag about and nothing to glory in, to those who know they are sinners. The message came to them because the Savior was coming for real sinners, not for those filled with pride and self-importance. God sent his angels to the real world where people struggle with loneliness, trouble, and sin. Zechariah prophesied that the Savior would "shine on those living in darkness" (Luke 1:79 NIV). So the angels appeared to the least of these, in literal darkness, to highlight the real darkness of our world, the darkness of real ignorance, real impurity, real sorrows, real death. It's into our dark world that Christ shines, enabling us to be different because of his Spirit.

December 23

"Because of the tender mercy of our God, whereby the sunrise shall visit us from on high to give light to those who sit in darkness and in the shadow of death, to guide our feet into the way of peace." Luke 1:78–79

The angel's announcement of a Savior came to the real world where people live in real darkness. Into this world, God moves with power. Zechariah prophesied that the sun would rise from heaven over those who live in darkness because of the tender mercy of our God (Luke 1:78). So into the real world, because of our God's mercy, comes a real Savior leading you through real problems and empowering you to master sins that are too much for you.

This isn't great news if all you need is a nudge, if you have most of the strength you need and all you want is for the Lord to prop you up a bit. If that's your religion, then you don't need a Savior. But the angels come with this glorious message to those who have the deepest needs of soul, to those who have an independent spirit and a willful heart. To those who want their own way, not God's way, and who have made a mess of their lives. To those people, the angel announces wonderful news. In the town of David the Savior has been born, the Christ, God has come in the flesh. He has come to do what no one else can—to change my heart and to change yours.

December 24

The angel said to them, "Fear not, for behold, I bring you good news of great joy that will be for all the people. For unto you is born this day in the city of David a Savior, who is Christ the Lord." Luke 2:10–11

A missionary linguist was working in a remote village in Laos. He was struggling to translate the word for Savior. So he asked the villagers what word would describe the person who saved someone from a tiger's attack? "*Pa*," they replied. Next, he asked what word would describe someone who rescued a child from falling off a cliff? Again they replied, "*Pa*." Some days later, the missionary set off on a raft with two women to cross a river. The water was turbulent and the raft flipped upside down. The missionary grabbed the women, who were drowning, and swam with them to shore. Afterwards, the missionary asked the villagers what word would describe that action of saving the women. They responded, "Not *pa*, but *che*. *Pa* is when you reach down to help someone from above and *che* is when you are in the water yourself." That's what Jesus did. He went into the depths of the water and pulled us out—a real Savior who became like us, lived with us, and gave his life for us.

December 25

When the angels went away from them into heaven,
the shepherds said to one another, "Let us go over to
Bethlehem and see this thing that has happened, which
the Lord has made known to us." Luke 2:15

The angels left and the shepherds said, "Let's go and see." These men simply go to Jesus. How many times do we pray lofty prayers without really going to our Savior? But the times you cry out, "Lord, be merciful to me a sinner," when you don't feel spiritual, when you feel vulnerable and weak, and when God seems far from you, it is then that God will reach in and touch you and change you and fill you with his vital life and power. Do you see how that works? God resists the proud; grace is for the humble (James 4:6). Grace flows for those who run to him. The humble go to Jesus and receive amazing power.

Perhaps your life is disappointing to you; the longings of your heart have not been fulfilled. God says, "Give me your heart. I want to meet you in your weakness." God wants you—in your weakness, disappointments, and sorrows—to run to Bethlehem. To run straight to Jesus. Do it as you pray, as you live, as you work. Do it out of weakness and you will receive strength from Jesus.

December 26

And when they saw it, they made known the saying
that had been told them concerning this child.
And all who heard it wondered at what the shepherds
told them. Luke 2:17–18

The shepherds didn't know the whole story of the gospel. They didn't know how Christ would live, die, rise from the dead, and rule from heaven's throne. All they knew was that a Savior had come to bring peace and light to a dark world. But notice that what little they knew, they couldn't wait to share. Did you ever see a child with a present he or she loved? Did they want to keep quiet about it? No, they had to show and tell all about it. You and I have this great gift. We don't have a small story, a small Christ, a small Holy Spirit; we have a great salvation! Go and tell the story. Go to your neighbors, coworkers, and friends; go overseas. Tell everyone the greatest story ever told. There will never be another like it. It's a glory story—not a myth or a dream, but the truth and the life.

After the shepherds tell the story they begin to sing—a shepherd choir glorifying and praising God (Luke 2:20). You too, regardless of how you feel, can tell the story and sing God's praises. It's the best news you've ever heard—and the best news the world has ever heard.

December 27

But now the righteousness of God has been manifested apart from the law, although the Law and the Prophets bear witness to it—the righteousness of God through faith in Jesus Christ for all who believe. Romans 3:21-22

In the first part of Romans Paul describes a cracked and shattered world filled with cracked and shattered people who can't see themselves or God clearly. Men and women have rejected God and his authority, and have tried to take God's place and run their own lives. That has opened the door to all kinds of evil. People have lost all respect for God, for themselves, and for others.

But there is hope for you, for me, for the world. We have a new future. There is a new way of living and seeing because the righteousness of God has been revealed in Jesus Christ through faith in him. Faith is not just for the Romans, it's for us too—for the cracked and shattered people of today. We can admit that we rebel against God, that we judge others, and that we try to get our own way. But now we have a different perspective because we see what God has done in Jesus Christ. We have a new life, a new record, and new eyes to see ourselves and God clearly. And we have a new, restored relationship with God. We are no longer condemned, no longer under God's wrath. We are free in Christ to love God and others.

December 28

Now the righteousness of God has been manifested apart from the law, although the Law and the Prophets bear witness to it—the righteousness of God through faith in Jesus Christ for all who believe. Romans 3:21-22

You can't understand justification by faith without seeing two things: your sin and the cleansing power of the cross of Christ. On the one hand, owning up to sin is hard because it means admitting what we really are. We want to hang on to what little righteousness we think we have. On the other hand, the cross holds up a mirror to our sin. Jesus says, "Look and see what needed to be done to pay for your sin."

With eyes of faith, we see how the cross of Christ has met our need. It's what God, out of love for us, has done to satisfy his justice. God's love moved into history in the person of Jesus Christ. Jesus is not on one side and God on the other; they are one. God is saving his people and that is our security. If God has done it, he is never going to take it back. He doesn't change his mind. You can face your sin with courage because you see how God loved you to the uttermost. No matter how deep into sin you have gone, God has gone deeper in the giving of his Son.

December 29

Now the righteousness of God has been manifested apart from the law, although the Law and the Prophets bear witness to it—the righteousness of God through faith in Jesus Christ for all who believe. Romans 3:21-22

The heart of the gospel is that God gave his perfectly obedient Son, Jesus, to die on the cross to take away our sins. Did you ever get your clothes so dirty that no matter how many times you washed them they didn't come clean? God says that's what our own righteousness is like—filthy clothes (Isaiah 64:6). There is nothing we can do that isn't tainted by our own self-centeredness and sin. But the righteousness from God is pure, clean, and ours through faith in Jesus Christ.

Now there is an umbrella of free justification over us that we receive by faith alone, without works. If you could add a single brick to it, your salvation would be insecure because it would depend on you. That's also why we have nothing to boast about. Isn't all boasting just trying to gain the acceptance that only God can give you? But now we can be free from trying to save ourselves, free from trying to earn the good opinion of others. We have the righteousness of Christ through faith as our unshakable new reality.

December 30

God presented him as a sacrifice of atonement, through
faith in his blood. Romans 3:25 NIV

Have you ever felt that there is no hope for you—
that you've made a mess out of your life? God says
to you, "Yes, you've made a mess, but I have made an
exchange—an atonement—for you. My Son, Jesus, has
died as an atoning sacrifice for your mess." The whole
idea of atonement is that the righteousness of Christ
has covered over, obliterated, our sin. Do you see how
radical Jesus's atonement is? God took away our sin and
guilt but more than that, Jesus's sacrifice satisfied God's
wrath. The fact that your sin has been atoned for means
that you are delivered from eternal punishment; you are
pardoned, forgiven, free.

A young man out on parole from prison lived with
us for a time. He hadn't been pardoned or forgiven; he
was on probation. He soon violated his parole by getting into trouble. The police came and led him, crying
and yelling, out the door. Watching that young man
being led away in handcuffs was one of the most terrible moments of my life. In Romans, Paul is saying
that you are not on parole; you are pardoned. God will
never lead you away crying and yelling. God doesn't
hold anything against you secretly. Your debt to God
has been paid in full. Because of Jesus Christ, God is
forever for you.

December 31

Then what becomes of our boasting? It is excluded. By
what kind of law? By a law of works? No, but by the law
of faith. For we hold that one is justified by faith apart
from works of the law. Or is God the God of Jews only?
Is he not the God of Gentiles also? Yes, of Gentiles also.
Romans 3:27–29

Our human tendency is to try to protect our own
record by boasting. But the grace of God says there
is nothing to boast in except the power and glory of the
cross. God forbid you should boast in anything else.
The cross of Christ puts to death all human strength
and righteousness. Through the cross we have Christ
and his wonderful forgiveness and we no longer need
protect our own record with boasting or despair.

When our boasting is in Christ, prejudices drop
away too. No matter who you are or where you have
been or what you have done or what color you are, anyone who has faith is my brother or sister. We don't have
anything to brag about except Jesus and the righteousness of God. When you find yourself boasting and full
of defensiveness and prejudice, turn to Jesus, ask for
forgiveness, and the power of God will flow into your
life. You will no longer have to lift up yourself; instead
you can boast in what Jesus has done in you and for
you.

Scripture Index